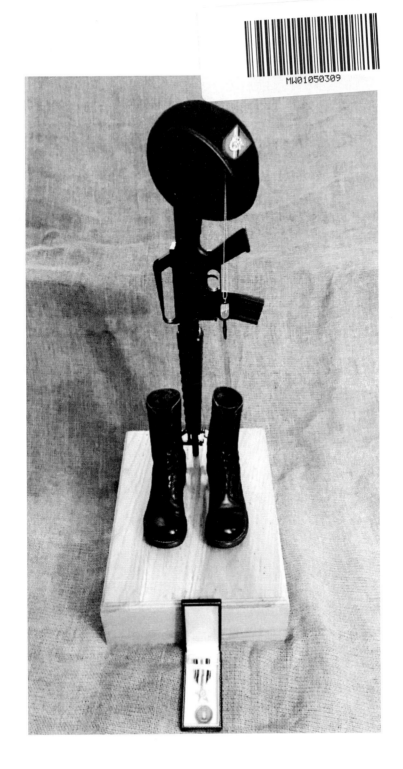

THE UNITED STATES OF AMERICA

TO ALL WHO SHALL SEE THESE PRESENTS, GREETING:

THIS IS TO CERTIFY THAT
THE PRESIDENT OF THE UNITED STATES OF AMERICA
AUTHORIZED BY ACT OF CONGRESS JULY 9, 1918
HAS AWARDED

THE SILVER STAR

TO

SERGEANT FIRST CLASS RONALD E. SMITH, UNITED STATES ARMY

FOR
GALLANTRY IN ACTION

IN VIETNAM ON 28 NOVEMBER 1970

GIVEN UNDER MY HAND IN THE CITY OF WASHINGTON
THIS   11TH   DAY OF   FEBRUARY   19 72

MAJOR GENERAL, USA
THE ADJUTANT GENERAL

SECRETARY OF THE ARMY

Still Waiting

A Sister's Story

By Linda Cope

Brenda,
Until they
all come home.
Thanks so much
my friend!
Love you,
Linda

Still Waiting

I have tried to recreate events, locales and conversations from my memories of them. I may have changed some identifying characteristics and details such as physical properties, occupations and places of residence. Some names and identifying details have been changed to protect the privacy of individuals.

Second Edition February 2017

Cover design by Jacob Kubon

Field cross photo by Brenda & Gary Stanley

ISBN 978-1-939294-44-9

Published by

splatteredinkpress.com

Dedication to Ron

Where do I start? You gave me so much in the twenty short years that I had you.

You were everything to us—Mom, Jim and me. You were our rock, our father, big brother, teacher, protector, our fun, laughter, and hero. You gave us guidance, education, morality and along with Mom, love and security.

I had you so high on a pedestal that no one could reach you in my heart or soul. To me you were the perfect son, husband, brother, policeman, Navy man, Army Green Beret, and you could do no wrong.

Then that damn war took you from us...

MISSING IN ACTION...KILLED IN ACTION/

BODY NOT RECOVERED

I put you on an even higher pedestal.

Now 45 years later I am telling the world of the torment, loss, heartache and injustice of what happened to you and how it was handled by our government. The only way I can stand the unimaginable anguish and agony is knowing I will see you again someday. May God bless you big brother.

Love you forever and always,

Sis

Acknowledgments

My first acknowledgement is to my big brother Ronald. He has been my hero since I was born and will continue to be into eternity.

My precious mother who endured tremendous heartache throughout her life, yet managed to be a fantastic mother.

My younger brother Jim, who became one of my best friends. We wasted years fighting, but thankfully realized what we had in each other.

My husband Randy, who has been one of my biggest promoters. He gave up hours of riding our Harley, opting to drive four wheels so I could write. He found my editor/publisher. He took my work to her, not me. He pushed when I needed. He listened to me cry as I poured over and relived the pain of losing Ron. He threw himself into the POW/MIA issue as if Ron was his brother. Thank you, my Harley Man.

My children, Angel and Matt. My niece and nephew, Scott and Crystal, who love their uncle Ron as if they had been with him from birth, even though Angel is the only one Ron lived to see.

My stepsons Joe and Charlie joined in with my kids honoring Ron. Charlie has been to DC nearly every year with the exception of when he was stationed in Afghanistan. Joe rode to DC with us one year. Both wear Ron's POW/MIA bracelet.

Rolling Thunder Indiana Chapter One, my other family. I went to The Wall with them the first time. They cry, laugh, and get angry with me while searching for answers to my endless quest about my brother's MIA status.

My beta readers, Darren, Brenda, Toni, Linda and Katie. Hugs, kisses, and eternal gratitude.

And Tricia, who started out being my publisher and now is a treasured friend.

Table of Contents

Prologue

From the first memory of my life to the present day, I have been waiting for my big brother to come home.

At three years of age, my first memory of life, I was waiting for my brother to come and rescue me from my not so loving grandma. As time went on, I was always waiting for him to come home from somewhere: school, dates, baseball practice, basketball practice, work and out with his friends.

When Ron was 15 years old he took the place of our father. Until I was old enough to stay at my friend's house and interact with older siblings, I thought all big brothers were like mine. I found out quickly that he was one of a kind.

He enlisted in the Navy right after high school and I began waiting for him to come home on leave. My mother, younger brother and I were lost without him.

Between five years in the Navy, 2 years on the police force and 5 years in the Army Special Forces, waiting for him to come home became a lifelong endeavor.

In 1970 he was sent to Vietnam. As he ran down the airport gateway, he waved and promised to see us in a year.

I am ... still waiting.

PART ONE

Tough Beginnings

On March 29, 1940, after fifty-six hours of labor, my mother gave birth to a ten-pound baby boy, my big brother, Ronald Eugene Smith. He didn't have the love of his father, who had abandoned my mother two months earlier, but my mom and her parents tried to make up for that loss.

My mother was a secret bride when she and my father were married by a Justice of the Peace on September 17, 1938, in Noblesville, Indiana. It was stylish in those days to sneak away, get married, then go back home and pretend you were still single. Months later you would announce to the world you had been secretly married. It was a quaint and romantic way to start a lifetime together and that was how Joseph Malcom Smith and Genieve Fauniel Spivey were united.

They had been engaged the last two years of Genie's high school years. Joe had graduated two years before, went to work in a mill and was waiting for his fiancé to graduate. After they were married, they rented a cottage in Perrysville, their small hometown on the banks of the Wabash River in central Indiana.

They were surrounded by family and friends as Genie had two younger brothers and two sisters, and Joe was the middle brother of three. Genie's best friend, Melba, was engaged to John Smith, Joe's younger brother.

Genie had married her high school sweetheart, her best friend was going to be her sister-in-law, and her family was close by, it seemed like a perfect world.

On July 19, 1939, Joe decided they should have a baby and Genie knew she became pregnant that very day.

When she was seven months along, Joe told her she was to give her baby to his brother and sister-in-law. When she refused, he left.

If Genie had been alone, she would have had choices, but there were only two months to prepare for this baby alone, with no husband and no father, and she would need access to some kind of medical care. Forget about mourning the loss of the love of her life, she had to survive for this baby. She had no idea where the money would come from to help pay for their survival so she was stuck - she had to go back home to her parents. This meant she would be brow-beaten, nagged, and complained about by her mother.

Genie's mother, Ruth, was not a happy woman. She could nag your ears off, make you want to run for the hills, sleep in the woods and eat worms to stay alive—

whatever you could do to get away from her continual complaints and controlling ways.

Her father, ST, was a lot easier to live with. He might want to use bodily harm on her now estranged husband, but at least he would be on her side and not complain about having her back home again.

By the time Ron was seven months old, he and Mom were living with a family she was working for. For three dollars a week and a small room for her and Ron, she made the family's life easier by cooking, cleaning, and doing laundry.

One afternoon my father showed up and Mom asked him if he would like to see his son. When he looked at his son for the first time, he said, "He'll do," and then he was gone again.

He joined the Army, left for World War II and Mom filed for a divorce. Legally my grandfather had to file for her, as being only 20 years old, she wasn't old enough. They had no money for attorney fees, so the lawyer received half of a butchered hog for his services.

For the next six years, Mom worked at whatever she could to care for herself and Ron. Her child support was set at $4.00 a week, but as expected, my father refused to pay. However, Mom had an edge. He had lied about his status when he joined the Army and listed himself as a single man with no children. She got word to my father, through his uncle, that if he didn't agree to pay his inadequate amount of support, she would report him to the Army. His uncle, a wonderful man Mom always told us, didn't want to see his nephew in trouble, so old Uncle Joe paid Ron's child support.

In 1943, three years after Ron was born, my Mom met and married her second husband, Edgar. They had two daughters, Joy and Carol. The girls were two and three years younger than Ron.

Along with physical abuse, their living conditions were horrendous. They lived in a third floor apartment, with no running water so Mom had to carry water to wash clothes, on a washing board, for three kids in diapers. The babies had dresser drawers for beds.

She knew she had to get out, for their safety and her sanity. Once again my grandfather rescued her and all three children, this time at gunpoint. I was never told, but I have wondered if my grandfather lost more of his livestock to get her divorced this time.

Mom and three kids were now living back with my grandparents. She was trying to work and take care of her children, but it seemed impossible to earn enough to live on her own. Her mother never let her forget that she was a burden on her and grandpa, and the girls were a constant reminder to my

Ron - three years old

grandma of another mistake my mother had made.

Grandma treasured Ron, so she treated him different than the other grandchildren. For Mom and the girls, being at grandma's mercy, living conditions were not pleasant.

They had been living with her parents for about a year when life got even worse. On one of the weekend visits with their father, Sunday evening came and her ex-husband didn't return with the girls. There was no amber alert. No evening news to report to the public that a parent had broken custody laws and taken his children from their mother. My mother had no money to hire professionals to find them, so she and grandpa searched for them, going to all family members, neighbors, and acquaintances. The police department was alerted, but of no help. Mom's daughters had vanished.

Mom took off many times on wild goose chases whenever she heard of any sign of them being back in the area, returning every time empty handed and broken-hearted. It was 25 years later before my mother saw her daughters again.

Ron – five years old

After the war, my father came home and started looking for Mom and Ron. He had decided once more that he wanted to be a husband and father. He found her living with her parents in Brownsburg,

Indiana, working at Eli Lilly, a pharmaceutical company. He contacted her while she was at work, not wanting to be confronted by my grandfather. He was sorry and wanted to get back with her. He promised that he would hire a lawyer and find her daughters. Magic words were spoken, back she went. The old song and dance was on once again.

On January 26, 1946, mother re-married our father. Not long after, he re-enlisted into the Army and was sent to Washington State, where he was stationed in Fort Madigan Hospital as a mess sergeant. In September of 1946, Mom and Ron drove out west in an old Ford coupe. Things between the three of them were ok then. He treated them good at first, sometimes taking Ron fishing, and acting like a father. He was never a loving man or showed much affection toward Ron, but he did treat him better in those first days back together than he did as time went on.

He never did follow through with his promise to help find Mom's daughters. No detectives were hired to search for them and no attorneys were hired to get the legal matters in order to get them back. Joe had done it again and gotten what he wanted with his lies. And now he had them in Washington State.

By the time Ron was eight years old, he had to stay alone in the evenings until my parents got home from work. One night Ron heard a noise outside. He turned the lights off and climbed onto the kitchen sink. Right outside the window were two guys stealing their coal.

There was nothing he could do, so he stayed inside, and kept quiet. Leaving kids of young age was more acceptable back then and although Ron was much older than his age and more responsible than some adults, it didn't change the fact that his childhood was sad and lonely. They lived near Ft. Lewis when Ron started school where he was getting beaten up and having his belongings taken from him daily by a group of kids.

In 1948, Mom thought she was going to have surgery on her back and would not be able to take care of Ron for a while, so my parents took him back to Indiana. I believe the real reason was that it was her way of getting him away from our father who was starting to resent Ron.

Ron lived at my grandparent's farm for two years. Grandpa was great and Ron was grandma's favorite, so he was treated well. My mom's youngest sister, Jeanette, was only two years older than Ron, so they had each other. They rode horses, raised pets, experienced farm life, and became very close. Ron had a bit of a problem adjusting at first. He had become such a little bully to survive in Washington that his self-defense attitude got him in trouble until he learned how to get along in a much different atmosphere. One incident I've heard through the years was the day he beat the tar out of his aunt's boyfriend. He thought the kid was way too friendly, so he took care of matters on his own.

Mom wanted Ron back in Washington, but my father didn't care if he was there or not. This time she got her way, went home on the train and brought him back. He was back in Washington by February 2, 1950, the day I arrived.

The day I was born, Tacoma was having the worst storm they'd had in nine years. Coming from Indiana, Ron was used to snowstorms, so he was having a ball. His school had been let out early and some of the kids were afraid to go out in the weather, as the visibility was extremely poor. So Ron led groups of kids' home through the blizzard. He would return to the school, get more kids and lead them safely home. Even on the day I was born, at ten years of age, he was busy being a hero.

Now we were a happy little family of four and several months later, Mom was pregnant again. My father wanted her to get an abortion, so she told him she would, if she could go back to Indiana to get it. That was the only way she could get money from him to go back home. She secretly packed some of her keepsakes and gave them to her friend Mary for her to ship after we left.

Mom, Ron and I left for Indiana in the dead of winter on a train.

Somewhere in Montana, the heating system broke down and it was fifty-one degrees below zero. Mom and Ron took turns walking me, so as not to freeze to death. At the next station, the conductor refused to take the train any further, saying he did not want to be responsible for the death of a baby. I would have frozen to death had the train gone any further.

Mom wrote my father after a while and informed him that she was not getting an abortion and not coming back to Washington. By now it should have been evident that the man wanted what he couldn't have.

He wanted her to come back, said he was sorry and he wanted the baby. So back she went.

Why? Why did she continue to subject herself and her children to his insanity? She would get her fill of his asinine behavior and leave him. Then after a little while, he would beg and she would go back. Surely by this time she knew it would not change. She was a wonderful, loving mother who almost killed herself working all kind of jobs to support us. She wasn't a college graduate, but she wasn't stupid either. Maybe it was just too hard to support us alone. To this day, it's the only thing that makes any kind of sense to me.

James Terry Smith, my younger brother, was born two months early on April 7, 1951, and was in the Army hospital for at least a month. Mom could only see him for one hour a day. She would bring Ron and me with her every day to see her newborn baby and spend that very short hour holding him. Ron would take care of me outside while Mom was inside with Jim.

Not long after Jim was home from the hospital, my father became angry about something and signed up to go to Korea. After he got over his tantrum, he couldn't get out of it. In 1952 he left for Korea. Mom, Ron, Jim and I went back home to Indiana.

We lived in a trailer on my grandparents' property and Ron went back to Hillsboro school. The next year we stayed with Mom's sister, Lettie, and my baby cousin, Regina, in Crawfordsville. My uncle was in the Navy, somewhere near Korea. While the men were in Korea, the women and kids stayed together. Mom had two jobs, one at a factory and the second at a dime store. My aunt took care of us kids. Ron would stay with us on the weekends and go back to grandpa and grandmas during the week for school.

When my father came home from Korea, we were off to Ft. Lee in Virginia. This was only a holding station and we did not know where we would end up. Again, Ron was shipped back to Indiana on the bus so he wouldn't miss any more school. South Carolina was next, and then we finally settled in Kentucky at Ft. Campbell. That was Army life.

Ron was back with us the summer after his freshman year. He worked all summer in a tobacco field, saving his money, only to have our father get drunk one night and take it.

My grandparents came for a visit and wouldn't go home without Ron. Mom said they pretended they needed him on the farm, but in reality they hated the way my father treated him. Our father didn't want any of us, but Ron was old enough to realize his father didn't care about him. I can't imagine how he must have felt. At least Jim and I were too young at that time to understand what was going on. By the time we knew the whole truth, we had no feelings for Mr. Smith (our father). Therefore, it didn't hurt us as much. Ron was gone again.

Not long after, my father decided he wanted to go to Panama and he wanted his family with him. Mom, Jim and I had to get all of the shots to leave the US. Ron was not going. He wanted to stay with our grandparents and attend the school he loved. After we had our papers in order and had gotten sick from all of the shots, our father decided he didn't want us to be with him. Thank goodness. How much worse would our lives have been if we had been there with only him? At least when he decided that he didn't want us in the states, we could get back to Indiana.

We were visiting Indiana one afternoon in 1953, when my mother left me with my grandma, and even at three years of age, I knew I was not wanted. Crouched into a corner of the big wraparound porch of that giant old farm house where my grandparents lived, I was crying and didn't want to be there with her. I also didn't want her to know I was crying, as I knew she would criticize me for being a cry baby. My loving grandma had the heart of a pickle, sour and cold.

I stayed very quiet until Ron came in from the field to rescue me. He was out in one of the fields, on some big tractor, but would be coming to the house some-time. I knew I would be ok as long as my big brother was near, as long as Bo was close by. Bo was Ron's family nickname. Mom would come back, but in the meantime, I waited for Ron and tried to stay out of my grandma's way. He was ten years older than me and being thirteen, he seemed like an adult to me.

My Mom, Ron, my younger brother Jim and I were back home living in a trailer behind grandpa and grandma's house, at the farm called Clarks Place. My grandparents rented it for a few years and we lived there during the times my father was at different Army bases where we couldn't go.

Clarks Place could be fun at times, as long as Mom or Ron was there with me. I loved the tricks the ghosts played on my grandma as they were constantly locking us out of the house. We would go out the back door and be locked out. The locks were not complicated locks, just an old screen door with a hook. It must have happened quite often for all the commotion it caused. I wasn't sure what a ghost was, but it liked playing games on us. I can still hear my grandma complaining about "that damn ghost." She would get to the door with a basket full of laundry she had taken off the line, or an arm full of vegetables from the garden, and have to traipse (my grandma's word) around the house to go in through the front door. No one would be inside, so how did the door get locked? I was convinced the ghost did it, whatever a ghost was.

I also loved playing with all the rabbits. There were probably 10 hutches lined up against one of the out-buildings full of big rabbits, middle sized rabbits and itty bitty babies being born every few weeks. Ron always let me help feed, water and change the bedding from hutch to hutch. I had my favorite rabbits and he would let me take them out and play with them. About the time they would be used to me and I would have named all of my favorites, a few would be missing. I would have to start all over petting, cooing and taming them, only to have them disappear again. I didn't understand what was happening for years, but I had been eating my best friends for Sunday dinner. The strangers who came to buy our rabbits were either having the same delicacy as my family or hopefully, enjoying them as pets.

Back to Indiana

By 1955 we were moving back to Indiana. My father had requested to be sent to the Panama Canal and as soon as he left, Mom bought a small lot in Hillsboro and had her brothers move our trailer there. Now Ron was with us all of the time since our father wasn't there to abuse him, and he wouldn't have to be sent to grandma and grandpa to escape. We could be a family now, just the four of us.

Ron was a junior in high school when I started first grade. My teacher was Miss Betty, one of Ron's friend's aunts. I loved her, she liked me and it was the only time in my life that I was the teacher's pet. Life was good, as I was in school with my big brother and had him all to myself.

Mom worked in Crawfordsville, which was about 25 miles away. She would drop Jim off at grandma and grandpas on her way to work and he would stay with them during her work hours. They would leave for Mom's job before Ron and I left for school.

We had a 1955 yellow and black Mercury and I thought it was funny when the family would tease her about driving the yellow streak and her lead foot. I wasn't sure why they referred to her foot as lead, but it must have had something to do with the police stopping her for speeding.

After Mom left in the morning, Ron and I were on our own until evening. Lunch was my favorite as I was released from class first. We lived only a half block from school, so I would walk home, get our lunch out and set the table. Then I would go back outside and step on the anthills on Ron's homemade dirt basketball court until he arrived home for lunch. I thought I was so important, doing a task that Ron had asked me to do.

We would eat lunch, clear our dishes and walk back to school together.

To some sibling's this would only be lunch; to me it was golden because I got to spend time with the person I adored.

Hillsboro school was very small and Ron had attended here on and off all his school life. He was very popular and everyone knew him. How could they not, since there were only 12 in his class.

First and second grade was sacred to me because Ron was always around. I felt so protected when I was with him, even with the neighborhood bullies and brats. Two classmates of mine, Allen and Denny, loved to torture Jim and me, especially Jim. He was 14 months younger and very shy. They were relentless with regard to his stuttering. He was an easy target for such little

20

creeps and most of the time I could handle them my-self. For instance, when they stuck gum in my pony tail or spit in my clean hair, I would just beat them up. But they never let up, making fun of Jim and playing dirty tricks on us. Since Mom or Ron couldn't be with us every minute, I had to protect my little brother. Once when I was in second grade and Jim was in first, I had him hold my doll while I beat up both of them. I blood-ied one of their noses and tore the other one's shirt. Jim hated the fact that his sister had to protect him, espe-cially since he grew up. He is now 6' 3, with no speech problems and hasn't taken crap from bullies for many years. After I didn't have to protect him and myself, I quit beating boys up.

I wasn't always able to take care of the boys, espe-cially when they teamed up with older bullies - four brothers who lived two blocks away. One Saturday, Jim and I were playing on the school playground alone, no teachers or witnesses. It was only half a block from our house, but the playground was blocked from view by another house.

The brothers decided to lock Jim and me in an old huge wooden box that sat outside the lunchroom entrance. I had walked by the harmless old box hun-dreds of times, even sat on it at recess, but now it looked like impending doom. The brothers told us that since it was Saturday, no would find us until Monday when the lunch room staff came to work. I was terrified as they were physically holding onto us. I was certain we were going to die, and I knew I couldn't take on all of these guys. Allen Jay and Denny were little brats who were not very big or smart for that matter, the older guys were another story. There were two of them, plus Allen and Denny to boot. How on earth was I going to get us out of this mess?

I needed my big brother, but he was working at the lumber yard where he worked after school and Saturdays. All I could do was threaten them with Ron.

"If you touch us my big brother Ron will get you," I screamed.

"Oh ha! He isn't here now, cry baby. " They laughed.

"He'll know who did this to us. We already told him how you treat us."

Something I threatened must have made sense to them, because they didn't put us in the box. After what seemed like hours, they let go of us and we ran home and later we told Mom and Ron. I was never told what happened, but my guess is that Ron had a serious talk with them or their parents because they never bothered us again.

I learned at a very young age to use whatever I could to protect myself and Jim. Threatening my adversaries with my big brother had worked many times. Even when Ron wasn't with us, he was near.

My little brother needed extra help with a lot of things like his school work, shoe tying, riding his bike, and street sense. Mom explained to me that because he was born two months early, he had to catch up with himself. The doctors had told her he would be ok, but it would take him several years to accomplish this. It also didn't help that our father treated him so poorly. Jim was unsure of himself and afraid to speak most of the time when our father was around.

Jim and I would wait for Ron to come home from a date or out with the guys, his job, or ball practice. Our trailer had a big front window and the couch sat in front of the window, making a good look-out tower. We would climb up on the back of the couch, hang onto the window ledge, then stare out the window and wait. As soon as a car would pull up we would stare out and wave, acting like complete dorks. On more than one occasion, Ron would tell us to stop acting like little "goof balls" in front of his friends. The poor guy was always stuck with us. This went on the entire three years we lived in Hillsboro, his sophomore, junior and senior year of high school.

I loved it when his girlfriends paid attention to me. I was Smitty's little sister and I felt special when they made a point of talking to me. I was sure, even then, they were trying to make points with him, but I didn't care. Anything that connected me to him was all right with me.

Money was something we didn't have much of, so snacks and frivolous items were not high on the grocery list. Ice cream was our favorite, but we didn't have it often. One evening Ron was home with Jim and me while Mom was out working a second job. Ron piled us into the car and drove to the gas station for a special splurge. Ice cream in hand, back home we went. Ron scooped up three heaping bowls and covered the ice cream with chocolate syrup. We ate the entire half gallon that night and I can still hear his laughter while telling us, "It's ok, we can do this once in a while."

I felt so mischievous eating that much ice cream, but safe at the same time. Ron was in charge and Mom was never mad at him or anything he did.

By my second grade year and Jim's first, our school had hot lunch and Mom worked as an assistant cook, so she was at school every day. Our father was still stationed in the Panama Canal.

I missed my Mom when she had to work at factories out of town, so I loved the fact that my little family was all at school together. Each class would walk single file to the lunchroom and take their tray back to their room and eat at their desks. After eating, we would take our trays back to the lunchroom. By this time the concession stand, run by the senior class would be open. We had to walk right by the stand to take our trays back. My big brother would be working in the stand almost every day. He would check Jim and my trays as we passed and if we didn't clean our plates and eat our vegetables, we didn't get a treat. I tried sneaking by, but that didn't work. Then I had a brainstorm. I would put my unfinished veggies on my friend's tray. It worked a couple of times, and then Ron figured it out. I was never mad at him, even though I pretended to. I just loved the attention from him.

Ron had homework every night. He was always writing papers or reading a big thick book. When he ran out of homework or books to read, he would read the dictionary and encyclopedias. He would lie on his stomach, prop his head up with his hands and read anything he could find.

Ron also helped Mom with our health care, otherwise known as wound and knee repair. I had the worse bike wreck of my life when I was in the first grade. I was riding on the gravel road next to our trailer, hit a big bump and fell off my seat, still straddling my bike. The momentum dragged me several feet on my knees. I had no skin left on any part of either knee, and gravel was embedded into both. Ron rescued me from the wreck site by first carrying me home, then removing the gravel from my knees. He washed the affected area, and then applied the dreaded red stuff - methylate. All wounds had to have the red stuff, and I hated the red stuff.

I knew I would never walk properly for the remainder of my life, and I had to go through the daily routine of knee repair for what seemed like months.

"It might get infected and we couldn't have that," Ron would explain. He would sit on the floor in front of me, put the methylate on my knees, and then blow as hard and fast as he could suck air back into his lungs.

These were the ways Ron took care of Jim, Mom and me - physically, emotionally, and monetarily. I thought all big brothers were like him and never gave any thought to what he did, as it was all I knew.

Enter Father

Out of nowhere, my father came home and I was elated. He was happy, taking us places and buying us presents for no apparent reason. It was great.

Dad, Mom, Jim and I went 35 miles away to Danville, Illinois just to go shopping. I got a new doll, a new blue velvet dress, and a poodle skirt, in the middle of the year. Jim got new clothes and a truck. Dad bought Mom a new dress and shoes. To this day when I smell a new doll, I can feel the false sense of happiness I had that day. I thought my world was complete because my Dad was home, happy and buying us presents. Mom seemed happy, too. *Is this what other kids and families do?* I thought.

After a few days, it was time for dad to go back to the Army and we were going to take him back to Fort Benning, Georgia. The night we had to leave, Ron had a basketball game. I was excited as we would get to watch Ron play ball, then take off on a trip for Georgia.

When we got to the gym we just sat in the car and I kept asking if we could go in to watch Ron.

"NO, we are not going in," my father said.

He seemed upset and cold, different than the prior days. I didn't understand, but I knew not to ask. Mom was wiping her nose and eyes and she wasn't talking. For what seemed like an eternity, we sat in the car while my brother played ball. I just played with my new doll, walked around the car and waited for Ron.

When he came out, he got into the car and we left. My father drove, Mom was crying, and no one said anything. I fell asleep and the next thing I knew it was daylight and we were pulling over to a bus stop and letting my father out. The last thing he said to us was that we were not allowed to stop at Rock City on the way home. Mom didn't say a word and Ron got into the driver's seat. My father walked away, I started to cry and Ron turned around to face Jim and me.

"You might as well stop crying," he said. "You are never going to see him again." Ron was upset, not sad, but stern.

Jim and I stared at our brother. I was confused, but also sensed that it wasn't the time to ask a bunch of questions. Mom was crying and I didn't understand what had happened to our happy family of two days ago. After a few minutes, Ron told us that dad wanted a divorce from Mom. I was barely old enough to understand what divorce was, and Jim just sat in silence.

"Don't worry about anything," he said. "Mom and I will take care of you both, just like we always have. We will be just fine. We have been ok, haven't we?"

Jim and I nodded our heads. Mom and Ron talked low to each other, while Jim and I sat like stones.

"Mom, it will be better without him and you know it. All he has ever caused you was pain and heartache," Ron said. "This last trick takes the cake. Coming home and acting like the big man, buying you, Sis and JT all that stuff, then pull this. What a load of crap. If he ever comes around again I will take care of him. It's done."

"You're right, Son," Mom said.

"We are going to Rock City, and Ruby Falls. So let's wipe those sad faces away and get ready to have some fun!" my brother said.

Mom laughed into her tissue and blew her nose one last time. Her smile gave me comfort and Ron's confidence let me know he was in charge. He would take care of us like he had been doing all along. They didn't think I heard this last comment, but I did.

"He really thinks he is going to tell us what we can and cannot do after that stunt, bull," my brother said, as he sped further away from the horror of what should have been our father.

We were going to Rock City and Ruby Falls. My thoughts swirled through my young mind. *This can't be so bad. Ron's happy and Mom's talking and smiling. We don't need a dad, we have Ron.*

Mom and Ron took us to the parks they had mentioned and kept joking about dad not being able to control us any longer.

"What a fool," my brother said.

Ron's graduation was approaching and he and his two best friends, Jay and Jack, had signed up to join the Marines and leave on the buddy system, soon after graduation. I could feel the uneasiness in my mother and even at seven years old, I knew this was serious. He would be a long way from home and

Ron's graduation

we wouldn't get to see him very often. I was afraid to be without Ron.

Mom was a great Mom, but she had to work so much and so hard to support us by herself. Ron made life better and he could be there when Mom was working nights. Without him, who would take care of us? Who would make life fun? And school without Ron? In my world, the excitement of his graduation was clouded by the doom that hung over our little family; the departure of our big brother.

Graduation came and it was time to take Ron to the Marines. As we drove him to Crawfordsville, Indiana to catch a bus Mom and I were crying, which frightened

Jim and he cried. Poor Ron, he probably felt like he had escaped.

Ron left for a physical, to get his hair shaved off and fill out a lot of paperwork. We went back home - without him. That little trailer, which was crowded, now seemed empty.

Three days later, Ron re-appeared. Jim and I were ecstatic, Mom looked confused. He had not passed his physical as he had a cyst on his tailbone. He needed to have surgery before he could go to boot camp. I was excited to have him back.

Ron was in the hospital as fast as he could make the arrangements. We brought him home after surgery and he had to sit backwards on the seat, on his knees. Jim and I got to help him with his recovery. We loved getting him beverages, snacks, books, turning the channel on the TV, anything we could do, we did. But all too soon he was back on his feet, ready to go to the Marines.

As it would end up, he could go into the Marines, but not with his friends as they were already halfway through boot camp. Ron was furious. He and his friends had planned this for over a year. They would be Marines together. Now because of a piece of something on his tailbone that he didn't know he had, he was held back. There was nothing he could do to alter the facts.

He started rethinking his decision. If he joined the Navy he could get more schooling, so he changed his mind. Before we knew it, he was gone again.

We missed him terribly and I counted the days when he would be home from boot camp.

Jim (8), Ron (19) & Linda (9) at Grandma's house.

I was so proud of him and loved to tell people he was in the Navy, but inside I was lost and scared without him. I couldn't imagine life without Ron.

It had begun - waiting for Ron to come home.

The Waiting Begins

Ron was gone and nothing felt the same. Home had a void as big as Texas and school was lonely. It didn't feel right to be there without Ron. I had liked school before, but I didn't this year. I was in third grade and Jim was in second and he was struggling. He had stopped stuttering once he knew his father was not coming back, but he needed his big brother to help him. Life was difficult for Jim, and Ron's presence had helped him in every aspect of his development.

School was monotonous, boring and a little scary without our brother for moral support and everything he helped us with regarding our school work. Mom was there, but she had to work and support us solely. We received no help or support from our dad. We had not seen him since we left him in Georgia over two years ago on his way to the Panama Canal. With Ron gone, she had to do everything on her own. We were so young we didn't understand any of Mom's burdens and we missed her when she had to work so much.

She had lost her job at the school when the politics had changed after the last elections, along with the entire lunchroom staff. She had gone back to the factory in Crawfordsville which meant longer hours. She also cleaned for our dentist and his family on Saturdays to supplement her income.

We had nice babysitters after school, but they weren't Ron. On weekends, we had to stay with grandma and grandpa whose farm was a couple miles outside Waynetown, about eight miles from Hillsboro and closer to Crawfordsville. Now there was no reason to stay in Hillsboro since Ron was out of school and Mom worked in Crawfordsville, so a move was in the making and our trailer was moved to their farm. It would make Mom's life easier since we could be with our grandparents while Mom worked, and she would have less driving time.

Changing schools didn't make me happy, as I had been with the same kids for three years. I did have friends, but not enough to be brokenhearted; I was only nine. I didn't really have any emotions about the move, but now we were living on the farm, way too close to my grandma.

"You look and act just like your damn dad," she would shout at me with disgust in her voice. I wasn't sure what I had done to make her mad, and existing seemed to be my biggest sin.

In our family, it was just understood that grandma was the boss, her word was the word and no one argued, not even grandpa. As a child, I grew up in this family dynamic just knowing that's how it was. As an adult, I understood why Mom didn't buck up against her mother. Number one, she was living on her property and grandma was helping take care of her children. Number two, no one ever won against grandma and Mom had grown up with that rule.

We were in a new school now and I hated it. I had entered into the middle of some juvenile fourth grade war between two groups of stupid petty nine year olds and I was their human volleyball. I was enticed by both groups to be their new friend and before I knew it, they were both fighting for me to be their new girl. For about two seconds, I thought I was just way too cool and everyone wanted me. Then I realized that this battle had been going on a long time before I came on the scene. I was only their pawn.

One group was the prissy do-good little rich girls. The other was the fun loving, down to earth, lower middle class to poor group. I was thrown back and forth until I didn't want to be with either. I just wanted to be back in Hillsboro school with my big brother and my Mom working in the lunch kitchen.

Jim and I had to ride the bus and since we were only a couple miles out of town, we were one of the last stops before school. When Jim and I got on the bus it was nearly full and there weren't a lot of seats left. Right away we were bullied by older boys. They would pull on our clothes, push us, and threaten to take our books, lunch and anything else we had. We were scared. Mom got involved this time by calling the school, but the bullying lasted off and on the entire year we rode the bus.

I hated everything about our new school. I didn't like living at the farm with my grandparents, and I missed my big brother. It was too long between his furloughs.

One afternoon while running across the barnyard, I stepped on a nail that was sticking up out of a two by four. It went through my shoe and into my heel about three inches. It was stuck in my foot so hard that I hobbled back to the house with the board stuck to my foot, bellowing my head off the entire way.

Mom was home so I didn't hear grandma's favorite response of, "Oh quit crying, it's a long way from your heart."

Mom and grandma pulled the board and rusty nail out of my foot, I had to endure a lot of home aid treatments, and the 'toe walking' began. I couldn't set my heel down flat because it hurt, so for the longest time I walked on my toe on that foot.

Mom's sister, Tootie, was still living at home at that time and her fiancé, Bob, was always around. He decided one day it was time for me to stop walking on my toe. He explained that the puncture was healed and it wouldn't hurt if I put my heel down, but I didn't want to put my heel down. The last time I did that, a big rusty nail dove into it and I had felt pain like I had never felt before, except maybe for the bike wreck in first grade.

I tried ignoring Bob, but he wouldn't leave me alone. Who did he think he was? My big brother was my first aid expert caretaker and I wanted Ron to rescue me because he would make everything all right. If it was time to walk on it, Ron would know better than this big goofy guy I was supposed to call Uncle Bob. It wasn't his foot and besides, I had learned to run on my toes.

"Put your heel down on the ground, Linda" he said. "It will not hurt, it's been too long. It's healed, just do it."

I set my heel down, cringing all the way. It felt strange and I was waiting to scream in pain. "Oh, it doesn't hurt," I said. *Wow, he's right*, I thought, but I didn't want him to be right. All I wanted was my big brother to be here fixing my foot and my world.

Ron's Leave

A few months after we moved to the farm, during the summer, Ron had a two week leave. He and several of his buddies started out from their base in California and drove across country, leaving each guy off at his home.

Since it was years before cell phones, his arrival time was a guess.

Mom and grandma had cooked for an entire day to prepare a feast. There was fried chicken, potatoes and gravy, green beans, garden fresh sweet corn and tomatoes, and homemade biscuits and pies. Our feast was ready and sitting on the old cook stove, just waiting for Ron.

Mom, Jim, our grandparents, and my mother's younger sister, Tootie, were gathered in the living room, waiting. I wanted to sit down by the road, but was told I couldn't.

The house was a large old farm house with an enormous yard. The yard was long and at the end was a fence covered with vines and bushes, making it impossible to see the driveway. You couldn't see if anyone was there until they came through the gateway.

I was sitting next to a window, my back to the front of the house and yard. After turning around to look out the window for what seemed like a thousand times, my grandma scolded me with a snarl.

"Stop looking out the window," she said. "A watched pot never boils."

I wanted to argue with her and ask her why I couldn't go outside and wait. I wanted to ask why I couldn't sit in the yard or on the porch and wait for him. I wanted to ask but of course I couldn't because it would have been construed as back talk. Any other day I would have been banned from the house. Grandma was always yelling, "Go outside and stay outside until I tell you to come in." We couldn't even get drinks inside and had to go to the pump. But today, I had to sit in the house and wait for Ron.

I sat there telling myself not to look, but there was no use, I couldn't stand it, and I didn't care how much trouble I got into with grumpy grandma. I turned, looked and there he was, about half way up the yard. I tore through the living room and the kitchen, and then streaked out the door screaming.

"Bo! He's here, he's here!"

I jumped off the porch and ran across the big yard as hard and fast as I could. I was in his arms, legs wrapped around his waist in seconds. I couldn't hug him hard enough. By the time he had hugged, kissed and twirled me around, everyone else was there for their hugs and the tearful reunion.

We surrounded him as we went into the house. Everyone was talking at once, wiping tears and stealing another hug. The excitement was electric. Jim and I couldn't stay close enough to him. We sat by him at dinner, hanging on every word and every story. I loved to hear everything he had to tell us, whether I understood it or not. I needed to soak up as much as I could, because I knew he would be gone way too soon.

Now the feast began and it was grandma who would shine for a while.

Ron would fuss over her dinner and say how much he missed her and Moms' cooking. It was totally the truth, no kissing up. Those two women could cook like no other. I tried to cook like them later in life and did ok, but I couldn't compare to Mom and grandma in their day.

The next two weeks flew by faster than Christmas vacation and we had to share Ron with so many people—his friends, aunts, uncles, cousins, and sometimes dates. Plus, he would always help grandpa with whatever farm thing was on the front burner. If it was work here on the farm, Jim and I would be close by, watching, or helping if it was something we were allowed to do. I continually asked Mom, "How many days are left?" She would get that sad painful look and give me a number. As the countdown got smaller, I felt scared again. I hated to watch him leave, so I would try not to think about it. Sometimes I would even pretend he was here for good. That only worked for so long, and then I would see the big Navy duffle bag stretched out somewhere, waiting to be filled with his clean clothes.

Jim had been out on the tractor with Ron a couple times on his last leave, plowing for Grandpa. He was barely eight so Ron had tied him on the fender of the tractor with his jacket. Jim was afraid of the big beast, so he and Ron sang, "She'll be coming around the mountain" to ease Jim's fear of the farm equipment.

All too soon, the night before Ron had to leave arrived. As he packed his things, Jim and I sat on the floor and watched him fold his clothes and pack that dreaded bag. We stayed up as long as allowed and then shuffled off to bed, dragging ourselves toward the bedroom like we were walking the green mile. We could hear the adults still laughing and talking into the night. I was so envious of spending the last few hours with Ron and we had to be in bed. I didn't want to go to sleep knowing that although I could hear his laughter and camaraderie with family now, tomorrow it would be empty again.

In the morning, Ron was packed and waiting for his Navy buddies to stop and pick him up. Grandma and Mom had made a big breakfast and all had enjoyed the food. The mood was quite different from the welcome home dinner we had shared just two weeks ago. Everyone was trying to be cheerful, talking about all different subjects and avoiding the obvious one. No one said "My God, I just hate this."

Ron's Navy buddies showed up and met the family with hand-shakes, hellos, and so glad to meet you by everyone. We walked Ron to the car and put his bag in the trunk, followed by hugs, kisses and tearful good-byes all around. I hated this, hated this and hated this. I always cried because it hurt so badly not to. In minutes, he was in the car and pulling away, still waving and shouting that he would see us soon.

The walk back up to the house was quiet, accompanied by sniffling and sighs.

Ron was gone.

Ron in the Navy

Goodbye to the Farm Life

Another school year was almost over and Mom was working two jobs while grandma was in charge of the house. Grandpa was doing all the planting and harvesting, taking care of the livestock and working nights on the county road crew. Everyone helped with the garden. Jim and I had daily chores of feeding the chickens, gathering eggs, raking leaves, helping with dishes, the laundry and anything else we were told to do.

Work was never ending on a farm.

Grandpa suffered a massive heart attack and everything came to a halt. For a while it wasn't certain if he would make it. After a few touch and go days and nights, he fought his way back. He had damage to his heart that wouldn't be able to be repaired, but he could live a fairly normal life, as long as he quit farming.

Who would take care of the farm? Their two sons, Theron and Harry, had their own families and jobs. Ron was in the Navy. There was no one to do the farm work. After much discussion and advice from doctors, it was decided that the farm had to be sold. My grandparents would retire and move to Crawfordsville where their fourth child, Arletta, and her family lived. Since Mom worked there, the decision was made to sell the farm, and move our trailer on the property in Crawfordsville. That way, everyone could help take care of grandpa.

I wasn't upset about the move, because I didn't like my school and had decided I wasn't very fond of farm life. In Crawfordsville I would be closer to my cousins and maybe a new school would be better. But I was afraid of grandpa, as dying was foreign to me and very frightening. He seemed so fragile and every time he made a noise or winced for any reason, I freaked out.

The entire summer we moved and re-built the dumpy little house my grandparents had bought. Uncles, cousins, and son-in-laws helped with the mountains of work that was required to make the house livable. Mom decided not to move our old trailer from the farm, and bought a new one. It was so exciting to have a brand new home to move into, even though it was a trailer.

Finally it all came together. Remodeling was finished, our new trailer was moved in and the farm was sold. Mom, Jim and I were tucked into the third back-yard of my grandparents.

Life with grandma had not changed. It was all work and no play for her, so she seemed to think that's how we should live. She harped and complained at us all the time. On one occasion, I had forgotten to take a paper to school and Mom was at work so she couldn't bring it to me. I was sent home to retrieve the homework and since it was quite a hike to school from our house, it took at least a half hour one way. I got home, found my paper and was ready to start back when I noticed it was raining. I knew it would be a long shot to ask grandma for a ride, but hoped that she would feel sorry for me having to walk in the rain.

Grandma's cousin and her husband were there and when I asked, Aunt

Gladys said, "Oh Ruth, go ahead and run her back, we will wait for you."

"No, she can walk. A little rain won't hurt, she won't melt. Go on and get back to school," she said.

I cried for a while as I walked in the rain, since no one would know because I was soaked anyway. *Mom would have taken me, Ron would have taken me,* I thought. I vowed that day if I ever had children or grandchildren, I would never make them feel the way she made me feel.

Around this time, Mom was introduced to Charlie through some cousins. He lived in Covington, about 35 miles away, and rumor was that he had money and lived on a large farm, in a beautiful ranch house.

He was very nice to Mom and took her to dinners and movies. He took us to the drive-in and to Dog n

Suds for dinner. He was polite and quiet, but didn't seem to have much of a personality. Even at nine years old I wondered what the heck Mom saw in him, because before we knew it, they were engaged.

They got married and the best part of the wedding was that Ron came home to give her away. It was a short visit, but at the time it was worth Mom marrying this strange little man to have Ron home for a visit.

We were moving again, this time away from grandma and into our own home. Mom and our new stepdad, Charlie, had bought a two story house, with a basement, a back yard, and a garage in Covington, 35 miles away. Jim and I had our own rooms, with doors and locks. I was so excited about the house being miles away from my grandma that I could have peed on myself.

School had already started, but it was still in the first grading period. I was in fifth and Jim in fourth grade. *What will this school be like?* I wondered whether these kids could be any worse than the battle zone group in Waynetown or the last school. I was not going to be fooled by fake friends again and would have my guard up.

Mom took us to school the first day to enroll, meet the principal and teachers. After school, she was waiting to drive us home. It almost scared me and I thought something was wrong, but it wasn't. Mom just wanted to pick us up after our first day since she wasn't working. What a treat!

The new school was rather nice, but I wasn't going to let that fool me. I was self-conscious about the way I looked because I was a bit overweight and my clothes didn't seem to measure up to the others. But the kids all talked to me and invited me to eat lunch with them, play at recess and even walk home with the ones who lived my direction. I felt myself wanting to let my guard down and get to know them, but then I would have a flashback of previous schools. I was not going to go through that again. If I really started believing they wanted to be friends, then the joke would be on me. I would just play along and wait for the ball to drop as I was sure it would.

The first week I decided the teachers must have threatened the kids to be nice, as that seemed to be the only answer. The popular group, the ones who wore better clothes, were smart, funny and all hanging together, had asked me to be with them at recess, and helped me with everything a new kid needed, like directions to the bathroom, lunch room, and where to be at recess. They kept asking me to play with them, walk to class with them, and eat lunch with them. *What the heck is going on here?* I didn't think for one minute it was sincere.

I kept waiting for the other shoe to drop, but it never did. Not in the fifth grade, or any of the following seven grades to graduation, when I was still totally in love with my school, my friends, and my little town.

Jim made friends, too. We both had found something we had never had before - a home and a school where we were accepted. The only thing missing from our life was our big brother.

Charlie, our new step-dad, seemed nice enough, but we were too young to understand, or even notice, what was going on between him and Mom. He was clueless when it came to discipline or raising children and was more like another kid for Mom, than a parent or a partner. He let us do anything we wanted to do, and on weekends he would take us and our friends to the drive in-movies, where he would pay for their admission and all snacks. Mom never went and this started to bother me as I worried that she was lonely. I didn't understand why didn't she go with us?

It wasn't long before our house became the hangout place for the neighborhood and all of our school friends. We would have marathon hide-n-seek sessions that would last for hours on end. On some evenings, the older brothers of our friends and our crazy step-dad would join in. Some of our hiding places were so good and the area we hid in was a three block area so they were never found and we would wait forever for the hider to realize the group had given up and gone on to another game. Our base was the enormous gas tank sitting in the back yard. As people were found, we would all sit up on the gas tank and talk or cheer on the person still seeking. These games would last into the night.

Our social status and success was in part due to Mom and our step-dad letting our house become the hub and safe haven for all our friends. This happened from the time we moved to Covington until each of us got married and left home. Our lives had done a complete 360 in one short year, so it was no surprise I felt I couldn't survive any other place on the earth. My life had changed so drastically when we moved to Covington, I was sure if I had to leave my little town, I would shrivel up and die of a broken heart.

I wanted Ron to see how our lives had changed, that we were not the pathetic little brother and sister he left behind. We were becoming siblings with personalities and interests outside of following him around like lost puppies. I wanted him to see how much I loved his music and had developed a taste of my own. I couldn't wait for him to see the life we were building. I wanted to have fun with him and do things he would enjoy and not just things he did to entertain us or take care of us.

I was so happy in Covington and I wanted him to make a life here with us. I couldn't imagine how life would be now, with him with us.

By this time Ron was stationed in Hawaii where he was an electrician on a subma-

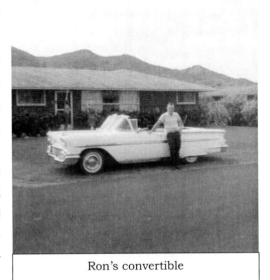

Ron's convertible

rine, the USS Bream. He loved Hawaii and his letters were full of stories and pictures of his temporary home. He hunted in his off time, had girlfriends and even bought a convertible to drive around the island. He was doing everything he could to take advantage of the time he was stationed in this paradise called Hawaii.

What he didn't tell us in his letters was that he was often out on missions in the Cold War. I learned of this much later when I overheard him telling Mom about a mission somewhere in the Pacific Ocean. The submarine had to sit on the bottom of the ocean for days, waiting for the enemy to go away so they could surface and it was running out of air. I didn't understand the story and it scared me, but at the time Ron was sitting in our kitchen all safe and sound.

USS Bream

Ron wrote letters to all of us and I loved getting my own personal letters from him, addressed just to me. I couldn't wait to answer his letter and write funny stuff on the envelope like he did. When it was airmail, he would print FLY IT really big on the outside of the envelope. I thought it was amusing since it was air mail, so of course they would fly it. When Jim and I were little, Ron would print all of our letters so we could read them ourselves. He could have just told Mom to tell us that he loved us, but he always wrote letters to each of us.

A few times Ron tried to fool us and come home on leave and surprise every-one, but he had a hard time pulling it off with Mom. The content of his letters would change since he was trying to be so careful and not give anything away, but he would start

Ron in Hawaii

communicating differently. She would always say, "He is either coming home or something is wrong."

He never forgot our birthdays and he would send a card and money or a present from where ever he was in the world. The gift might be late, but it always came. If the present was going to be late, he would send a letter or short note and tell us it was coming. He even sent us valentine cards and I kept them all.

Life Changes

As I said, Jim and I had made friends at school almost immediately. I had become friends with a girl named Marla who lived the next block over. We walked to school, did homework, roller-skated, played hop scotch, and started liking boys together. I was old enough and living in town so I could go to the little movie theater, slumber parties and swimming at the park pool. I joined brownies and sold cookies. I went to the library and checked out books. I felt like I'd never lived until I moved to Covington.

The most wonderful part of our new life was Mom being home with us. She would be there most every day when we returned from school, and the aroma of her fabulous cooking would greet us when we walked in the door. On some days homemade chocolate chip cookies would just be coming out of the oven as we bounced inside.

Our grandparents were no longer our authoritative figures, but that didn't stop grandma from giving her views on everything. She criticized how we got a drink, whether we should be allowed to have friends, what clothes we wore, and how many times we wore them before we were allowed to put them into the dirty laundry. I dreaded seeing her.

Marla and I were walking home from school one day, laughing, eating a candy bar and talking about the day's events. She lived three blocks from school, I lived four. If I went to her house, I could cut through the alley and mine was almost straight from hers, both in the middle of the block. But instead, most of the time we would stay on the sidewalk going straight toward my house, get almost there, then walk back to hers, then back to mine, going back and forth giggling like crazy. Who was going to be the last to go on and leave the other to walk by herself?

This particular afternoon when we cleared the corner and my house came into view, I saw the dreaded black rambler and knew that my grandparents were visiting.

"Oh no," I said. I sat smack down on the sidewalk and began to cry.

"Why is she here?"

"I'll go with you," Marla said. "She can't be so bad if some else is there!"

"Bet me, buckwheat." I said. "She doesn't care who is around. She thinks she is the boss of the world." I wiped at my tears. "I'll get griped at because you are with me."

"Why would she care? It's not any of her business if your Mom doesn't care," Marla said. "Let's ask your

Mom if you can come to my house. We'll tell her we have a big homework project and we're going to do it at my house."

"It's no use," I said, still in tears. But out of desperation, I thought it was worth trying. Anything was worth trying to get out of listening to her pick on everything I did, said or ate. I gathered my books, brushed myself off and we started toward my house. Mom greeted us at the front door and I asked her if I could go to Marla's.

"Don't you have chores to do, without company?" grandma said, giving her two cents worth. "Then you can help your mother with dishes after supper. I'm sure you can do your homework by yourself!"

Mom gave me an expression of 'please just do it so I don't have to listen to her.'

I turned and guided Marla out the door and away from my grandma before she insulted Marla.

"Told you," I said, holding back tears. I walked back into the house as soon as my face wasn't red from crying so I would have to hear what a big cry baby I was. I went to the cabinet to get a glass for a drink of water and it started, "You don't need to get a clean glass every time you get a drink," she said.

Where am I supposed to get it from, the bottom of the sink with all the dirty dishes? Then I remembered they would leave after supper and go back to their house, 35 miles away. The thought made me smile. That gave me the strength to get through the rest of the evening letting her complaining remarks slide right off.

By my sixth year of school I was so absorbed in my friends, school, and new town that I couldn't imagine living any other place on earth. Mom was still home with us and Jim was doing ok with everything, just not loving school. Our stepdad worked at the International Tractor parts store and still liked hanging out with our friends, rather than Mom. He was starting to give me the creeps and I wasn't sure why. Ron's Navy career was keeping him stationed in Hawaii.

Even though I was a thousand times happier, missing my big brother had not changed. I looked forward to his furloughs and couldn't wait to show him off to my friends. He only had another couple months and he would be out of the service. I couldn't wait to have him home with us. I had plans to get him to fall in love with Covington so when he got out of the Navy he would want to live with us. I worried he might want to live in Hillsboro, where he had spent a lot of his childhood and teen years, and where some his friends still lived.

"Leave?" Mom said out loud one day while reading a letter. "He only has a few months left, why are they letting him come home so close to his discharge date?" A look of knowing came over her face, her shoulders dropped and she let the letter fall to the table.

"What did he say?" Jim and I asked her.

"He has signed up for more time."

"Did he say that? " Jim asked.

"Not in so many words. But that's the only reason he would be coming home so close to his discharge date."

He was home in a couple weeks and we were thrilled to see him. I wanted to blurt out the white elephant questions immediately after our reunion hugs, but I kept my promise to Mom. She had made Jim and I swear not to mention anything about her suspicions.

"He will tell us in his own time," she had said.

After supper and conversation, Jim and I were sent off to bed and we knew it was time for adult conversation. We hugged and squeezed our big brother, then nodded our heads with anticipation of the promises he made of what we would do together the next day.

As soon as I got into my room and closed the door, I dropped to the floor and put my ear to the heat vent. My room was above Mom's bedroom, off the kitchen where they would be talking. Mom's kitchen was the hub of the house, and the coffee pot was always on.

It took me a minute to get my ear situated so I could hear them. I had been using my register to eavesdrop on private conversations since we moved to this house. I would lie on my stomach; head turned sideways and ear on the register.

Mom and Ron were still discussing the plans for tomorrow. I hadn't missed anything.

They made small talk for a few minutes before Ron told Mom he had something to tell her.

"I know you do," she said.

There was a pause and I could hear him pour another cup of coffee, then pull out a chair. I knew he was sitting down in front of Mom.

"I signed up for another year," he said. "I couldn't pass up the bonus, besides I can get another year of schooling and it will give me more of an edge on jobs when I get out."

"I knew what you were going to tell me."

There was silence.

"It's ok Mom," Ron said. "I'll get to stay in Hawaii and its only one more year. It will be over before you know it." I heard the chair scrape along the floor. "Sis and JT are doing ok, and Charlie will be here taking care of you guys."

"I know Son, I know. It's not your responsibilities anyway. I want you to do this if it's what you want. The money will be great for you and you are safe in Hawaii. We'll be fine, I was just looking forward to you being here with us," Mom said. "I knew it anyway. I knew the only way you could come home so close to your discharge was if you had signed up for more time. You can't fool your ole Mom, you know that." She blew her nose.

I heard the chair move and assumed that Ron had gotten up and hugged her. Tears covered my face and I needed to get tissues to wipe them and my running nose. I got up, grabbed the box, slipped under my covers and cried myself to sleep.

The next day Jim and I were told of Ron's re-up and I had to act like I was surprised or get busted for eaves-dropping. I would tell myself that the goodbyes would get easier, but the next two weeks flew by and he was leaving again. I would always end up crying and Ron would be positive, smiling and promising that he would see us soon. It was never soon enough for me.

The only difference was that now I was much happier in my life than all the years before we moved to Covington. So instead of missing Ron while wallowing in the misery of living on the farm with my grandparents, I had my friends to help take away some of the sadness.

Time moved on and I left behind my little girl world of dolls, hop scotch and jump rope and entered into the magic world of music. I loved rock and roll and for Christmas that year I begged for a transistor radio so I hear all the great songs coming out of a station in Chicago, WLS. Ron had introduced me to these addictive tunes in his last two years of high school (sock hops were big in his teen years), and I was already a big fan of The Everly Brothers, Elvis, and all the doo wop groups. Ron had even taught me to do The Hop, a dance named after the song of the same name that you had to do in your socks.

Jim and I had grown apart as we grew up. I no longer felt the need to watch over him as he could take care of himself. Sadly, he and I fought constantly if we were in the same room, which drove Mom crazy.

Another bonus of living in Covington was having my favorite cousin, Brenda, living only ten miles away. She was four years older than me, a sophomore in high school.

In those years, family recreation was going to each other's house for the evening or Sunday dinner. Brenda's brother, Gary, the oldest by two years, was a daredevil, rough neck farm boy who wasn't afraid of anything. He was always daring Jim and me to do something we had been warned against, concerning the farm and animals. I hated being called a baby or scaredy cat, so I would take on his dares and either get into trouble or be scared half out of my mind 90% of the time we spent with them.

Grandpa had pigs on the farm and always warned us to stay away from the mother pigs with new babies.

"Don't go near those old sows," he said. "If you get near their babies, they will rip your legs off and eat anything they can get. They are mean."

This didn't seem to scare Gary and one day he, Shirt (Shirley's nickname), Jim and I were playing in the barn. Gary was acting like a monkey crossing the beam above the sows' pens, arms stretched out balancing himself.

"Hey, grandpa said we're not supposed to be up there. If you fall the mother pigs will eat you," I said.

"OK little cry baby, why don't you come up here and try it yourself," he said.

"No way! I don't want to get eaten by a pig or be in trouble with grandpa."

"They won't hurt you, baby face." He continued to taunt me.

So I made the walk across the pig pen, shaking all the way, knowing it could be the day of my death—by pigs. I was stupid to let him badger me into such crazy stuff, but it continued for several years.

Then one day, I walked into Brenda's house and announced that I was done putting up with Gary's stunts. I asked if I could hang out with her and she welcomed me with open arms.

Brenda and I attended the same school, even though she was four years ahead of me. She had band practice once a week after school, and on those nights she got to stay all night at our house. We would talk Mom into letting us to go to the movies, even on a school night, especially if an Elvis movie was playing. We both loved Elvis and I had every one of his records.

On movie nights we would pop a grocery bag full of popcorn, hide it in one of my mother's old purses, and head to the theater four blocks away.

It cost a quarter to get in and a dime for a pop.

If we didn't go to the movies, we would talk Mom into letting us make spaghetti. That meant a trip to the IGA where Brenda would poke her finger through the hamburger package and eat raw hamburger. I would nearly puke, then laugh, then nearly pee myself. We have spent a lifetime laughing and crying, but we do it together, which makes everything ok.

Mom's Health

Mom began experiencing late night episodes where she would have excruciating pain in her stomach. She had tests done and when the results came back, she was scheduled for gall bladder surgery. Plans were made for grandma to come and stay with us so she could help with cooking, laundry and making sure Jim and I got to school. Not only was I scared about Mom's surgery, but I dreaded grandma coming.

My first concern was Mom, and I prayed for her to be ok. She came through the surgery ok, but was in the hospital for about a week. Her recuperation took several weeks, grandma stayed for most of that time, and I was miserable.

It started the minute I stepped in the door the first day she was at our house. I couldn't walk across the floor to suit her. I laid my things in the wrong place. I couldn't talk to my friends on the phone. I was not allowed to do anything or have anyone over when she was there.

Just about the time I thought I couldn't handle grandma anymore, Mom started re-gaining her strength and grandma could go home. But within a few months Mom was scheduled for surgery again. We didn't know why and no one was telling us the reason.

Jim and I begged Mom to let Brenda come and stay instead of grandma. She agreed, but only if we followed all of her rules. I didn't care how many or how ridiculous I thought Mom's rules might be, if it could replace grandma during Mom's surgery, I would have done anything. Mom was back into the hospital, but Jim and I were not allowed to miss school to be with her so we had to wait until we got home before we knew if she was ok. When we got home grandma and Aunt Tootie were there and the mood was pretty serious. Jim and I asked how Mom was doing.

"She will be ok in time," Aunt Tootie said.

"When can she come home?" I asked.

"It will be about a week," my grandma said. "But you two need to listen to me and remember what I am saying. Your mother is very sick and will need help when she gets home. The two of you need to straighten up and quit your fussing and fighting."

"Ok, grandma."

"I'm serious. If she dies it will be your fault for fighting all the time," she said.

I got cold chills over my body. *Mom might die and it'll be my fault?*

Brenda, Jim and I stood motionless staring at grandma and Aunt Tootie.

"What's wrong with her?" I asked.

"She had to have a surgery, and that's all you need to know," Grandma spat the words at us.

Aunt Tootie didn't say anything while grandma gave orders and said she would be back in a day or so to see Mom.

"You better behave yourselves," she repeated.

After they left, Jim, Brenda and I stood in the kitchen and stared at each other.

"Do you know what she was talking about?" I asked Brenda.

"I have no idea."

"Can you make someone die from fighting with your brother?" I asked.

"I never heard of that," Jim said.

"I never have either," Brenda said.

"Man, we have to be the worse kids ever," I said. I dropped my head to the kitchen table. "We will have to never fight again, Jim."

"No kidding," Jim said, as he also slouched into a chair. "We're awful kids. Mom must really be sick, but I didn't know you could get that sick from your kids fighting."

"We better do our homework and clean something," I said.

"Yeah, that's a good idea," Brenda said.

"Ok," Jim said.

We did our homework, straightened the house and washed the dishes.

Then we locked the doors and got ready for bed. Charlie had been with Mom and when he came home, we asked him how she was. He told us she would be ok in time and that was about as much help as nothing.

I had a hard time falling asleep that night. I was so worried and scared about Mom. *How did we make her sick? What if she dies?* I couldn't live without my Mom, and if I helped to kill her, I wouldn't even want to live. She was so good to us, how could I be so horrible and make her sick by fighting with Jim.

What's going to happen when Ron finds out Jim and I made Mom sick fighting over dumb stuff? We were in so much trouble.

Brenda, Jim and I got through the next few days without a hitch and as predicted, Mom came home in a week. Jim and I did as much as possible to help her recover and were on our good behavior for weeks. Brenda had to go home a couple days after Mom came home, so grandma and grandpa came and stayed for about a week. My life went into the toilet, but it didn't matter this time. All I cared about was Mom.

She was weak for a long time and looked so bad I was scared to death.

But in time she began to regain her strength and started to look like Mom again.

Our grandparents left a week later and grandma gave us an hour lecture on chores we had to do every day, and reminded us that we better not argue about anything. As bad as I hated to admit that I needed or wanted her there, Jim and I benefitted from them staying to help with Mom, housework, laundry and cooking. Having an adult there to make sure Mom was ok gave me comfort since we didn't even know what was wrong with her. Mom recovered from her surgery and our lives migrated back to our old habits.

A couple of months later, Mom received a call stating that our teachers wanted to talk with her. They were concerned that something was bothering Jim and me as our grades had dropped and our attention was elsewhere. They indicated it had started when Mom was in the hospital, but they had waited to call until they heard that she was ok.

Grandma's comment had scared Jim and me into believing we had caused Mom to be so sick. We did need someone to shake a knot in our tails, as Ron would have stated, and tell us we were going to kill our mother was a bit over the line.

It wasn't until about ten years later, that Mom and I had a conversation about her illness. She told me that she had uterine cancer and had asked all of the adults to not tell us, so we wouldn't worry. She had a complete hysterectomy, which was a total success.

When I told her what grandma had told Jim and I, there was a look of horror on her face. If grandma had not already passed, I think my Mom might have finally put her in her place. Standing motionless with a potato in one hand and the peeler in the other, Mom apologized as tears ran down her face.

"No wonder the teachers called me to school," she said.

"What?" I asked as I folded clothes.

"Your teachers, they called me to school to ask what was wrong with you and Jim."

"I didn't know that. What did you tell them?"

"All I could think of was you were worried about me and our household was upside down with me in the hospital. I told them to let me know if you didn't start getting better after a little time passed."

"I never knew about any of this. I didn't even realize the teachers noticed, or that we were acting any differently. Did they call you again?"

"No, and your grades went back to normal. I'm still here so I guess you quit worrying."

We started laughing, but Mom would look at me every so often and shake her head. "I can't believe she told you fellers that."

"She did. You can ask Brenda, she was there, too."

"Oh, I believe you. Why didn't you ever tell me?"

"She threatened us not to upset you and we were scared to death that we were going to kill you."

"Oh Sis, I am so sorry."

"It's ok, Mom. It wasn't your fault and its long past now. She can't do that crap anymore."

As I looked at my mother, I wondered how on earth she turned out so great with a mother like that.

As a teenager, I became very close friends with two other girls in my class, Deb English and Nance Parke. Marla was still around, but her involvement with boys was a little too advanced for my taste, so we parted ways.

Deb and her family had moved to Covington from a town in Illinois when we were in 8th grade. She had one brother and two sisters, all younger. She had a baby sister that had been killed when her uncle had accidently ran over her in their driveway years before we met. This tragedy was the most horrible thing I had ever heard of in my life and I couldn't believe it was true. How had they managed to live through such a horror? They had gotten up every day and went on with their lives, and I couldn't understand that kind of loss or pain.

Deb's house was about four blocks from me, farther from school. When I learned this I asked her to stop at my house and walk with a group of us who walked to school together. I remembered how I felt when everyone was so great to me when I was the new girl, so I offered friendship and she accepted.

She was the prettiest girl I'd ever seen with eyes so blue they sparkled and hair that was shiny and bounced as she walked. I thought she would be stuck up, but she seemed rather naive.

Nance had been going to Covington school since kindergarten. I knew her, but never had any personal connection until one summer day when she stopped to talk to Deb and I while we were in my yard. She was babysitting at a house up the street and wondered if she could borrow a couple records to listen to for the afternoon. Deb went inside and got a Beatles and

71

Herman Hermit's album. Nance accepted the loan and rode off on her rickety bike that we later named the carnival crud. There was something about Nance that drew Deb and me to her. She was very smart in school and knew the Bible inside out, but I wasn't sure about her common sense. Was she slow, sly or joking? It was hard to tell the difference for quite some time.

Before the summer was over we were inseparable. We took turns staying at Deb's and my house every weekend, weekdays if we could get by with it. We didn't stay at Nance's house as her parents were strict and very religious. Her mom didn't approve of Deb or me as she didn't approve of anyone unless they spent all their time with church. Deb and I went to the First Baptist church, same as Nance and her family, but we didn't measure up. She tried to push certain kids on Nance who she thought were holy enough, but most of the kids she approved of were not what they seemed. They just knew how to fake it with adults. Still Nance couldn't convince her Mom that Deb and I were the better choice of friends.

With Jim and his friends, we continued our neighborhood camaraderie. There were enough of us to have softball games on the empty lot up the block, and the hide and seek marathons were starting to fade. We would also organize a group, usually five or six of us, pack lunches and take canteens of water. Then we would take off early on a summer day and ride our bikes 10 miles south of Covington to an old abandoned saw mill named Snoddy's Mill. Ten miles was absolutely forever and would take us about three hours or more to get there. By the time we climbed hills, took breaks, got chased by dogs and stopped for repairs, we would arrive to the welcoming site of the swimming hole.

Snoddy's Mill had a dam to jump off and a water hole big enough to swim. We would spend hours swimming and nosing around the old mill that we were not supposed to go into. Mom would show up in the late afternoon to take us home, as we were all too tired to ride back. We would load all the bikes in the truck, then some of us would pile in the front and some in the truck bed, and back to Covington we went.

On days we couldn't go to the mill, we would have cops and robbers bike games, boys against girls. We would ride and chase each other all over town for the entire day. There was also a very nice city park with a huge pool. We just had to be home by the time the street lights came on.

Life was good and we only had a year before Ron would be home for good.

Ron Comes Home

It had been five long years, but summer of 1963 was here, Ron was being discharged out of the Navy, and he was coming home for good. I was so excited for him to see how grown up I thought I had become.

He would be flying from Hawaii to California, and then Mom and Charlie would pick him up and vacation a little on the way back. While they were away, I stayed with Mom's sister, and Jim stayed with Charlie's sister, patiently awaiting our big brothers return.

We had been six and seven when he left, and now were twelve and thirteen. A lot had changed while he was away, and even though he had been home several times, being with us full time would show him how much we had changed.

He was 23 years old and had been all over the world, flying in airplanes and sitting on the bottom of the oceans in a submarine. He had been in several countries in the Orient, stationed in Hawaii and other parts of the United States. He was now a grown man, but I didn't have one fleeting moment of doubt that he would be the same super big brother he had been before he went to the Navy.

I couldn't wait to get him home and show him how much I had grown up. I wanted to play my records for him, introduce him to my friends and let him see I wasn't a baby any longer. I was excited at the prospect that we could be friends, have fun together, listen to music, go to movies, and maybe I could do things for him now. After all, he wouldn't have to take care of me any longer.

The reunion was as grand as always. There was family everywhere, laughing, hugging, kissing, eating, and a serene feeling I had never experienced in Ron's previous homecomings. It was the comfort of knowing that in two weeks or a month he would still be here.

He had presents for us—Mom, Jim, me, Charlie, our aunts, grandma, and grandpa. All the females received a beautiful musical jewelry box from Hong Kong, silk scarves and bracelets. The guys got carved pocket knives from Hong Kong, cigarette lighters, and a ring for Jim. He also brought Mom silk pillowcases and head scarves with embroidered sentiments. It felt like Christmas, only better, because we had Ron instead of Santa Claus.

Ron had sold his convertible before he left Hawaii and another convertible was the object of his pursuit as he started job and car shopping the next day. *I can see us riding around in a hot looking convertible with Ron at the wheel.* He hadn't bought the car yet and I was already picturing my friends being envious of Jim and me.

Number one on his job quest was being a state trooper. When it did not happen fast enough, he accepted a job at the General Electric factory in Danville, Illinois, about 13 miles from Covington.

"It will do until the police thing comes into play," he said to Mom.

After getting home from the Marines, Ron's high school friend Jay, got a job at the same factory, so many nights he would stay at our house instead of going another 25 miles to Hillsboro where he was living with his family. So I had my big brother and Jay (who I had a secret crush on) at home all the time.

Ron and Jay were double dating, riding around in each of their convertibles, and hanging out at our house. I had learned to cook a little and it was my greatest thrill to cook dinner when they were going to be there. My specialty was Italian spaghetti. Mom had taught me to cook the sauce like my dad who had been a mess sergeant in the Army. Mom said he made the best sauce she had ever eaten. I couldn't stand him, but for

Ron's convertible

some reason, I relished in the feat of creating his sauce. The other thing I enjoyed cooking was burnt weenies on the grill. They teased me because I usually ended up with most of them black, but what I didn't tell them was that I liked them that way. It was a joke for years that if I was cooking on the grill, someone would say, "Sis is burning weenies for supper."

During that time, Ron worked on our house, the yard, and with Jim and me.

He was right back helping Jim with school, and helping me with my diet. At one point he promised me a new wardrobe if lost a certain amount of weight.

After working at GE for a few months, Ron gave up trying to get a job with the state police. The reason he was not hired was that he was not tall enough. What were they talking about? Couldn't they see that he was ten feet tall? *What a loss for them!* He had muscles on top of muscles.

I had seen him working on the farm, picking up heavy farm equipment, and shoveling mountains of stuff from one place to another. He could throw enormous bales of hay from the truck to wagons and to the hay mow. He would do 12 hour stretches plowing or planting, sleep a few hours and be back at it by dawn. Ron and grandpa always had to do things with the livestock, even things I didn't understand then. Ron could hold down pigs three times bigger than he was, while grandpa castrated them, while the pigs fought, squealed and scared me to death.

He could dig deep holes and put big fence posts into the ground, then stretch wire and make long fences to keep the livestock inside. And all of this was before he had joined the Navy, now he was worldly and knowledgeable. I believe their denial of his employment insulted me as much as it did him. I knew his worth and I didn't care about regulations. I felt bad for him as this was the first thing I had seen him attempt that he was not able to accomplish.

There was a silver lining to this cloud, as he joined our town's police force. I was ecstatic as this meant he might be there forever, even though he talked of living out west and working for the DNR in Colorado. My life was too good to think about him leaving, so I decided not to think of him leaving again, and would pretend this is forever.

The first year Ron was on the force he had to drive his own car, a ford convertible, on the job. If he needed to pull someone over he would pick up the red cop light magnet and slam

Ron in the Covington Police Force 1966

it on the dash of his car. The red light would flash and my brother's car would be turned into a police cruiser. There were three officers and the chief of police, all well-known and recognizable. On and off duty, everyone knew the police cars, even though they were their personal cars.

Some of the officers had family members who were in the habit of getting into trouble and expecting their relative cop to get them out. It made my brother furious. He informed Jim and I there would be no special treatment for us.

"Do not get into anything that Mom and I have taught you not to," he said. "I will not use my job to break the law to protect you, not even curfew. So don't do it, don't put me in that position."

"We won't Ron, we promise."

"I will not be like the other officers who are covering up their nieces, nephews, brothers and sisters law breaking habits," he said. "In fact, you two will need to be better than the others, set an example. I don't want our family to be the talk of the town like what's going on now." He said as he buckled his gun belt.

"Ok Bo, I promise, we wouldn't do that to you," I said.

"Me too, we won't do anything you don't want us to," Jim said.

"Ok, just so we are straight on this. I know you won't let me down. I just need to be sure we are on the same page. I can't have my little brother and sister doing anything that I am so against," he said. "You guys have always been good, so I'm not really worried about you. I just need to let you know how important this to me. I need to have you guys on the right side, with me."

He gave Jim a slap on the back and me a squeeze on my shoulders as he went on to talk to Mom where he relayed his complaints to Mom. He was dead serious about his warning. If his intention was to get our attention, he had succeeded.

One Friday night, in Ron's second year on the force, he knew he was facing a long night. He had been around long enough to have made some enemies and there were a handful of delinquents bragging that they were going to get Smith. Ron had arrested them for break-ins, traffic related tickets, drug busts and numerous offenses.

He stopped at the house early in the evening to get something he had forgotten. Deb was spending the night and he made a point of telling Mom that Jim or I had better not be out after curfew.

"If you need to do anything or get anything, do it before 11:00," as he checked something he stuffed into his back pocket.

"Ok Bo," I said. "We are staying here tonight."

"Good, see to it that you do. I don't need to be worrying about the two of you with all the crap that is going on out there tonight."

"Ok, son," Mom said.

We had no intentions of breaking our promise as we never disobeyed Ron. It wasn't even in our thought process. Then about 10:50 p.m., Deb and I were getting ready to play some albums.

"Crap, Deb, where is the Beatles album you were going to bring?" I asked, looking through her stuff.

"It's in my bag," she said.

"No, it is not!" My voice raised in panic.

"We have to go get it," we said at the same time. We could not get through a Friday night without it or the whole night would be ruined.

We flew down the stairs screaming at my Mom as we slid into the kitchen on one of her throw rugs.

"Do we have time to go to Deb's? We have to get a record!"

The three of us looked at the infamous clock on the kitchen wall, the clock that would be crucial in so many of our endeavors. It was the only thing on the entire wall, and it nearly screamed the time of 10:58 at us.

"Mom, we have to get to Deb's, we have to. We have to have the new Beatles record here. It has the words to all the songs and pictures," I said.

"Linda Jo, you know perfectly well what your brother told you about curfew. I am not going to get him mad at me for letting out after what he said only a couple of hours ago."

"Then you can take us, ok?"

"Have you forgotten? The car is in the garage and Charlie is on a Chicago run for parts, so the truck is gone also. Looks like you fellers are out of luck," she said.

"We can set the clock back and pretend we thought it was 10:30," I said.

My mother looked at me over the top of her glasses and rolled her eyes. It wasn't even good enough to get a reply.

"Mom, Ron will never know. We can go through the alley, run across Liberty Street, through the cemetery and come up Deb's alley and into her backyard. We can be there in five minutes, get the record, back in about 12 minutes."

"You are going to go through the cemetery?" she asked with surprise.

"Uh yeah, I think that is the fastest way," I said with hesitation.

"No, you may not," she said, as if coming to her senses. "I don't want your brother mad at me after we just promised him you would be here and not out after curfew. NO," she said with last word finality.

I went into my begging mode, pleading and promising we would not get caught. How could we? Ron would be on the street and we would be in the alleys and shadows. I knew how to wear my mother down and we did just that. By 11:30, Deb and I were sneaking down the alley that went beside our house. We stood in the shadows waiting for a break in traffic, until no cars were coming in either direction. When the cars were far enough in the distance that we could not be recognized, we started for the street, where we would cross the highway into the cemetery and be out of sight.

Just as we got to the street, a car came screeching around the corner and pulled up right in front of us. Crap, it looked like Ron's car. Crap, it was. Before we could retreat, he stuck his arm out the window and pointed right at us.

"Get your butts home, now!"

"Crap, damn, crap," I said under my breath. When we could move our feet, we ran back to the house. Crap with a capital C. Now I was in trouble with Ron, and Mom would be, too. My failure was not only the absence of the new Beatles record for Friday night, but now I had to face Ron. He would be mad at me and worst of all; I would see the disappointment in his eyes.

I had pressured Mom into this bad decision and now Ron would be upset with her. Then an ugly, selfish thought crept into my head. I had lost credibility for the next time I wanted to cheat the rulebook. I failed all the way around.

He was way too busy to come back to scold me that night, but I got a tongue lashing the next day and was grounded for a week.

We relayed our adventures to Nance the next day and I pretended to be mad at Ron for always bossing me around. The truth was, I was never mad at him, but I felt like I had to pretend to be so I would be normal. By this time, I had encountered too many sibling relationships to know ours was not the norm. All the others got tired of their older sibling telling them what to do. I didn't care if Ron told me what to do or how to do it. I had missed him so much for so long I didn't care how many times he told me to get my butt home, because I knew it meant he loved me. Even at 14 years old, I knew that but I didn't know how to explain it to my friends, so I just pretended to be aggravated.

Since Mom and Ron were so close, he shared a lot of the frustrating, amusing and irritating events of his job with her. I'm sure I wasn't supposed to hear most of it and I know I missed some, but I did overhear a lot.

He told Mom the job was not what he envisioned and some days he felt like he was babysitting for our small town. He found couples parked in the alleys that were not married to each other and discovered a Key Club. I had to do a little research to find out what a key club was. I learned that they were couples who got together at each other's houses and would throw their keys into a pile. Each woman would grab a set, and whoever owned the keys took that woman behind closed doors and had sex. I thought my brother must have been mistaken or I misunderstood him. I was positive people did not do such horrible things, especially in our little town.

Every weekend the police would get domestic abuse calls. They would rush to some woman's distress only to have her drop the charges the next morning or later that night, and bring her drunk, battering husband home.

It had been rumored that one of the more colorful families in our city had been affiliated with the mafia in years past. The father and head of the Jones family had moved his family to Covington, away from Chicago, to keep them safe. He had purchased three massive aging mansions all close in proximity to each other. They were connected by tunnels, some already in place from the Underground Railroad and some he built. The tunnels connected the houses and made an escape route down to the Wabash River in the event the FBI found his cozy little getaway where he had hid his wife and children.

Another interesting family was the Jackman family. They were very wealthy and occupied a rundown mansion close to the center of town. One of the two sons lived in or near the big house and I had seen him walking around town alone nearly every day since we moved to Covington. If he owned a car, he never drove it and I never saw him talk to anyone. I thought he was just some poor weird guy who was half crazy and he scared me.

For some reason, he took an interest in my brother, but instead of talking to him or trying to be friends, he harassed him. Late one night, Ron was sitting at his desk in the police station finishing his paperwork. All of a sudden, a giant trash can crashed through the window and landed on his desk, spilling garbage and broken glass all over him. He grabbed his nightstick and went to look for his attacker. There stood Don Jackman grinning at Ron in the alley.

"What the hell is wrong with you, Jackman?" Ron said.

"I don't like cops, Smith."

"Well, now you can spend the night disliking us more in jail!"

Ron handcuffed Don and took him to jail for the night.

Ron was Don's new interest and as the months went on, Don pulled a few more stunts.

The court house was the center of town, and the four streets surrounding it were lined with most of the businesses. One of the stores was an all-night coffee and donut shop, only four doors from the corner where the cops parked. The coffee at the shop was hot, the donuts were warm and a pretty little blonde named Carolyn worked the night shift.

One night Ron had parked his car and walked to the shop. He was sitting at the counter, taking his first sip when he looked out the window and his car was passing by, being driven by Don.

"Oh shit, there goes my car!" He spit his coffee as he yelled and ran out the door. It didn't take but a second to see that Don was not trying to get away. "Jackman, get your ass back here or I swear I will shoot you!"

Don laughed and kept driving, taunting my brother. He drove around the block and took the car back to its starting place under the clock. Ron had chased him on foot around the block. Don didn't even seem to care that he was headed back to jail, only that he had taught Smitty a lesson—don't leave your keys in the car.

Don's next escapade was one for the books. He perched himself on top of his massive three story house and sat there for four days, holding a gun.

When the police force got him down, he was headed back to jail again.

By this time I was quizzing Ron about this poor insane idiot. I wanted them to put him away for good and was ticked that he had made my brother look foolish. I was also afraid of him and worried for Ron. What if he decided to shoot Ron? I thought he was capable of anything.

"Aren't you mad at him?" I asked Ron.

"Well I'm not happy, but he's harmless," Ron said as he shined his boots.

"Harmless. How can you say that?"

"Oh Sis, he is just lonely and wants attention," he said, half smiling.

"He threw garbage on you, stole your car, and sat on his roof for days with a gun!" I was raising my voice by now.

"I know, but the gun wasn't loaded, he brought my car back and he apologized, and the garbage, well that did stink and was a hell of a mess," he said, making a funny face as if remembering the stench.

I couldn't believe my brother was amused at this stupid guy and I was still afraid of him. I tried to stir Ron up so he would feel the same way.

"Ron, he could have taken your car and wrecked it or drove it away and sold it."

"Oh Sis, he doesn't need the money." He continued working on the shine on his boots.

"What? Doesn't need the money? Are you serious? He doesn't have anything. He walks every place and he wears crappy clothes, plus that giant old house is falling down."

"Sis, he has a ton of money, hidden in places all over in that old falling down house, and under it and buried on the grounds. He could own anything in town if he wanted."

"What? Have you lost it? He is the next thing to a bum."

"Yeah in a way, he just doesn't care about things we do."

"You mean clean clothes and acting like he has a brain?"

"Pretty much." He chuckled as he put the lid on the boot polish. "His mother had all kinds of money and farm land. They made a lot of very smart investments. That's probably why he goes to all the banks, sits in the lobby and reads Forbes Magazines," Ron said. "Didn't you ever notice he doesn't work? He's one eccentric character, I give you that, but harmless, I think. He's lonely and too strange to befriend anyone."

I stared at my brother, trying to wrap my brain around what he had shared with me. If anyone else had said these things I would have laughed at them and dismissed the entire idea. But Ron had said it, so it had substance. Was he right? Was this peculiar creature I had watched skulking around town for the past four years really a misunderstood lonely man? I had believed the crazy stories of dead bodies buried under his house. I was afraid to say hi or look him in the eye. Did he do these things to Ron because he wanted to be his friend? Was he like the mysterious ladies in the movies who lived in forbidding houses at the end of the scary tree-lined street on the edge of town? Just misunderstood souls? How did Ron know this stuff?

Wanting to be the extension of my brother's knowledge and great wisdom, I decided to be nice to Don. Maybe I could change things for him and make the town see he wasn't fearsome, he just needed a friend. So the next time I saw him I waved and said hi. I got nothing. Hmm, that's disappointing, I thought. So I talked all of my friends into waving and yelling hi to him as we saw him around town. He started waving back at us and I'll bet he wondered why, after years of being ignored by most of our town, all of a sudden these teenagers were waving and yelling his name.

Not long after this conversation with Ron I was re-laying the story to Jim.

"Well," he said in a slow methodical response. "I guess Ron must not be too mad at him or worried about him doing anymore stupid stuff."

"Why do you say that?" I asked.

"Because I saw them having coffee together at the Wabash café a couple days ago."

"What?" I looked at Jim like he was mistaken, or crazy, or blind. "He wouldn't."

"Well unless he has a twin, yes he would. I saw them, and I think it's been more than once. Don shows up at the café or pool hall when Ron is in there after his shift. I think he likes talking to him."

I guessed that Ron had been right, and Don was just trying to get his attention. But having coffee with him after all the stuff he did? In my eyes, my big brother had climbed another round on the pedestal I had him on.

Ron Has a Love Interest

Ron's interest had moved from the coffee at the donut shop across the square to the Wabash Café, as the
cute blonde who worked at the shop now worked at the
café. She was a shy quiet little thing and had a boyfriend who seemed to be a big dumb oaf.

As usual, I overheard Ron telling Mom some of the
rumors floating around town about this so-called
boyfriend. At my immature age he sounded like a dork
to me and after I scoped him out, I found he was ugly to
boot. I was confident that if Ron wanted to date this
girl, all he would have to do was smile and say hi. How
could any girl resist my brother, especially when she
had an ugly stupid boyfriend?

At first she didn't give Ron much encouragement,
but he was persistent when he wanted something. Not
much time passed before she agreed to go out with him.

Immediately the boyfriend was out of the picture,
mad as the devil but a thing of the past. She was not
engaged or even going steady, so she was available in

the game of love and war. Ron and Carolyn began dating on regular basis, and it was only a few weeks before they became a couple.

Ron brought her to the house to meet the family and I wanted her to like me, because she meant a lot to Ron and that meant she would be special to me.

I was jealous of her looks and size, as she weighed about 95 pounds and was five foot tall. *Why couldn't I have been born like that instead of the fluffy kid I am?*

Since I was old enough to have jobs and was always looking to make money, Ron asked if I wanted to work with Carolyn at the restaurant. Someone was on vacation and they needed help, so I got to work with her for a few days. She did everything with such ease, and I felt like a complete klutz as I tried to do everything she did. Would I ever be able to be so efficient in a job? She could laugh and tease with the customers and serve them all at the same time. Plus, she looked adorable doing it.

In my estimation, she had the world by the tail and was the luckiest girl in the state of Indiana. She was cute as a button and so tiny it made me want to puke. She had to wear kid's clothes because size 0 in teens was too big. To add to the cuteness, she had this funny little excited giggle that even made me laugh, let alone all the guys who swarmed over her.

She was everything I wanted to be and she was stealing my big brother away. I was surprised I didn't hate her. As an adult I know that the love Ron had for me was different from what he felt for her, but at 14, being rational was not on the front burner. I'm not sure why I didn't have a jealous streak building toward her, but maybe it was watching how happy she made Ron, or because she was so easy to love. Best of all, I was becoming friends with my brother's girlfriend and I felt so grown up.

It wasn't long before rings were being whispered about and we knew Ron was serious about Carolyn. I overheard a conversion between Mom and Ron about talking to Carolyn's dad about something. Ron said he wouldn't even speak to him. I did not understand this even a little bit.

He told Mom that he sat next to her dad the week before at the pool hall in a game of cards and the man wouldn't acknowledge him. Ron and Carolyn had been dating several months and her parents had refused to meet my brother. When he picked her up for a date, they would hide until he was gone.

I didn't understand. What could they have against Ron? He walked on water in our lives. What was the matter with these people? Why wouldn't they at least meet him and find out what he was like? I thought it was weird. We all loved Carolyn, and if even if we didn't, we would have faked it for Ron.

One afternoon Ron and Carolyn were walking down the street on the square and saw her dad sitting in her parent's car. They saw this as their chance and Ron and Carolyn started for the car. Her dad immediately started to get out on the other side.

"Not going to work this time old man," my brother said under his breath. He and Carolyn split up and walked to both sides of the car, trapping him inside. Now he would have to meet my brother.

Ron introduced himself and the old man made some rude remark about Ron taking Carolyn away from her boyfriend. Apparently her parents didn't like the fact that she had broken up with the guy she was dating.

Carolyn had eight siblings and her sisters and some of her brothers were excited to meet Ron. All of them had nicknames that didn't seem to have any relevance to their real name. Carolyn's was Little Woman and her twin Marilyn's was Jane.

I guess all families have funny quirks, but it was the parents' refusal to meet Ron that did it for me. If they had met him and then didn't like him, I would still have thought they were crazy, but her parents didn't even give him a chance. In my estimation they didn't deserve such a fantastic son-in-law. But it didn't matter as the wedding and shower plans began.

I was thrilled to be a part of such a happy time in Ron's life. He cherished this little lady and I watched how he treated her, reacted to her, and respected her. I thought it was the first true love I had ever witnessed and was what I would hold out for in my life. I didn't realize it then, but it ruled and gauged my relationships forever, sometimes not always turning out very realistic.

When Carolyn asked me to be one of her brides-maids I thought I would burst with pride. I was going to be in Ron's wedding! Jim was going to be a groomsman and I saw it as another sign that we were growing up.

The only downside to being in the wedding was that I was going to have to stand next to the tiny relatives of Carolyn. Oh yuck, why hadn't I lost the weight my entire family had been after me to lose? *Can I lose 40 pounds in three months*? Even if I didn't eat anything but a banana a day I couldn't do it by the time I had a dress fitting. Crap! I was surprised Ron even wanted me in his wedding since I looked so bad. He never said anything like that to me, but I always felt like people would like me more if I was skinny. My grandma had hounded me about my weight, but she wasn't kind like my mother or Ron. Mom would talk to me and even took me to the doctor once. Ron had promised me a new wardrobe if I lost weight. I would always lose some, and then I would gain it back. I hated the way I looked, but seemed to be unable to do anything drastic about it. I promised myself that by the next big event I would be skinny.

Ron & Carolyn wedding

Ron and Carolyn were so happy on their wedding day and he had a big smile as she fed him the bite of cake at the reception. She would

97

giggle; he would squeeze her, and then give her a big kiss. She had an almost childlike personality and a tiny high pitched voice to match. Ron was an ecstatic groom and she was the blissful bride and no one could change or influence her, not even her parents who did not attend the wedding.

After the honeymoon to Niagara Falls they moved into a small upstairs apartment about six blocks away. Ron, Jim, Carolyn, Jay and I almost killed ourselves moving all of their things and wedding presents up the two flights of stairs. We laughed, joked and wore ourselves out lugging boxes and furniture up the stairs.

Ron, as usual, made even the upstairs move fun. He would tease Carolyn about something and she would giggle. How could anybody be so cute I would question my poor fat brain. I had never been around a couple who were so in love and had so much fun doing nothing and everything. I loved their love. I knew I would not settle for anything less. It also validated my already set-in-stone mindset that men only loved skinny girls and I had no hope whatsoever if I didn't lose weight.

About six months later I came home from school one afternoon and found Mom and Ron deep in a heavy conversation. I paused a moment, said hi to my big brother and disappeared. I flew up the stairs with the full intention of using the heat register as my usual listening device, but they had already walked outside to Ron's car. I watched out the window and Ron looked about as sad as I had ever seen him. Mom had that worried look she always got when one of us was in trouble or hurting.

She hugged him as he left. *Oh crap, something is wrong. Big time wrong.*

I listened for her to come inside the house, and then went down to begin my interrogation. I waited for Mom to speak, but she was wiping tears and blowing her nose. *Oh God, it's bad.*

"Mom, you have to tell me."

"I promised your brother, Linda Jo," she said, as she continued wiping her tears.

"I don't care. I am promising you that I won't let him know you told me. I am not a baby anymore. You guys are scaring me," I said. "You can't let me just wonder what I walked into. What the hell is wrong with my brother?" I cursed at my mother for effect.

"Linda Jo Smith, watch your mouth!" she said.

"Mom, you can't let me wonder and worry like that. I know something is so wrong. Is Ron sick, or Carolyn?"

"Oh honey no, nothing like that."

"Well what then? I can tell it is bad and you just can't let me be afraid. You have to tell me. I promise on everything in the world I won't let him know."

I could tell I had gotten through to her and she was going to tell me. But now I was even more scared. In a few minutes I was going to find out what had made my big brother so sad and upset.

My mother blew her nose again and looked me square in the eyes. "You have to promise me as you have never promised me before; keep this to yourself until Ron is ready for people to know."

"I promise, I promise, I promise!! What?"

"Ron is moving back home."

"What did you say?" I stared at her like she was from outer space. Maybe I misunderstood, surely I did.

"You heard me."

"What are you talking about? I don't understand. What, what? Is Carolyn coming with him? Did something happen to their apartment?"

"No Linda, she is not, he is leaving her."

"What did you say? What is wrong? I don't understand!"

"He doesn't either, I'm afraid. This time she hasn't talked to him for 13 days. He can't get her to say one word." Mom wiped at her eyes again. "She won't cook, won't do laundry, she won't even look at him. She totally shut down and he has no idea why."

"You said this time. Has she done this before?"

"This has been going on ever since they got back from their honeymoon. He has no idea what is wrong and why she won't talk. He begged her to go to counseling, but she won't respond. She can go for days and not say a word. He cooked, did the laundry and cleaned the house to see if that was the problem. She is still mad. She didn't utter a word when he told her he was moving out."

"Mom, I still don't understand. He has to have an idea what is wrong with her, none of this makes any sense at all."

"That's the problem, she just shut down and he can't find out why. He is sick and tired of begging her to talk to him. He decided to leave and see if that makes a difference."

"Oh man, they were so happy. How can you go from being so in love to this in a few short months? Ron looks like his heart is broken."

"It is Sis, it is. Just don't talk about it until he does."

"I won't Mom. I promised you, and I won't hurt Ron anymore. I'll tell you now; I will never be nice to her again. She is stupid."

"Don't say that yet, you don't know how this will turn out. If they work it out, we will act as if nothing ever happened."

"What? No I will not! I am going to treat her like she treated him. She is acting like her weird family."

"Exactly Sis, maybe that's all she knows. If they can work it out, you will treat her just like you did before. Put yourself in Ron's place. He is crazy about her and if they can get things straightened out, the last thing he needs is for you to start something. Hopefully if she ever comes back here it will mean she wants to make things right. She will probably be embarrassed. Ron needs us to be there for him and treat her like nothing happened so they won't have our family to fight about. Do you understand?"

"I guess," I said, plopping into a chair. I wanted nothing more than to march myself up to her stupid little butt and slug her. I wanted to tell her she was acting like an immature brat like her parents, who she had been so upset with. But I wouldn't, for Ron, and I had promised Mom.

I kept thinking about Ron's situation. He looked so sad and lonely, and I wondered when he would be coming home. I would do everything I could do to make him happy. I would cook his favorite foods, help with his laundry, even though he never asked or needed anyone to do all that stuff for him. I was going to make sure I acted surprised when I found out for real what was going on.

Life sure could kick you in the gut sometimes. He treated her with such respect and tenderness, like she was the most precious thing in the world to him. *What the heck was wrong with her?* Mom could tell me how to act, but she couldn't tell me how to feel.

Ron moved home and I was totally disillusioned with my brother's fairy tale marriage. If they couldn't make it, no one could. I was never going to get married. Why bother, it would never last. Mom's personal life with men and marriages had been a disaster at best. I wanted no part of all that heartache and total chaotic relationships. Ron and Carolyn had renewed my young anticipation in finding the perfect marriage. Now this?

Their marital problems lasted for the entire first year and Ron moved out 13 times. I was too young for him to confide in me, but he did become very close to our cousin, Brenda. She even helped him move out a couple of times. Still no one could find out what was wrong, as Carolyn wouldn't talk.

By this time Ron gave up as he was convinced it was over. There was nothing left to do but move on.

Ron decided to pursue his ambition of becoming a Green Beret, so he went to the Army recruiting office and signed up to go back into the service. By the time he got back home, apprehension had begun to cloud his decision. He couldn't just sign up to be a Green Beret, he had to join the Army, and then start the process of getting into the Special Forces. If a recruit didn't make it, he would still be serving the Army for two years. Ron didn't want to be in the Army if he couldn't be a Green Beret. He wrestled with this for a few days then came to the conclusion that since there was no turning back, he would just be certain he made it into the Special Forces.

The minute Carolyn found out he had enlisted in the Army, she did a complete 360 and wanted to be his wife again. It was like someone flipped a switch. She loved him and wanted to be married to him. The only thing I ever heard Mom say was that Carolyn told her she just didn't know how to communicate with Ron. She didn't know how to cook and didn't know how to fix their problems, so she shut down, just like her family. When he joined the Army and would be gone, she knew she was about to lose him and had to let him know how she felt. I wanted to smack her. Maybe if she hadn't acted like that, Ron wouldn't have joined the Army.

Before I knew what was happening, he was off to boot camp for the second time. Oh God, here we go again. I hate this. Carolyn would stay behind and wait until he was through with boot camp, and then she would go with him.

I couldn't believe he was in the military again, and now we were in a war.

This Vietnam thing was really scary and we were losing thousands of soldiers and for what? I sort of agreed with these crazy protestors all over the country. I didn't understand why we had to police the world. Who cared about some little country on the other side of the world I had never heard of until some politician decided we should stick our nose in and save these people? I did have compassion for the people, but why did we have to send Americans to get killed? And now my brother was going to be back in the military and might end up there.

Carolyn lived with us, not her parents, while Ron was in boot camp and it didn't take long to see that she was a cleaning freak. It was nice for Mom to have help, but Carolyn ran the house like it was hers. I was 15 by this time, had a very strong will, and she didn't mind giving her opinion when she didn't agree with what I was doing. I probably did get away with too much sometimes, but nothing illegal or immoral. I just stayed out too late and didn't always put school first. My friends hung out at our house all the time, since Mom had allowed it and I didn't think it was any of Carolyn's business one way or another.

I'm sure part of my resentment toward her was that I blamed her for Ron being gone. I also didn't like her interfering in my life. I knew whatever I did she would tell Ron, putting her slant on the given situation and I didn't care for her intrusion. Mom was an easy touch and could be talked into our antics easily. She had no idea sometimes what kids were up to because of the times she grew up in. Convincing my Mom that something we wanted to do was ok or not too dangerous, was not difficult. Carolyn had different opinions and she was ruining some of my freedom and fun. I had a good thing going and she was throwing a wrench into it.

I complained to my friends a lot and to Mom who was sympathetic, and I believe understood, but she wasn't willing to buck up to Carolyn or put her in her place. I think Mom was afraid to rock the boat after all the problems they had in their marriage. She wanted to do everything she could to get them on a better footing, even if that meant letting Carolyn take over our house.

Finally, the time had come for Carolyn to go live with Ron and them being together made Ron happy. That made me happy and being without her input into my business made me even happier. Although I'm sure being a mischievous teenager had nothing to do with my lack of tolerance for her at times.

Mom and Charlie took her to Fort Bragg where she and Ron would live for a year. I felt a sigh of relief because at least he wouldn't be in Vietnam for a year and I prayed that our troops would come home in the meantime. Now life could get back to normal around our house, only I wasn't enjoying it as much as I had as Ron's void was immeasurable. Not only was he absent from our house, but from our town, our police force, and our daily lives.

Ron was gone.

Teenage Life

It was my freshman year of high school, Jim was in the 7th grade and Mom was still at home as her only job outside the house was selling Avon. Charlie had started stopping at the bar and drinking way too much which at first was funny because he was a goofy little man and did some really weird stuff when he was drunk. It seemed harmless enough the first few times, but as it progressed things weren't so funny.

Deb, Nance and I were still inseparable, when I wasn't with my cousin, Brenda, who, after graduating, had moved to Crawfordsville to work at a book manufacturing company. She was now only 35 miles from Covington. Brenda had rented an adorable little house and was supporting herself. I was proud of her as she was Miss Independence and worked very hard to do it all on her own. For a long time she worked two jobs to make her rent, car payment, and living expenses.

I would spend the weekend with her every chance I got and on one of my weekend overnights, I went to a party with Brenda and her younger sister. The crowd was a little old for a high school freshman, but Brenda always watched out for me. I was out of my element, but I had too much fun and decided the older life was what I wanted.

The only problem was that I didn't think I fit in with the cute skinny girls. How could I attract older gorgeous guys looking the way I looked? I decided I was done being fat and something clicked inside my brain. I nearly quit eating from that weekend on. I was losing weight and couldn't lose it fast enough. I didn't lose the weight by being healthy, but the pounds melted off.

This was late winter and by summer I lost 45 pounds and had the most wonderful summer of my life. Going to the pool and not hiding behind a towel was a new high for me. I bought all new clothes and grew my hair out. All of a sudden I had all the boyfriends I could handle, which reinforced in my brain that only skinny girls got boyfriends.

I was again counting the days until my big brother could be home to see my whole new life. My saving grace was by the time I had lost the weight I wanted and planned to be more a part of Brenda's older crowd, I lost the desire to spend every minute I could with them. Instead, I was enjoying my own friends again. A passing phase, but it served its purpose. It had given me the desire and willpower to lose the weight I wanted.

Starting my sophomore year, I received overwhelming attention about my new body. I took my uniform in for alterations and the band director didn't recognize me. The guys were more than complimentary and the attention I had longed for was coming full force. Unfortunately, I was too young and this came too fast to learn how to handle the unfamiliar attention. The guys who had been my buddies and confidants, now wanted to date me and I was in heaven. I was supposed to be insulted with some of it, but I wasn't. I had no intention of becoming an easy mark for these horn toads, as Deb, Nance and I called them. I was just excited they were looking at me in a new light. I was now the object of their lust, but the joke was on them. They fed my ego and I gave them a need for cold showers as I had no intention of giving in to their sexual desires.

New clothes became addictive and I couldn't have enough new outfits. By this time I had started working at one of the most popular restaurants in the area, The Beef House. Ninety percent of my check went to clothes and I always had something on layaway.

I couldn't wait for Ron to see me as he had been one of my biggest supporters to lose weight and I knew he would be proud. This was the year he gave me the nickname of The Bee Bopper. It had to do with the fact that I never sat still, was always on the go and Brenda and I would say we were going bopping around. It was the same as cruising is now.

Mom, Jim and I took a four day trip to Fort Bragg to see Ron and Carolyn during fall break. I was on my way to see my big brother, had a cute boyfriend back home, was wearing jeans four sizes smaller, and was, because

I had my learners permit, behind the wheel. Life felt good.

I was used to Ron being back in the military and as long as he was stateside, I was ok. Missing him was always there, but being a teenager and not living at my grandparents took a lot of the desperate loneliness I had felt when he was in the Navy.

By this time, he had made it into the Green Berets. He was a proud man, but I might have been even more proud of him. The camaraderie between his fellow Special Forces buddies was exhilarating to watch and the bond between them unmistakable. They were almost arrogant about what they had accomplished and I loved listening to them joke around with each other. One joke I loved was Pick a Number. Their training had taught them 12 ways to kill with their bare hands and Pick a Number meant which of the 12 ways they wanted to die.

Ron as a Green Beret

The Green Berets were talked about in the news, and movies were being made about them. There was a mystic sentiment regarding this group of soldiers, insinuating they were super human. To me, it fit my brother to a tee. It was all I could do to restrain myself when Special Forces or Green Berets were mentioned. I wanted to scream it to the heavens, skywrite it for the world to see. My brother was one of those super human tough guys with the cooler than hell green beret on his head. I had always known he was more special than most, now he had proven it to the world.

On base you would see several platoons running drills and chanting as they ran. The verses rhymed and were complimentary to their selves. It was so exciting to watch these large groups of men training and chanting.

Ron bought each of us Green Beret Special Forces windbreakers and I was so proud of that jacket. I knew we would be the only family in Covington wearing them.

Ron and Carolyn were just as they had been when they were dating and just married. She seemed to have gotten over her problem with communication and all their trouble was a dim memory. You would never have known anything had happened and I started to look at them as the perfect couple again.

Linda, Ron & Jim

As I expected, my big brother was very proud of my accomplishment and teased me about boys all weekend. He told Mom to make sure those young punks were behaving or he would come back to Covington and pound them into the ground. *God, I love him!*

Carolyn and I got along great, as our differences had also melted away. She had become a wonderful cook and spoiled us with great meals all weekend. I watched what I ate, but splurged, knowing I would have to make up for the extras the following week. By this time, my brain was like a calculator when it came to counting calories.

Ron drove us around and showed us parts of the base where we were allowed. Everywhere you looked there were hot looking soldiers—boot camp guys marching and chanting. I was ready to move there.

"Hey Bo, look at those guys. Let me out of the car, I want to talk to them," I teased.

"No way, you are way too young. They are not allowed to look at you or talk to you," he said. "Besides, those guys are just legs, not worthy of my sister."

"What are legs?" I asked.

"Regular army, not SF," he said.

"Oh, I get it. I can only date a Green Beret?"

"You're not dating any of these guys, you are too young."

"I'm sixteen, I drove halfway down here and I can date now."

"Yeah well, not now, not here. Case closed."

I laughed at his brotherly protective attitude. Carolyn turned and winked at me.

Just like when I was six years old and we had lunch together in our trailer in Hillsboro, these exchanges with my big brother were golden to me.

Our weekend passed too quickly and it was time for us to start home. This was different—us leaving Ron. It never stopped hurting to leave him, but it had become different as I got older. I handled it better. He had Carolyn and I could see how happy he was. I had a life to go back to, not like it had been before we moved to Covington. I could get through it as long as he was at Fort Bragg. *Please God keep him here. Don't let them send him to Vietnam. Please, not there.* I knew the Special Forces had to do secret, dangerous missions and many didn't come back. I knew our family couldn't survive without Ron. It took my breath away to even imagine not having him.

I knew God wouldn't let that happen.

Ron at Fort Bragg

Only Two Years Left

My junior year of high school was fast approaching and I had a steady boyfriend, Gary, a guy who attended a neighboring high school. Deb, Nance and I were still fast and furious friends, while Jim and I got along worse than a cat and dog. Mom was taking care of the home fires and Charlie (my step dad) was getting sloppy fall-down-can't-drive drunk several times a month. I'm pretty sure Mom had missed How to Pick a Good Husband 101.

Ron and Carolyn came home for a month before going to Germany and it was heaven to have Ron in the house. We had big family dinners and relatives and friends stopped by to see him before he left. Charlie was on his best behavior, as he wouldn't get drunk in front of Ron, and Jim and I even got along. We knew better as Ron would have kicked our butts if he had heard some of our ridiculous arguments.

God had answered my prayers and Ron had been stationed in Germany. We could breathe easy for at least a year. Carolyn stayed with us again, waiting for Ron to send for her and it was pretty much a re-run. She took over the house and made it her own, but I didn't mind this time because I wasn't home much. I had my drivers' license and the use of my step-grandfather's old Ford Falcon, because he had started driving on the sidewalks.

Between school, band, dating, and working at The Beef House, there wasn't a lot of time spent at home. Carolyn could clean, do laundry, and have a ball. When I was home to do my share of household tasks, she redid everything after me anyway. When I washed dishes she would rewash all the pans and counters I had just cleaned. She would re-do anything we cleaned and some of her antics were hilarious. She would carry an ash tray around and sit it in another ash tray so she wouldn't soil the one sitting on the stand. If anyone set down a glass, she would grab it and wash it. You had to hang onto your glass so she wouldn't take it away.

I didn't understand why she acted like this. I knew she was lonely and worried, so maybe it had something to do with living without Ron. I never came to any definite conclusion; I just knew she wasn't that extreme when Ron was home.

Within a couple months after leaving for Germany, Ron had an apartment for the two of them. Carolyn and Trixie, their Pomeranian, were off to Germany and I was happy for both of us.

My 11th grade year was packed with classes, ball games, band, friends, dating and work. Scholastic endeavors were not my first priority as being social was more important and a lot more fun. Boys were way too high on the list, and of course, carving out time for Brenda was squeezed into every chance I got.

I was still going steady with Gary and we went everywhere together: church, each other's family dinners, proms, ball games and double dating. We were in love, breaking up, dating other people, and getting back together. I felt I was a bit more serious about him than he was me at times, or maybe all 17-year old boys were like that.

As far as school, band was my favorite activity and class. I was in concert, marching, pep, and swing bands. I played the sax, alto and baritone. I had followed in Brenda's footsteps.

I still worked as a waitress at The Beef House and Deb and Nance also worked there. We couldn't even work apart from each other. This restaurant was one of the most popular in the area, but our boss was not the easiest person to get along with. A few tears, some swearing and consoling each other helped make the job fun most of the time.

Mom's youngest sister, Tootie, now lived about four hours away in Elkhart, Indiana. Mom and her other sister, Lettie, would take off every couple months for the weekend and visit their younger sister. This meant two or three days of un-chaperoned fun for us. Charlie was there, but we had no respect for him or anything he might have said. Besides, he would get drunk at the bar

117

most nights Mom was gone. If he did stay home, he would be asleep by 7:00 p.m.

One weekend, Mom left on Friday morning and wouldn't be returning until Monday. Deb, Nance and Annette, a band friend, were all going to spend as many nights at my house as we could talk their parents into for the weekend. We just had to get through Friday at school and the fun would begin.

During third hour, Annette and I decided we couldn't wait until school was out at 3:00 p.m. We needed to start early and skipping school was the only answer. We had never tried it and were dying to do the deed. We needed a plan to get out and not raise suspicion. The school was so small, the teachers and office personal knew everyone and who their friends were. Attendance was taken each morning and afternoon and if anyone was absent the same time as their friends, they would get caught unless there was some sort of brilliance in the planning.

We told Deb and Nance our plan, hoping they would come along but they opted out, stating that if all four of us left for the afternoon there would be no way we wouldn't get caught. They told us good luck and would see us after school at my house.

We couldn't leave at the same time so one of us would leave at the end of third hour. I had the car, so I would go play sick after the bell rang, go home and wait. Annette would leave during band, fourth hour, claiming she had cramps and start walking toward home. I would pick her up when she was far enough away from school no one would see us.

It worked like a charm as she was walking exactly where we had planned and I pulled over. She jumped in and we raced out of town on the back streets.

As soon as we were out of town we started laughing and complementing our brainwork.

"We did it! Deb and Nance will be so ticked they didn't at least try," I said, as we sped toward Danville, the next bigger town over the state line.

We were going to have lunch there.

"We sure did. I just hope school doesn't call our house, my Mom is there," Annette said.

"Well, if they call mine no one will answer."

"I don't know if that's good or not. If you're sick at home you should answer."

"I'll tell them I was in the bathroom," I said. "It'll be ok. We left at different times. We have never skipped and no one should suspect. Don't worry, it'll be fine. Let's have fun and not ruin this."

"You're right, this is so cool. We have two and a half days to go wherever we want. My mom doesn't know your mom is gone, so I can stay all night, both nights. I told her we had a project to get done."

"Cool. Now where do you want to eat lunch, McDonalds or Marty K's?"

Shopping had been next on the list, but we chickened out. What if someone saw us that knew our parents and wondered why we were not in school? New clothes were out.

After we ate lunch, we decided to go to Attica, a town about 25 miles away. We drove by the school my boyfriend attended and saw no one because they were in class, so that was boring. Next we decided to go to Veedersburg, alias Veederstucky, the next town five miles from Covington. That was about the same because everyone we knew was still in class. It was ok, we were still having fun, how could we not? We had skipped school and got away with it.

We had shot the entire afternoon driving all over the county by ourselves and it was getting time to meet Deb and Nance at my house.

We pulled into my driveway and ran behind the yard fence so one would see us together. We unlocked the door and went into my Mom's bedroom, where we were to wait for a call from Deb or Nance. We flopped onto Mom's bed and gloated over our success. Two minutes later the phone rang.

"Boy, we timed that right" I said. "Hello."

"Smitty, is Annette there?" Annette's mother said. She had a stern heavy southern accent.

"Uhhh, yeah, just a minute." I covered the receiver with my hand. "Oh crap, it's your Mom," I whispered. "We are dead meat! Crap."

"I knew it. I will be grounded for life."

"Hello," Annette said.

I could hear Annette's mother order us to get to her house immediately. Annette hung up the phone and explained that the school took one look at the absent list and called our parents.

At Annette's house we received a lecture about how really dumb it was to think we could get by with leaving the same day, on a Friday.

"Now, you are both going to the principal's office and face the music today," she said.

"What?" we both said.

"Yes, you are both going to get it over with now. Why would you want to wait and think about it all weekend?"

We didn't have a good answer and I would have to do as Annette's mom said, even though my mom didn't know.

As we headed for the school, I didn't feel so smart and Annette was whining and fretting about what was going to happen.

"Oh Annette, how bad can it be? We'll get detention and Williams will yell at us. Who cares?"

Principal Williams was standing in the doorway to his office and motioned for us to come in and closed the door. He gave us the talk, told us how ashamed of us he was and we promised to never skip school again. Annette was fake crying and I had to bite my lip to keep from laughing. I had to get out of there before I got us into more trouble by cracking up. Did she really think crying was going to get her out of trouble?

I was instructed to have my Mom call when she returned home to let the office know I had told on myself. *Oh brother.*

Our punishment was six hours of detention, for three and a half hours of missed school. I had learned my lesson and would never do that again. I would never sit in detention again because the next time, I would make sure I covered my tracks before I skipped school.

Junior year was winding down and proms were approaching. I would be attending Covington and Attica's proms since Gary and I were still going steady. There was no way I could wear the same dress, so the question was how would I get two dresses? There would be some of the same kids at both proms and I would rather stay home, than be seen in the same dress. Our family income couldn't afford two dresses, but Mom figured it out.

This was the year Deb, Nance, Annette and I made appointments in Danville to have our hair done for prom. Deb had her car by this time so she drove. Three hours later we were finished and started home. I was having a fit because I hated my hair. It looked like some old farts beehive do and I would have to go home and re-do it. I had wasted the whole $5.50 on it. I must have distracted Deb because she started to turn down a one way street. Before we could get our mouths open and stop her some guy rolled his window down and yelled at us. Deb corrected her mistake before she faced into oncoming traffic and we went on home.

She dropped each of us off and went home to finish getting ready for our big night. Five minutes later she called upset because she walked in her house and her mom already knew she had made the mistake in traffic.

Shirley, Deb's mom always knew. The woman must have had ESP or had Deb followed because she always knew what we were doing. It was eerie how many times this happened. Even after we were adults she would never tell us how she always knew.

Prom, after-prom and breakfast kept us up all night and our parents made sure we had a night to remember. Exhausted and too sleepy to be driving, we planned to take off for the Indianapolis 500 time trials after prom. This was how my crowd celebrated the end of a school year.

We would take a picnic basket full of food that our parents prepared. Some years Mom would fry chicken and we would make a ton of bologna sandwiches. Our cooler would be full of food, pop, and illegal beer.

We would be there early and get in line to get into the in-field. We took blankets or sat on top of the cars so we could see. By noon we would be breaking out the food along with the beer we were not supposed to be drinking. Since no one had slept all night, by about three or earlier we fell asleep on the blankets. Every year I went home with a sunburned face.

As we walked by one the section of bleachers I had a flashback and a giant stab into my heart. The year before Ron left for the Army, I had been at the trials with Ron, his boss, Max, the Chief of Police, and a bunch of my friends. He and Max were sitting behind a pyramid of cans, enjoying the time trials, and a few cold beers.

This was another treat for me to love racing like my big brother. Now, he was halfway around the world, not here enjoying the Indy track. *How many years will it be before he would be back here?*

Life around our house hadn't changed much. Mom's only job outside the home was still Avon. Charlie was as big a disappointment as my dad had been, only in different ways. Jim and I had come to the realization that we hated each other. Deb, Nance and I were still the best of the best of friends.

Ron and Carolyn were enjoying being in Germany, although Ron was gone a lot, out on training missions and some real ones. He kept this information from us. This was a world apart from being in Vietnam and I was convinced my prayers were helping.

It was my senior year, and then what? I always seemed to be in a hurry to get to the next stage of my life, but now I wanted time to slow down. I had only nine months to spend with my classmates as the class of 68. We swore, vowed and promised we would never be like other classes. We would never lose track of each other. We would stay close, have parties and get-togethers. The class of 68 was great and we were damn well going to leave our mark.

Somehow our class had acquired a bit of a reputation, and instead of working to clean it up, we played on it. We weren't delinquents or druggies, most of us earned pretty decent grades and a few were brilliant.

We had a streak of rebellion running through our veins, not altogether unheard of in the sixties.

We partied harder, drove faster, stayed out later, played our music louder and defied our teachers. We were not always justified in our troubling making and we deserved to have our backsides tanned many times.

As much as I missed my big brother, I knew if he had been in Covington I would have been in trouble a lot more, or I would not have been a part of some of my class's antics. I would rather have had him home, but since he wasn't, I took advantage of my mother's easy going nature and lack of knowledge of what we were up to most of the time.

Graduation was upon us and there was distribution of caps and gowns, practice for commencement and graduation ceremony, and tying up of loose ends. We partied, stayed out late, drove by the school and honked at the kids still in class. We thought we were the smartest and coolest group of seniors ever, when in truth we were naive, green, and unprepared.

I wondered if Ron felt this way. He always seemed so grown up to me and I could never be as brave as he had been at this very age. He left our small town and went through boot camp, and travelled all over the world on boats and submarines. My biggest concern was how and who I would be partying with, and how much fun we could get by with on our big night. I felt pangs of guilt, but I let it pass as soon as one of my friends brought me back to the present.

The annual Indy time trials trip this year was the day before graduation. Mom was not in favor of this trip being so close to the big day, as there were too many things to do.

"Mom, this is our last time to go together," I said.

"You had better not come back all tired and think you can sleep around the clock like all the other years. You will be up early for graduation, then your open house. I assume you will be out half the night then at some party you were talking about a few days ago."

"Well, um yeah," I admitted. "I promise not to let it interfere with my open house or graduation."

I kept my promise, was up early doing whatever Mom had planned, then off to our commencement. There was only one problem, I had fallen asleep with the help of a couple of beers, on a blanket, in the infield of the Indy track and sunburned half of my face. Exactly right down the middle of my face, like a line had been drawn precisely down my forehead, nose and chin. I was beat red on one half of my face and wasn't thrilled about it, but my Mom was livid.

"Your pictures are going to look ridiculous," she said.

"It's ok Mom, I'll just look to one side every time I see a camera." I giggled to myself.

"You are not funny, Linda Jo. How on earth could you sleep while your face was burning so badly?"

"Uh, cause I had been up all day and night, I guess."
And the beer didn't help.

"Well, I hope you are proud of yourself. I'm sure your big brother will think you look cute when he gets your pictures." Ron went to the track all the time, so he would know what happened. He wasn't as naive as Mom and would ask her why I looked half baked. I figured I better come up with something good or hide my face all day.

Our graduation ceremony was held in our enormous gymnasium with the stage at one end, then our class seated in front. I looked out over the crowd one last time.

"Smitty, who are you looking for?" Deb asked.

"Uh, no one, just checking out how many people came to see us be set free," I lied. I was half expecting to see Ron out there, surprising me with his presence. I searched for a Green Beret, but saw only my family members I had already seen at the house. My heart fell, but it was only a dream anyway, the Army wouldn't let him come home for me. So I sucked it up and never let on that my heart had broken a little more.

Our principal had warned us that we were, under no circumstances, allowed to throw our caps or yell anything as we exited the big doors out into the sidewalk.

Of course this did not please most of us, so we plotted and planned that we would do as we pleased. What could he do? We would be leaving with diploma in hand. We were done. He could not take away our diploma for yelling outside the building. He had bullied us, made up insane rules and drove everyone crazy the entire year.

As I walked down the aisle, I held back the tears knowing this was my last walk through our gym as a student and member of the class of 1968. As I walked through the door and was past anyone who could see who the big mouth belonged to, I threw my cap into the air and screamed. "Yeehaaaa. We did it"

I was out of sight when I yelled, but my Mom recognized my voice since the scream came two seconds after I exited the building. As the evening wore on we teased her into a smirk as we bragged about our outburst of joy and defying the principal one last time.

The only thing missing was my big brother. Oh God, how I wished he could have been there. I was sure he wouldn't have been mad at me for my mischievous graduation behavior. Ron and his friends did plenty of crazy things in the name of fun. He didn't believe in breaking the law, he expected Jim and I to get good grades and take care of Mom. But he was no stranger to fun. I got away with a lot more with Mom than I would have with him, but he wasn't a boring guy. I had seen the pictures of him and his friends on their senior trip to Niagara Falls. They had snuck out of the hotel and went to the falls where they climbed the fence to put the tips of their fingers in the water. They sank up to their knees in mud.

I saw the pictures of him and the guys backstage of their junior class play in their underwear. Ron played a man, playing a woman and was dressed in a bra and girdle. They laughed for a solid month while attending play practice. Ron was the only guy brave enough, and secure in his manhood, to wear ladies underwear, gowns and play the part of a woman.

He had a brilliant sense of humor and his personality was charismatic. His smile was warm and captivating and he lit up a room when he entered. He blew the theories that claim children who are abused, neglected and unloved by their father will grow up to be the same or damaged in some way. It had the opposite effect on Ron. He couldn't have been more different from our father. I was surrounded by family and friends at my graduation, but the void he left was unmistakable.

A Summer to Remember or Not

Mom left for Germany the day after we got back from my senior trip, we had six weeks without adult supervision. This meant a house to hang out at and have parties. Of course, Charlie would be there to take care of us and make sure we were obeying the rules. What a joke! Did Mom really think he paid any attention to us when she was gone? She must have believed this or she wouldn't have taken the trip as we had been taught right from wrong years ago and hadn't caused too much trouble in our short lives.

I took a short term babysitting job with one of my previous babysitting families while waiting for a call from one of the places I had left applications. Jim was working for a farmer, bailing hay and other farm duties. Charlie worked five and half days a week. He only got drunk a couple days a week at first, and then it escalated to five.

At first, everything was much the same—working, laundry and some cooking. My girlfriends were staying all night often, which was not different from before. Then as summer was in full swing things got a little crazier. My older guy friends who knew Mom was gone began hanging out more often and staying later. No big parties or brawls, just hanging out, playing cards, listening to music, sometimes drinking beer and sometimes just having soft drinks and pizza.

Six weeks passed and it was time for Mom to come home. Instead, she sent word she was staying longer. Ron had been shipped out to the Canary Islands when Mom arrived and that had spoiled his plan for taking her and Carolyn on a vacation to several countries.

Six more weeks without Mom and trying to stay out of trouble. In truth, I felt tired.

Charlie was getting drunk regularly, which was nothing new. He had no idea what Jim and I were ever up to, good or bad. He had taken an interest in us when we were younger, but not now. His alcoholism had taken over and our disrespect for him was obvious. The only thing he said to me while Mom was gone was that I needed to do the laundry and I was driving Mom's car too much. He was right on both accounts, so I tried to get the laundry caught up and parked Mom's car, for a few day anyway.

Mom had a 1967 Chevy Super Sport Impala, black and white. We had a muscle car before we knew what a muscle car was. I had driven it when my car was out of gas and just kept driving it. It was so much nicer than the Falcon I had inherited. Mom had not said that I could not drive the Impala, it was just understood that I would drive the Falcon.

By this time I knew things were out of control, but I didn't have the willpower or desire to stop the insanity. Some nights we were staying out all night and we were having friends over constantly. The laundry was piled high, dirty dishes were stacked in both sinks, and the house needed immediate attention.

Every morning I told myself I would settle down, clean the house like never before and stop running around. I had every intention of reforming, but when evening came and friends arrived with ideas of yet another adventure we couldn't pass up, I would cave.

There were moments when I was ready for Mom to come home and life to get back to normal. Clearly I wasn't ready for all this freedom and I was starting to feel it, but I wouldn't have admitted it then.

I also knew that if Ron found out about the parties, Mom's car and that I wasn't keeping the house up as I had promised, I would be in trouble. I respected my brother so much and seldom disobeyed him or wanted him to be disappointed in me, so why was I taking this chance? I didn't understand myself.

It was finally time for Mom to come home. I had a week to get the house in order and get the speedometer hooked back up on her car. My friend Jack had disconnected it for me so Mom wouldn't know how much I had been driving it while she was gone.

The car was an easy fix by just having Jack reverse his handy work. Cleaning everything that had been neglected for three months was another story. I did laundry, washed dishes for hours, mopped floors, washed windows, and tried to make it look like it did when she left. I kept asking myself if all the craziness was worth the cleaning. Definitely no—well maybe.

I was uneasy about what Mom would know when she got home. No one had been arrested, not even speeding tickets. No one got pregnant, though half the town thought all we did was have orgies. I didn't even have a serious boyfriend the entire summer. No sex at all, but that wasn't the story that was going around town. We really did nothing different, same as when Mom was home, just more of it and later into the night. That's what made me angry about the gossips in our small town. I was guilty of not keeping the house up, putting too many miles on Mom's car and staying out late. Since most of us were 18, what was the big deal?

We picked Mom up from the airport the next day and it was good to see her and hear all the stories about Ron, Carolyn and her trip through Europe. She had bought a lot of souvenirs but had them shipped home, so we would have to wait a couple weeks to see her treasures.

I thought Mom would be pleased at the clean house, but she wasn't. She complained about the towels looking dingy as she was the most particular person in the world about her laundry.

What she was most upset about was that I had decided to start smoking while she was gone. Nance and Deb had been smoking for at least a year. Annette and I didn't. Annette and Nance battled about smoking in my car nearly every time they were in it together. Annette's parents didn't smoke, so she was more sensitive to the smell. She had complained about her green fuzzy coat smelling like smoke the entire past winter. Many of my family members smoked so I had no idea I smelled like an ash tray most of my life.

I had tried smoking a couple of times but hated it. It smelled disgusting, tasted repulsive and made me nauseated. This time was going to be different. I was 18, out of school, my own boss and I was going to smoke. Mom didn't hide her feelings even though she smoked and I wasted no time informing her of that fact. She had no rebuttal.

I had survived the summer without Mom, didn't get arrested or wreck any cars, didn't get pregnant, or get any diseases. I saw myself as a grown up now and my new plan was to find a job in Crawfordsville and live near Brenda.

Time to Grow Up

Life at our house in 1968 was back to as normal as it could be, considering the people who inhabited it.

Mom was selling Avon, playing laundry lady, and cleaning everything in sight. Jim was in his junior year at school and running the streets with his friends as much as Mom would allow. I was working at the Beef House and having fun with my new friends.

Charlie was getting so drunk that bartenders would call and we would have to retrieve him from either his bar stool, or passed out in his truck or on the court house lawn. I could barely stand to look at him, let alone pick him up and drag him home, wet and stinking. Charlie never got drunk when Ron was around and I wished Ron could come home. Charlie was making Mom miserable and Jim and I wanted to strangle him. Our real dad had been an alcoholic and now our step dad was a sickening drunk.

Mom would threaten to kick him out and he would promise to stop. He would try for a few days, and then fall off the wagon. I felt bad for my Mom, but I had no idea how miserable she was. I didn't realize how lonely she was for a partner, a friend, a husband. The only thing he was good for was a small paycheck. It sounded cold and heartless, but it was true. Mom's health was not good enough for her to punch a time clock again and she didn't want another divorce under her belt.

Ron and Carolyn were still in Germany where they were making lifetime friends. I would listen to the stories, when Mom came home from Germany and through their letters I would try to imagine what their life was like. The army had NCO clubs where they met celebrities, listened to bands, had dinner and drinks, and hung out with Ron's buddies and their wives. The bond and love these men created was obvious. I had never witnessed anything like the relationship they shared as Special Ops, Special Forces or Navy Seals. They have a connection like none other. I wanted to be a part of that life, and lived it through the stories they brought home and in their letters.

The most important factor remained first and foremost, he was not in Vietnam. I felt eternally grateful to whatever was keeping him out of that horrendous country. He was on missions a lot, but that was kept from us most of the time, or he would say it was something not dangerous.

As summer ended, I felt unsettled and thought that maybe I missed Gary. Yes, I decided, that was the problem. I missed my old boyfriend.

I wrote him a letter and told him how I felt. I figured he was still mad at me, but it was worth a try. To my surprise he replied right away. That was almost too easy, I thought. If he had made me wait and wonder, it probably would have been to his benefit.

We got back together and fell into the same routine. He wanted to get married and I was dragging my feet. It didn't take long to realize that Gary was not the answer to my restlessness. I didn't have the heart to break it off again, too quickly. I did miss him, so I just went along with it for the time being, hoping he would get bored with my distant attitude.

On Thanksgiving, we got together for dinner at my grandparents' house in Crawfordsville. The entire family was there except for Ron and Carolyn and I did not want to be there. I wanted to be at home for a party at my friend Ooley's apartment. I was antsy all day, wanting to leave as soon as dinner was over. As soon as we got home, I raced upstairs to change into a new leather dress I couldn't wait to wear. I reapplied my make-up, ran a brush through my hair, sprayed fresh perfume, brushed my teeth and I was out of there.

"We will be at Ooley's, be home by 2:00," I mumbled as ran by her, hoping she would not catch what I had said.

"Oh no, be home by 1:00," she said.

"Mommm," I protested. "Why? What makes the difference, if I'm gonna do something wrong, I can do it before 1:00." I repeated my usual reasoning.

"You drive me crazy, oh ok, 1:30 and behave yourself."

The place was already packed when I arrived and I had to squeeze past wall to wall bodies just to make my way into the kitchen to get a beverage.

Everyone talked, laughed, listened to music and drank. Someone turned the music louder, Born to Be Wild by Steppenwolf was blaring. It was one of my favorites, but then it was a favorite of anyone under the age of 20.

I jumped up on a chair and danced to the crazy loud rock and roll music. As the song ended, I grabbed someone's hand to jump down and caught the eye of some new stranger.

My heart did a little lurch and I felt self-conscious. He was staring at me and would not break eye contact. I looked away because he was making me feel funny, or good, or something.

He was tall with coal black hair, dark brown eyes and was hot. I looked back every once in a while and he was still staring. I looked behind me to see if he was looking at someone else. Nope, no one was behind me. This guy was bold or weird, or maybe drunk? He didn't seem drunk in the least, but he was making me feel uncomfortable.

I started to the kitchen to get another beer and change the dynamics of the situation. I had barely turned around from the fridge when I looked straight into his eyes. He made a comment, and never took his eyes off me. We talked a little and I realized who he was. Crap, he had taken Nance out. He was the new guy in town, Les something, just out of the Air Force, he was from the south somewhere, and had a hot beefed up shiny red GTX.

Nance had said he was ok, but she wasn't impressed with him and probably wouldn't go out with him again. I sure hoped she meant it. Maybe she had been blindfolded while on the date. Then again, was I missing something? I couldn't see one tiny thing wrong with him. He made it clear he was interested in getting to know me. I told him Nance was my best friend and making a connection would be impossible.

"What has that got to do with anything?" he asked.

"You took her out, didn't you?" I asked.

"Well, yeah, but I don't understand, it was one date."

"You guys don't get it." I took a drink.

"I guess we don't. We didn't get married or anything close to it. It was one evening and I am not asking her out again. No big deal," he said as he moved closer to me.

"She is my best friend and we don't date each other's boyfriends. We have been through this before. I promised her I would never go out with anyone she had dated, ever again."

"But I'm not her boyfriend."

My mouth was saying all the right things, but my eyes were telling him to come closer as I really wanted him to kiss me.

He sat his beer down and moved in slowly. We never took our eyes off each other as he leaned down and kissed me. The world and my surroundings disappeared.

I don't know how long we stood kissing until I was aware of another person getting into the fridge for a beer. We backed up from each other and regained control.

"Oh, hi Steve," I said to our host. He laughed and told us to carry on.

"Let's get back to the party," I told the tall, dark, sexy hunk I had just kissed till I was dizzy.

"If we have to," he said.

We went back into the living room and I walked to the opposite side of the room where Les was headed. I sat on the arm of the couch and tried to make intelligent conversations with my friends, but I had no idea what anyone was saying to me. Les and I stared at each like we had been hypnotized. The music blared. Midnight Confessions played and I knew I would die if I could not be with this new guy.

As the records played about a love struck pair who couldn't be together because they were tied to someone else, I knew I was in trouble. I rewrote my own song. I was the restless 18 year old, bored with her life and her boyfriend. Let her run into a 21 year old stranger, fresh out of the Air Force and Vietnam and tell them they can't be together. Put a little booze into the mix and you have some raging emotions.

About the time I thought I was going to burst into flames someone in the hall stairs starting yelling that the cops were on their way up. Someone grabbed Les and another guy and shoved them toward the kitchen.

"You guys have to get out of here, now. I know you didn't buy this stuff, but both of you are over 21 and you will get the blame," Ooley said.

"Where are you pushing them, there is no door back there!" I screamed.

"They gotta go out the window and climb down. It's that or go to jail."

They were already climbing out and down the back fire stairs and jumping down onto the ground. Another friend of mine, Diane, was yelling instructions to Dean, her boyfriend.

"We will meet you later in the alley and come back to get your cars when the coast is clear," she said.

When we walked back into the living room the police were talking to Steve and shining their flashlights into everyone's eyes.

"Where's Dean and the new guy?" the police asked. "Their cars are out there."

This was the down fall to small town living. Everyone knew your car, police included. Being new was no better, maybe even worse. Les' car was like a neon light, new in town, fire engine red and race track ready.

We told the police they weren't there and although they probably didn't buy it, there was nothing they could do as Dean and Les were not in the apartment. I wasn't sure why the remainder of the party group didn't get arrested because we were all under age. Underage drinking was handled much differently in those days.

To our advantage, no one was falling down drunk and we were showing no interest in driving around. Maybe that's why they didn't haul everyone to jail. The cops were more interested in catching Dean and Les for buying booze for underage kids.

Covington's finest left with strict instructions that they didn't want to see any of us in our cars until morning. Where did they think we were all going to sleep?

The official visit put a big wet blanket on the festive mood. Even though no one got arrested, we knew we would have to be ingenious to get into our cars and home without getting arrested. There would not be any more alcohol. We waited and left one and two at a time to avoid getting busted.

Diane and I left after a short while, found Dean and Les, and brought them back to their cars. Les followed me to my house.

When he pulled up behind me, I walked to his window. He asked me to get into his car so we could talk.

I explained that not only was Nance to be considered, I was still dating Gary. I had convinced him that going steady was childish, so I was not technically cheating on him. About the time those words left my mouth, Gary drove by my house.

Under most circumstances that would have put a damper on our feelings, not so. We talked, kissed, and stared at each other for four hours. All the while, Gary drove by about every half hour.

Around 2:00 am, my sweet concerned mother started flashing the front porch light.

"Ok, it's time for me to go in and let my Mom go to bed. She won't quit until I come in. I was supposed to be home by 1:30."

Technically I was home by my curfew, I just wasn't inside.

Les repeated that he had never felt the way he felt on this night about anyone else. I told him the same. He told me not to see anyone else and asked if I would take care of the guy in the 57 Chevy who kept driving by.

I told him I would.

Mom met me at the door as I went in.

"It's about time you got yourself in here," she said. I walked past her with a dazed look on my face. "What is the matter with you?"

"I'm going to marry that guy someday," I said.

"Who? What are you talking about?" She was looking out the door by now, trying to figure out what I was babbling about. "Married? To who? I know that wasn't Gary's car you've been sitting in for the past four hours. Married? Didn't you say, just two days ago, that you were never getting married?"

"You don't know him, he is new in town. He just got out of the Air Force, his name is Les."

"Les who? What on earth are you talking about?"

"Les, he is Max's cousin. Ain't that a hoot?"

"How long have you known him?"

"Uhhh, about six or seven hours."

"What? And you think that is long enough to know you are going to marry him? Linda Jo, that's just ridiculous. Have you been drinking? Are you listening to me?"

"What?"

"You haven't heard a word I have said."

"Sorry Mom, you can yell at me or ground me, but right now nothing can ruin how I feel. I have never felt like this about a guy. Can I go to bed now?"

"You might as well. You look like a love sick puppy. Go wash your face and go to bed."

She knew me so well. Nothing she said was penetrating into my silly teenage dreamy brain. I washed my face with stinky Noxzema and went up to my room.

I tuned WLS on my transistor radio, stepped out of my leather dress, threw it across my green chair that doubled as a closet and slipped on my oversized 68 is Great t-shirt. I reached under my bed until I felt my big fuzzy socks, pulled them up to my knees and sank into bed.

I was exhausted, but sleep didn't come until after I had re-lived the entire evening starting with when I met Les.

It Wasn't a Dream

I awoke slow and dreamy the next morning as the memory of the night before hadn't worn off. For a split second I thought it was a dream, but then the realization of the new guy and our romantic discovery of each other blasted my body and soul.

"Oh wow," I said aloud. I relived the entire night. Wow was all I could think of to describe what had happened to me. I didn't doubt for a minute that he was sincere. I could feel it.

Les and I had made plans to see each other that evening, so I decided to get up and get moving. As I rolled out of bed, I looked straight into my prom picture and Gary's eyes. It was a reminder of what I had to do.

"Ohhhhhhh nnoooooo," I moaned. I had to tell Gary it was over, again.

"Oh, double crap, Nance too."

Even though she said she didn't want to go out with Les again, she was still not going to like this. Oh boy, this was not going to be a fun day. The only driving force behind my motivation to get through the sticky situations I had put myself in with my best friend and my boyfriend, was the fact I was going to be with Les later in the evening.

My mother brought me back to the matter at hand with one of her bellowing calls up the stairway. "Linda Jo, get down here, you have company."

"Geez Mom, tell the whole town."

I threw on some jeans and a sweatshirt and down the stairs I started. About half way down I saw Gary and my pace slowed. I was in no hurry to face him.

"Hi," I said.

He didn't have a greeting or a smile.

"I take it you saw me last night?" I asked.

"Yeah, who's the guy?"

"His name is Les and he's new in town. It's over between us Gary, I'm sorry."

"Just like that? Didn't you just meet him?"

"Yes, but it doesn't matter, it's what I want."

"Ok, I'll get my things later." He turned and shut the door in my face.

I felt bad for him, but so relieved he didn't draw it out. We had been each other's first love and he was special to me. I had tried to make myself fall in love with him again, but it was no use, especially after I met Les.

I tried to make myself feel better by focusing on some of the less than admirable things Gary had done when we were together. I had been the one more invested in our relationship in the beginning. The past two years, he had been the one agonizing. I still didn't like hurting anyone, let alone my first love, but it had been over for a long time, new guy or not. I was going to end it; Les just put it in fourth gear.

Ok, I sighed, one down, Nance to go. This would take a lot longer, because I would not be breaking up with her. She would be my friend always, no questioning that. I just needed her to understand. I went back up to my room to call her and start the process. I knew she would feel that I had betrayed her.

I called and asked if she would come to my house because I had something to talk about. She was not about to move one foot out the door until I told her what the big mystery was.

After much discussion, we finally decided I could date Les and I was relieved. What would I have done if I couldn't persuade her to give me the go-ahead? I knew I wasn't walking away from new red car sexy Air Force guy.

Les came to get me that evening and nothing had changed. We were both so infatuated with each other that the rest of the world seemed to disappear. He asked me to marry him the second night we were together. Who had any commonsense? Of course I said yes. Then he wanted to set our wedding date in January. I told him I would ask my mother, but I doubted if she could pull off a wedding in one month.

"Are you crazy?" Mom said. "Number one, you don't know him. Number two, I can't get a wedding together in one month. Number three, are you crazy? Who is this guy anyway? And don't tell me he's Max's cousin. That doesn't mean anything to me. What do you think your big brother is going to say?"

"Oh yeah," I said, as my bubble burst and I sank into the big rocking chair. Crap, was my first thought. Crap again; I wanted Ron to be here for my wedding. "I want Ron to give me away."

"Give you away? I'm not talking who is going to give you away. I'm talking about what he will say about you wanting to get married to a perfect stranger."

"Mom, he's not a stranger, he is Max's cousin."

"Linda Jo, he never set foot in this town before one month ago. That makes him a stranger, Max's cousin or not."

"But Max is Ron's really good friend and was his boss on the force and is still the chief of police."

"Linda Jo. Write to your brother and see what he has to say."

"Guess I better get a letter out to him today. I want him to give me away. I wonder when he will be coming home."

"That's probably first on the agenda, but I'm telling you they won't give him a leave for your wedding." Mom barked out her opinion as she slammed another handful of silverware into the dish drainer.

"Mom, I hate to remind you, but I am 18. I can marry him even if no one wants me to."

"I know that. That's the only reason I haven't told you that you are absolutely not going to get married to this guy. I know how bullheaded you are. If I told you

150

no, you would just run away with him. Maybe this way you will wake up before the date gets here. I just hope Ron can talk some sense into you."

Oh man, why does she do that? She knew how I felt about Ron's opinion.

Damn, I wish he was here so I could make him see this wasn't a mistake. People can fall in love this fast, I know, because I did. It was real; I knew it and I could make Ron understand.

I wrote to my brother, explaining everything. His letter arrived a couple weeks later and to my surprise, he didn't make a big deal over our short engagement. The bad news was he had no idea when he could come home. It might be summer or it might be the next summer.

"A year and a half!" I said out loud as I read Ron's letter. I was sitting at the kitchen table and Mom was cooking. She turned and stared at me.

"What are yelling about?" she asked.

"Ron may not be home for a year and half. Maybe this coming summer, but maybe not till the next. This sucks."

"Well that's ok, you can just wait," she tried to hide the smile forming on her lips as she turned back to the stove.

"Les isn't going to like this, but I want Ron to be here. I'll talk to him tonight."

I could tell by the look on her face she was counting on my love for my big brother to keep me from getting married too soon. She had gotten to know Les and she liked him, but she still wanted us to wait.

Les was not at all happy with the news from Ron. He didn't want to wait and had already given in to waiting past January.

"Is it that important that your brother be here?"

"Yes, I want him to be here on the most important day of my life." I tried to impress upon him how important my big brother was to me. He had already missed my graduation, now my wedding?

"I don't want to wait," he said.

He was stubborn on the subject and I took it as a compliment, instead of a control issue. It was about this same time that he informed me I would quit smoking, even though he was a smoker. All I said was ok as I was secretly relieved I wouldn't have to smoke anymore. I never questioned for a minute why he would order me to do something he never intended to do himself. Love was blinding me from seeing red flags.

I was not at all happy, but I let Les have his way about not waiting for Ron to get home. I wrote to my brother and explained how my fiancé felt, and asked again if he was sure about when he could come home. If there was any chance, even a small one, I wanted to wait. Ron explained that when he would get leave, it would be short notice and we couldn't get a wedding planned. He said to go ahead if I was sure I really loved the guy.

I felt relieved in a way, but my heart was sad. Too many important events in my life were coming and going and one of the most important people was always absent. I was so confused about what to do. What if Les changed his mind if I made him wait? The wedding date was set for three months away on March 8th, 1969.

My big brother would not be walking me down the aisle.

The next three months were a blur of church reservations, dress fittings, tux rentals, florist visits, cake tastings, and decisions regarding our bridal party.

The best man would be Lloyd, alias Brownie, who Les had become friends with due to the fact that he was a car freak like Les. His two groomsmen were Steve, and my brother Jim. My maid of honor was Brenda and my bridesmaid was Gina, both my cousins. This created some hurt feelings with my friends, but I couldn't please everyone. I felt like I was being torn in two during this blur of preparations.

I wrote to Ron to announce my engagement and asked again if he could come home to my wedding. My answer came back in about two weeks. He congratulated me, remarked this guy better measure up, and he couldn't get leave for my wedding. He told me how sorry he was and how much he wanted to be there, but he had no idea when he would get leave. It might be in the summer, but could be the year after. Nothing had changed.

The fact that I was so in love with Les and couldn't wait to get married was the only reason I could bear letting my step-dad give me away. I wanted to share this time in my life with my big brother. Now I could relate to how he loved Carolyn. Maybe that was the reason he didn't have any negative remarks, or why he didn't talk Mom into making me wait to get married.

After much discussion I decided to invite my dad. I didn't care if he came or not. I extended the invitation for his wife, Ruby, who was trying to make us a family. She said they wouldn't miss it for the world, but I wasn't convinced.

Les and I were trying to find an apartment to rent, but the ones we could afford made me sick to my stomach. One we looked at had stains on the walls that I didn't even want to identify. I could barely see through the windows, and the bathroom had a smell that 10 gallons of bleach wouldn't touch. I could never live in anything so revolting.

Mom came to my rescue. Being an Army wife, she had lived in many trailers, and thought we should give them a look. So we went trailer shopping.

Used ones didn't cut it either, so we went to look at new ones, thinking we would never be able to afford a brand new trailer. Once we started looking inside the new ones, we were hooked. We looked at dozens and it was addicting. Each one was cooler than the last. I would never live in one of those nasty smelly apartments after walking through dozens of brand new, never lived in trailers. Now we had to figure how out how to come up with a down payment. Our parents loaned us enough to seal the deal, splitting the amount.

We picked the best one for the least dollar amount, and then found a lot to rent just outside Covington.

I was in heaven. I had a new gorgeous husband-to-be, a brand new house, and my wedding was coming together. Only one thing could make this better, my big brother making an appearance, then making my big day perfect by giving me away. At this point my only hope was that he was planning one of his surprise homecomings. I hoped it was his plan, but Mom put a big negative on my wishful dream.

"I wish for your sake that he would surprise you, but it is very doubtful. He knows all the planning that goes into a wedding. A surprise visit would not make things run smoothly," she said.

We had just dropped Les off after we signed papers for our new home and driving back to Mom's house.

"I don't care. I don't care if he walks into the middle of my ceremony, or if he gets there barely in time to walk me down the aisle. I just want Ron to be there. I want him to be in his dress greens and his Green Beret," I said. "Instead I get Charlie, the pride of my teenage years."

"I know you do, but you could have waited for your brother, if you weren't in such a hurry to get married. Are you having second thoughts? Too bad you didn't come to this conclusion before the invitations went out." She gave me the I-told-you-so-look.

"I know, but what if I made Les wait and he changed his mind about getting married to me," I said, half under my breath.

"What did you say?" she hit the brakes and almost stopped in the street.

"Oh nothing, it doesn't matter." I wasn't about to repeat it and I couldn't believe I had said it out loud, but it was true. I let Les have his way about not waiting for Ron to get home because I was afraid of losing him. So now I had to live with the consequences—my wedding without my big brother.

My wedding day, March 8th, had arrived and the only surprise I received was a snowstorm. It was supposed to be a cool spring day, but instead it was a freezing and snowy. Even with the cold and white stuff, the day was wonderful and I was so happy I thought I would burst. I had no doubts or apprehension what–soever about my choice of a husband. The only downside was the absence of my brother. Just like my graduation, I secretly hoped he would show up at the last minute and walk me down the aisle.

My father showed up, stayed during the ceremony, and then left. When he came through the reception line, he shook Les' hand and told him that I came from good blood. He always seemed to have some arrogant comment, and I was glad to see him go. He had left me when I was so young, that I barely remembered living with him. What I did remember was mostly bad. I had taken the high road and invited him, but it was over for me.

After the ceremony and reception, we took the traditional drive around town with friends following us honking and carrying on. I loved it and had to pinch myself because it didn't feel real. Four months ago I didn't know this man existed, and now he was my husband.

Linda & Les wedding

Is This Married Life?

The first few weeks together were like playing grown-up games and still didn't feel real. Les went to work and I took care of our house, did the laundry and grocery shopping.

We had only been married a few weeks when Les started going out most nights. One evening, after I pulled off his boots, served him his dinner and washed the dishes, he announced he was going into town. When I told him to give me a minute to get ready, he informed me I wasn't going.

"Where are you going?" I asked.

"Why? You act like you don't trust me."

"It's not a matter of trust. Why can't I go?"

He walked out.

I called Mom and asked her come to come get me. I knew where he might be hanging out with our friends, my friends. I was embarrassed, but I had her drive me through the hangout where I was sure he had gone.

We pulled in and there he was parked in the line of girls and guys I had introduced him to when we started dating. This group of kids were my friends and now he thought he should be going out at night without me.

He was standing about three cars over when I got out of Mom's car, walked over to our car and got in. He looked at me for a minute, walked over and got into the car. He drove me home without speaking, told me to get out and then left again. I called Mom and she came back and got me.

This time we found him at the bar where he stayed for hours, and then came home still mad. He wouldn't talk, so I had no idea what he thought or felt. By this time I was sure he did not want to be married and I felt he had changed his mind about me. I wanted to understand him so I apologized, even though I didn't know why. I didn't want to fight. I didn't want to sit at home while he acted like he was single.

We got along great sometimes, sometimes not. Les was like two different people.

Sometimes cold, uncaring and secretive, other times he was loving, caring and adorable. I felt like I was a yo-yo, yet I was determined to make my marriage work. I would not be a rerun of my mother's life. One of my friends told me the talk around town was that my marriage wouldn't last.

Most everyone who knew me had noticed a change in me and predicted the marriage would be over as fast as it had happened. I vowed that I would make my marriage last at all costs.

Is This Married Life?

Four months after our wedding, Les and I were sound asleep when the phone rang. I barely regained consciousness since it was usually my husband's work when the phone rang in the middle of the night. I reached for the phone and mumbled a response.

"Ron and Carolyn are coming home!" Mom shouted.

"What?" I was awake and on my feet. "Are you serious? No way, oh God, oh man, ok." I was rambling; my brain was so far ahead of our conversation.

"You and Les have to go to Chicago and meet their plane, they will be there in five hours," Mom said.

My big brother was coming home! Almost as soon as the excitement hit, so did regret. I had been married barely three months and he was on his way home. *Damn, why didn't I wait?* I felt sick to my stomach for a few minutes, then shook my head and pushed regret aside for the moment.

In less than half an hour we were on our way to O'Hare airport to meet Ron and Carolyn. I was so excited I could barely contain myself. It had been over two years and now I was going to see my brother. I had changed so much since he had last seen me. I was a married woman and couldn't wait for him to meet my husband.

Les was excited for me and seemed eager to meet Ron and Carolyn. As we were making our way to Chicago, I was secretly making plans to entertain Ron and Carolyn while they were home. I had visions of barbeques, movie nights, huge family dinners, card mara-

161

thons, and just hanging out. Then it hit me—would this be his leave before going to Vietnam?

"Are they sending him to Vietnam?" I asked Les, trying not to panic.

"I don't know," he said.

"Well, what do you think? Is that why he gets to come home, when six months ago they had no idea when he could have leave?"

"I don't know. No one can second guess the Army. Your Mom didn't say anything about it when you talked to her?"

"No, she didn't say anything. I'm scared. I bet that's where he is headed." I stared out the window. "I can't stand the thought of him being there.

Oh God, Please don't let this happen.

"Don't start worrying about it before you know."

I didn't say anything more about Ron's destination, but it never left my mind.

We got to the airport close to 3:00 am, found the flight gate and waited for them to arrive. I couldn't sit still and was up and down, looking out the enormous windows every time a plane landed. Les and I walked over and looked at the flight arrival and departure listings. I heard voices, turned and looked into my brother's face about 20 yards down the corridor.

"There they are!" I yelled, grabbing Les' arm.

I ran into my brother's arms, laughing and crying as we hugged. I hugged Carolyn, then turned to Les and nearly shoved him into my brother's handshake. Ron started laughing as soon as we got through introductions.

"I wondered who my newly married sister was hanging onto," Ron said.

I looked at him, and then at Les. I didn't understand.

"The beard, he didn't have a beard in the wedding pictures. I didn't know it was Les and I couldn't understand why you would be with another guy. I nearly punched him out." We all laughed. "I saw you Sis and thought, hmm, guess her new husband must be working, maybe one of Les' brothers brought her. Then you leaned into him and started holding his hand. I thought wow, that's just a little cozy for a brother-in-law."

We laughed and hugged again. I was on top of the world.

My beloved big brother and my new husband, who I was crazy about, were walking through the airport among hundreds of travelers. I knew without a doubt that no one was happier than me.

We picked up Ron and Carolyn's luggage, made our way to the car and headed to Covington.

There wasn't a quiet moment all the way home as Ron and I had an equal an amount of questions for each other. He wanted to hear all about our wedding and as usual, I hung on his every word. Carolyn had many stories about her experiences in Germany, and we laughed at her request to hit the first McDonald's.

"Where are you going after your leave?" I asked, crossing my fingers and praying while I waited for him to answer.

"Back to Germany for at least a year," he said.

Oh Thank You God, Thank You God, Thank You God. My pact with God was still in place.

"That's the best news I've ever heard," I said with a long breath of relief.

When we arrived at Mom's near daylight, everyone was waiting up for us.

There were hugs, kisses and laughter all around as Ron's homecomings were my family's favorite time. We had a month to spend with him and I was determined to get my fair share.

It was almost full daylight when we unloaded their luggage and we decided we should all get a little sleep. I hugged my brother again and promised to see him a little later in the morning. Les and I went home to get some rest. He went right to sleep, but I didn't. I was still in high gear and sleep would not come. Ron was home for a month! I knew the 30 days would fly past fast, but right now, nothing on this earth could bring me down.

I wanted to go back to Mom's house and see what Ron and Carolyn were doing, but I had to force myself to behave like an adult instead of a little girl. I got out of bed and decided to make sure my house was spotless.

Ron had teased me about doing a white glove inspection when he came to see our new trailer. I knew he was teasing, but I wanted him to see that I was a fantastic housekeeper. I washed all the dishes, dusted, rearranged things, and then put everything back. I waited for Les to wake up before I ran the vacuum. When I was satisfied it was spotless, I stood in my small house and imagined Ron and Carolyn's reaction. I couldn't wait any longer to be with my family. I called Mom to see if everyone was awake from our early morning nap and she said Ron and Carolyn were on their way to check out my new house.

Excitement ran through my veins, as I realized that any minute my brother would arrive. I was watching out the window as they drove up and had to stop myself from jumping up and down like a five-year-old. I met them at the door, smiling and welcoming them to my home. Carolyn told me how adorable our trailer was, but I was waiting to see what my brother's reaction would be. He pulled a white glove onto his hand.

"Oh no, you really have a white glove?" I asked.

He ran his white glove clad fingers over the top of my doorway, and then brought them up for everyone to see. There was no dirt on those clean white gloves, I had passed.

We laughed at Ron's joke, but I was thrilled the glove had no sign of dust. Would I ever outgrow the need for his approval? It was doubtful.

The first couple of days were filled with family and friends as Mom had invited everyone over to see Ron and Carolyn. We listened intently to the stories of

Germany, their friends and what little he told us about his Special Forces career.

After a few days, the steady flow of people slowed. This made me happy because although it was fun to be a part of the excitement, after the rush there was more time for us.

Les and I were at Mom's every day. Either I had laundry to do or she would invite us for dinner. I made sure I was there whether I had a reason or not. I knew this precious time would end all too soon and Ron would be gone again.

On several evenings, we had euchre games. My family had euchre running through their veins and Les was a card player, so this was right up his alley. I didn't always play, but I liked sitting in the background watching and listening to the camaraderie within my family. It reminded me of years past when Ron was on leave from the Navy. We would be at my grandparent's farm where the family gathered, having big dinners, card marathons, and celebrating Ron being home.

Les and I were getting along better, I was so happy I wasn't concentrating on everything he did that I didn't like or understand. Being around my brother and his wife seemed to have a positive effect on us. One evening, while watching Ron interact with Carolyn, I realized how much I longed for Les to treat me the way Ron treated Carolyn. He treated her as if she was the most precious thing in his life. His pet name for her, Sam, was even cute to me. He considered her in everything he did, with friends or family. His teasing was playful, not ever mean or hurtful. He always had something sweet or teasing to say to her, or give her a kiss when he walked by, or tickle her as she was washing dishes.

Having the Military in common, Ron and Les seemed to be getting along well. Les had been in the Air Force for four years and in Vietnam. Les didn't talk about Vietnam with me, but that was not unusual for him or Vietnam Veterans. I don't know if he and Ron talked about Vietnam, but if so, they kept it between themselves.

One afternoon, while folding clothes in the living room, I could hear Mom and Ron talking in the kitchen over coffee and cigarettes. This was a memory that usually brought me comfort, reminding me of when I would hear them talking late into the night while I was supposed to be asleep. Today it gave me chills and made me want to lock him in the basement so he could never go back to the Army.

"Son, do you ever hear from Ski?" she asked. Ski was Ron's team leader in Germany before he went to Vietnam.

"Yeah, a couple months ago I got a letter from him. His version of what is going on in Vietnam was upsetting," he said as he poured another cup of coffee.

"What do you mean?" she asked.

"Ski said whoever was running this war sure as hell didn't have a brain in their head. He said we could have won the damn thing years ago, had our men home and saved a hell of a lot of American lives," Ron said. "He told me that in one battle his team took a hill seven times only to have orders to back off and let the NV take it over again. Then order us to take it again, losing several of our men each time. He said he was becoming extremely disillusioned with the entire mess."

"Oh son, that is horrible. Why would our officers do such a thing? I don't understand."

"I'm not sure I do either, Mom. Ski is not the first one of the guys saying these things. It makes no sense to me, but that is what happens when the wrong people in Washington run the war."

"Ron, is there any way you can stay out of there?"

"I can't if they tell me to go, but it makes me skeptical on whether I want to volunteer to go."

"Oh Ron, please don't do that. I am begging you," Mom said. I heard her pull a tissue out of the box.

"I won't, Mom. I wouldn't do that to Sam, she is scared enough. But that doesn't mean I won't get sent there. And you know there is nothing in the world that I can do about it."

"I know Son, I know the drill."

Mom and Ron scooted their chairs back and ended the conversation as I sat there with the basket of towels in front of me, tears dripping down my face. I slipped out the front door and walked around the house where I could go back in without them knowing I had overheard.

I didn't doubt for one second that what Ron had said was the absolute truth. I had listened to stories about Ski for years and he was another hero in my mind. Anyone who had my brother's respect had to be right on. *How can this be happening in the US?* We were supposed to be the best, the most honorable, and the most dedicated to our service men and women.

I wiped my face and went back into the house, pushing my fear back and pretending everything was ok. I didn't think my feelings about Vietnam could get any worse and now they had. I began asking God again to keep our pact and never let my brother go to that horrid place.

A few days later Ron, Carolyn, Les and I decided to go to our local theater and watch True Grit. Ron was a big movie buff and loved westerns,

James Bond movies, military shows and anything action packed. It was such a simple outing, a movie, but to me it was incredible. All the years when I was young I watched him go out with his friends, while Jim and I stayed home. I begrudged the time he spent with them, the laughter, the joking and the friendship. Now, it was my turn, I was going out with him and Carolyn. It was just a movie, but to me it was better than the prom.

The following weeks passed like someone had pushed the fast forward button and now Ron only had a few days left at home. The parade of family and friends would start over, only now it was tearful good-byes instead of joyful reunions just one short month before. I busied myself so I wouldn't have to watch everyone say goodbye. It hurt and I knew I would be the one crying all too soon.

Departure day arrived and although I hated it, I wouldn't miss being with Ron to the very last minute. I didn't want to be a baby, but I had spent my entire life saying goodbye to my big brother.

The ride to the airport was quiet compared to the ride home one month ago and we arrived in a little over three hours. Like robots, their luggage was checked and we made our way to the gate and waited for the intercom to announce the flight boarding.

Ron looked handsome in his dress greens and beret. This was years before half of the service personnel wore berets. Back then when you saw a military guy in a Green Beret you knew he was US Army Special Forces. People would often stare at him and I wondered who was more proud, me or him?

Minutes later, the dreaded announcement came. We shared hugs, kisses, handshakes, and promises to write soon. Next was the vow to take care of Mom we always gave Ron. My tears were falling as they walked through the gateway and out of sight. My heart was breaking again.

Les and I made our way through the airport and out to our car. I replayed the entire month through my aching head. Especially the night one month ago, right here at the same airport. I had been giddy with the anticipation of spending a month with my big brother. My mood was now at the opposite end of the spectrum.

The one bright spot was that he was going back to Germany and not Vietnam. I wiped my tears again, looked up to the heavens and thanked God once more for keeping him out of that horrible country. I could endure his absence if he was safe somewhere and not on a suicide mission I felt our troops were on in Vietnam.

The Emptiness Returns

As usual, the first few days after Ron left I felt empty and unsettled. I went through the motions, but his absence left me depressed. I didn't think it would be as bad this time because I had Les now, but it hadn't changed.

Mom was having a hard time and I would find her crying when I stopped by unannounced. I would ask what was wrong and she would say nothing, but I knew. She felt the same as I did, lost and sad.

Ron was now relatively safe in Germany, but I knew he was on borrowed time. How much longer could he escape Vietnam? As the days passed, we got used to being without him again and returned to letters and pictures, waiting for his next leave.

It didn't take too many days for insecurities to creep back into my head regarding my relationship with my new husband. Every other day I was certain he wanted out of our marriage, so when he announced that we should have a baby, I was in disbelief. We had only been married four months and he spent much of his spare time with his friends, not me. I was so surprised and thrilled that I couldn't think of anything but the fact that he did not want a divorce.

I was so happy I didn't consider how young we were, or the fact that I had only known Les for seven months. I wasn't happy with his idea of how a marriage should be. I had no say in how the money was spent, I was not allowed to see my friends, drive our car, or think for myself—I just wanted him to love me. I didn't care, or think, about how all these problems were going to be solved.

I ran his words over and over in my head. Having a baby would tie him to me forever. This was what I wanted, no matter what I had to go through. I loved him so hard it hurt. A baby, yes that is what I would give him, even though I didn't understand why he wanted a baby or why he wanted one with me. He didn't seem to be happy with most things about me. I needed to lose weight, I talked too much, I was too friendly with people, and he didn't want me to have anything to do with my friends or male cousins.

Having a baby would mean he would have to stay home and be a family man. I convinced myself he was ready to act like he was married to me. I wasn't nervous to become a mom, as I had my mother to guide and teach me.

I went off the pill and two months later, I was pregnant. We were both thrilled and Mom shared in our joy.

She and Les were quite close during the first several years of our marriage.

I wrote to Ron and Carolyn announcing that they were going to be an aunt and uncle. They sent their love and congratulations. Ron gave orders to send pictures as soon as I was showing.

The next three months were not the most pleasant. Morning sickness plagued me throughout the days and nights. Les was pretty sweet during most of my pregnancy, except for the times he told me my nausea was all in my head. I wanted to puke on his head and then ask him if it was all in his head.

By my fifth month I felt better and was obsessed with fixing the baby's room with pink and blue things. Mom and I couldn't stay out of the baby department. Every week the room had new pictures, clothes and anything baby related. It had to be unisex things because this was before determining the sex of babies before they arrived.

My family had a baby shower for me and we were blessed with a stroller, baby seat, a swing, diaper bags, bottles, clothes and everything we would need for this much anticipated baby.

The crib was set up, the clothes were in the drawers and my bags were packed for the hospital four months ahead of my due date. We had the family bassinet set up ready for the first few weeks when the baby would be next to us in our room.

Les had decided we were going to have a girl. This was surprising to me as he was into hunting, sports, shooting, motorcycles, cars, and was a veteran. I figured he would want a boy. He wouldn't even talk about having a boy as his mind was made up. He had four brothers, four nephews, and one niece. I had no faith that we would have a girl.

A letter arrived from Ron with strict instructions not to buy a bassinet for his new niece or nephew. I couldn't wait to tell Mom, I called her immediately.

"Oh wow, Ron is sending something for the baby!" I said as I tried to find the part in the letter so I could read it to her.

"You aren't surprised are you?" Mom said.

"No, not really but I can't wait. I bet it's different from anything around here," I said.

"It will be something German. They have really different wooden made cradles. You will have to wait and see. Whatever it is, it will be nice," she assured me. I had no doubt about that.

I was at the post office every day, checking to see if I had a delivery. Ron had spoiled me with special gifts from all over the world. Jewelry boxes from Japan, charms from Italy for my charm bracelet, a labor chair from Italy, goat skin rugs from Spain, the list was endless. Now he was sending something for my baby.

About a month later it arrived and I couldn't get it opened fast enough. The wrapping was endless as Ron was the world's best packer, probably because he did it so often.

After an hour we had all parts unpacked and unwrapped, with the contents spread all over the living room floor. I stared at the pieces. It wasn't anything at all what I had envisioned. I expected a cradle made with dark wood and sitting low to the ground. Nothing in this pile of wood, metal and material resembled what I thought a German cradle would look like.

Les reached for the instructions and began to assemble the baby bed. Soon enough it began to come to life and it was the most beautiful baby cradle I had ever seen. It was red painted wood with a white lace canopy. It had a wooden peg that could be removed to let the cradle rock. I stared, touched and rocked the empty bed that would hold my brother's first niece or nephew.

Ron and Carolyn had included a letter in with the cradle and asked for one stipulation—they would use the cradle for their babies when they came home and started a family. I couldn't think of anything more wonderful than to have all of the family babies sleep in this wonderful gift from my big brother. Tears filled my eyes and heart. I missed him and wanted to share this time in my life with him. I wanted him to be here when I gave birth. The realization hit me that he would not see me pregnant and I had no idea when he would hold my baby in his arms. I sat in the middle of the floor crying. Les looked up, and said nothing.

After my pity party, I washed my face and buried my sadness. I arranged and re-arranged my special new cradle in different places so everyone could see it. Next, I sat down and created a thank you letter to Ron and Carolyn. I wanted to call them, but in 1970 we didn't make overseas phone calls to say thank you or we miss you. Those calls were for emergencies only. We wrote letters, many letters.

It's Baby Time!

My due date was fast approaching and I felt like a giant pumpkin with legs. With two weeks to go, my doctor put me on bed rest as the baby was resting on a nerve and it was hard to walk, sit, or sleep. Les and I moved into Mom's house so I wouldn't be alone while he was at work.

On May 7th, Mom fell while walking into the kitchen and landed with her foot underneath her butt. Not only was her ankle broken, it was crushed.

She was taken to the hospital by ambulance.

I was supposed to be home resting but I couldn't, not with Mom on her way to the ER. I felt responsible for her accident as she was doing my laundry when she fell. The doctors told us it was a very bad break and she might never walk properly again. She would have to have surgery, inserting pins to hold her ankle and foot together.

Mom had surgery the morning after the fall. Les, Jim, Charlie, her sister Lettie, my grandparents and I gathered at the hospital to wait. The presence of our big brother would have been welcomed at times like this, but Jim and I were going to have to learn to be adults without leaning on him for every decision and crisis. I was a married woman and about to become a Mom. I would have to handle things like this on my own, without Ron. He had been gone off and on for many years, and Mom was our rock. Now she was out of commission and he was out of the country. I had Les to lean on and Jim was about to graduate from high school. We would take care of Mom in Ron's absence.

The surgery took several hours and the outcome wasn't what we had hoped for. The metal pins would hold her ankle for now, but she had some kind of bone deteriorating disease. Her ankle would never be the same, she would always have pain, and we would start to see other parts of her body start to have problems. I felt like someone had punched me in the stomach and I was having cramps. *Wait, are these labor pains?*

A nurse paged my doctor to ask if he wanted to check me before I went home for the night. I was sent to the maternity floor and checked by one of the RN's. She reported that I was dilated very little, so I was ordered to go home and rest, mother in the hospital or not. Les and I talked with the nursing staff, made them promise to call if Mom needed us, and then left for home. I was exhausted and scared for my Mom and myself. I could not imagine having this baby without her taking care of us.

"I can't do this without my Mom," I said to Les.

"I don't think you have much of a choice at this point."

"Thanks. Why did she have to fall? Why did it have to be so bad? I need Ron to be here."

"They won't let him come home for this, it's not life or death," he said.

"I know. I've been living with the military thing all my life. I know the rules."

I dried my eyes and told myself to grow up. This could be something so much worse. What if it was cancer, like before? I would have to toughen it up. I tried to get some sleep and rest, but it didn't happen. I was uncomfortable since the baby had dropped, worrying about Mom, and feeling guilty about her injury since it had happened while she was doing my laundry.

Les and I went back to the hospital the next day, as soon as he was home from work. I had called the hospital several times and couldn't wait to see how she was doing.

We walked into Mom's room and Les stopped. All color had left his face, and he had a tortured look. He excused himself and told me he would be outside.

I kissed Mom, asked about her pain and if I could get her anything. After I had checked her out, I told her I would be right back and left to find Les. I had to find out what was wrong with him. I had never seen him look or act so strange. He had looked physically sick. I found him outside her room leaning against the wall.

"What is wrong with you? You look terrible," I said.

"I'm sorry. I can't go back in there."

"Ok, you don't have to, but why, what is wrong?"

He fidgeted, stalled and he ran his hands through his hair. I stared at him, waiting for an explanation.

"Her cast smells exactly like the dead bodies I had to bring back from Vietnam on the plane."

He had kept all that ugliness from me and I felt instant nausea. He had been a load master on a C130. He had shared with me some of his duties and I knew they hauled all kinds of things in and out of Vietnam, tanks, jeeps, food and supplies. He left out the fact that he had been in charge of bringing our dead soldiers home in body bags. He explained that they would pile them up in layers, blood running across the plane floor.

"Oh my God, I am so sorry. You don't have to go back, but I'm not telling Mom the reason. I can't tell her what you told me. Ron may end up there before we get troops out and I won't let her hear that. I'll tell her you don't feel well."

How could I go back in there and pretend? I thought I might be sick as I pictured what Les had told me about the body bags of American soldiers. I held my hand over my mouth and forced myself not to throw up.

Someone's son, brother or husband lying in a plastic bag, stacked on each other, on the floor of a plane. I knew they died over there, but I had never been told how they got back home. This was barbaric. The image of flag-draped coffins and staunch military personnel lining the way for a fallen soldier flashed through my mind and I knew I would have to pursue this question at a later time.

I went back to Mom and explained that Les didn't feel well and not to worry. Les did come back into the room, but kept his distance from Mom, so as not to inhale the smell from her blood soaked cast.

As the evening wore on, I had to be checked again to see if I should bother to go home or stay and have a baby. This time they said I should stay, even though it wasn't going to be anytime soon. By this time the doctor and nursing staff knew I was spending too much time at the hospital with my Mom. We lived 30 minutes away and they didn't want to take the chance I would give birth on my way back.

After telling Mom goodnight, Les and I went back to maternity floor and checked in. It was baby time.

I had to push the image of American soldiers, dead, bleeding, bagged and stacked on a plane from Vietnam. I felt guilty and selfish as I begged God never to let this happen to my big brother. My stomach lurched again. *Was this labor or the picture I had stuck in my head?*

Having my first baby was a long drawn out labor. I was checked in by 10:00 p.m. and then the whole process slowed down. Sometime after midnight they gave me something to let me rest a little better, and around 7:00 a.m. the baby decided to make an entrance.

"Les, get the nurse, the baby is coming now," I said.

He came back with a nurse.

"You have a long way to go Mrs. Winters, but I will check to make you feel better."

"No, it's coming now."

"No, this is your first baby. You have been very slow with your dilation, it will be quite a while," she paused and then ran toward the door. "I'll get the doctor."

"I told her it was time," I said to Les.

Within a couple minutes I was being rolled into the delivery room and at 8:50 am, I gave birth to Angel Joette. She was 7lbs 8oz and 21 inches long. I loved this baby before I gave birth to her, but now I felt a devotion I had never known. I thought of my Mom and all she had gone through with my brothers and me. I felt a new respect for her.

My brother and his friend Walt were at the hospital a few hours after I gave birth. They checked her out then went to report to Mom that she was the cutest baby in the nursery.

The birth of our daughter was the highest point of my life and I couldn't imagine anything ever topping this. She was beautiful and perfect and I thought I might burst. The only thing that could have made it better was if Ron had been there to share in our joy.

Four days later, Les took Mom and I both home from the hospital. I was happy, but uneasy about Mom not being able stay at our house as we had planned. Instead Les' Mom and Dad had invited themselves to stay and help out.

The next four days seemed like four weeks. I was nervous without Mom and didn't trust my mother-in-law's advice regarding anything baby related. Then, just as quickly as they appeared, they left.

My grandparents had been staying with Mom, but they were not up to taking care of her. It was decided that Les and I would move into Mom's to take care of her. I felt so much better knowing I would be with Mom, even though she couldn't help with the baby, we would be together.

By now it was the end of May and Jim was graduating from high school. It would be difficult, but we would get Mom to his graduation. She would have to be taken in a wheel chair, but she would be there. The entire family was there to watch Jim receive his diploma. I'm sure he missed the same thing I did at my big night. Ron was unable to attend, Germany and the Army kept him away.

My days were a maze of new baby care, bottles, diapers, laundry, cooking, cleaning and waiting on Mom for everything. My nights were spent up with a new baby that had her days and nights mixed up.

Since I was Mom's caregiver, there was no time for naps when Angel was sleeping during the day. It wasn't long before I was exhausted.

About a week after we moved in with Mom, we received a letter from Ron and Carolyn. They were coming home in three weeks. Mom and I looked at each other with surprise and panic. It had barely been a year since he had been home, so this could not be good. I kept reading, searching for one word. My eyes raced down the page until I found what I was looking for, Vietnam.

He was going to come home for a month because he was being sent to hell.

"Oh my God Mom, he's going. He is going to Vietnam. This is why he is coming home."

As soon as the words were out, I wished I hadn't let my feelings escape, but the news had caught me off guard. Tears were spilling onto Mom's cheeks and I handed her a box of tissues. It looked like the pact I had with God had run out.

My sweet baby girl had barely entered into our lives and this was supposed to be the most precious and happy time of our lives. Now it would be clouded by fear of what could happen to Ron. This was not going to be an easy year.

Uncle Ron Meets Angel

My days and nights blurred into each other for the next three weeks as caring for Angel and Mom had me on the go nearly 24/7. Having to grow up was now in the past. I had grown up fast and hard. High school and running around with my friends seemed like a distant dream. It had been a conscious choice, so I wasn't complaining—I was just tired and wondered why I had been in such a hurry. Then all I had to do was look at my sweet Angel or watch Les holding our baby daughter and my frustrations melted away.

Ron and Carolyn were expected home the second week in July. They would stay at Mom's. Les and I were going to move back to our home. Carolyn was going to stay with Mom again, while Ron was gone. She had agreed to care for Mom and the house. She could clean, wash clothes and obsess all day long. I didn't care this time, I needed a break.

Trixie, Ron and Carolyn's Pomeranian child, would arrive in Indy in one week. She had been Carolyn's birthday gift from Ron. She had white, fluffy, beautifully groomed fur and was the funniest, most spoiled dog in the world. She had flown to Germany with Carolyn and now she would fly home a couple weeks before them. I had agreed to take care of her.

Everyone loved Trix, as she was the child Ron and Carolyn didn't have.

I was scared out of my mind thinking of Ron being in Vietnam. The Special Forces were highly trained for secret special ops missions the public had no knowledge of. Ron always down played any danger he might be in, but I knew differently.

Our guys were being sent home in body bags daily, by the hundreds. I didn't want to know what the statistics were for his return. Prayer was all I could do. Surely God wouldn't let anything happen to him. He was so vital to our family, so loved, and too important to lose. That was it, he would come home. God would return him safe and sound to his adoring family. It had to be that way. Any other scenario was inconceivable.

The next three weeks dragged. Mom's recovery was slow and she could barely get out of bed. Jim and I were not having the best time either, since he wasn't any help when he got home from working in the hot sun all day. I tried to boss him into helping, but that didn't work. Charlie was on somewhat of a good behavior pattern, maybe rehearsing for when Ron got here.

Trixie was more work than fun as she wouldn't eat and barely drank. She would walk around her bowl of food and water and cry or bark at it. We couldn't figure it out.

"Mom, what the heck is the matter with her?" I asked as I stood over Trix and tried to get her to eat. "Do you think she misses them?"

"I have no idea. She acts like she is starving," Mom said.

"Did she do this when you were in Germany?" I asked. I pushed her bowl toward her.

"No, never."

All I could come up with was she was homesick for Ron and Carolyn. But if she didn't eat she was going to get sick or die.

"Mom, I have to make her eat. If something happens to her, Carolyn will kill me."

That night we had fried chicken, mashed potatoes, gravy, green beans, and rolls for dinner. I cut up some chicken and spooned some potatoes and gravy onto Trixie's dish. She whined and paced around it.

"What the heck is her problem?" I asked as we all watched her peculiar behavior.

Finally I picked her up and laid her on her back like a baby in my arms. I got a bit of potatoes and gravy on my spoon and fed it to her. She ate the food and the entire family roared with laughter.

"Are you kidding me?" I asked.

No one answered because they were still cracking up.

"I don't have time to hold this dog and feed her like a newborn. I have a real baby to take care of," I said. I sat her on the floor and put her food in her bowl. "Surely she will eat now that she has tasted her chicken and gravy."

She paced, whined, and refused to eat out of her bowl. Everyone was still laughing, but this time trying to coax her to eat her people food. She refused to eat out of her bowl. Out of fear that she would get sick or starve, I picked her up and fed her. Her cuteness had vanished for me.

The countdown to Ron and Carolyn's arrival was 24 hours. I had cleaned the house, done the laundry, changed all the sheets, washed the dishes and cooked dinner for the family. I fussed with Angel, changing her outfits several times. I wanted her to look perfect to meet her uncle and aunt for the first time. I placed the cradle so Ron could see it as soon as he came into the house. I couldn't wait for him to see Angel.

One short year ago when he came home I was a new bride, now I was a new mother. If I could only put the brakes on and slow the world down to a crawl, we could spend more time with him.

I was laying Angel down when my younger cousin Mona cried out, "They're here! Bo and Carolyn are in the driveway."

They were driving their car as Ron had had it shipped home and it was waiting for them when they were stateside.

I picked up Angel and headed out the back door with Jim, Charlie, Aunt Lettie, Uncle Gene, Gina, Mona, Lisa, my grandparents and Les, everyone except Mom.

I was standing inside the yard gate, holding my prize, ready to hand her over to my big brother. He was all smiles as he took her in his arms, held her up, and then gave her a big kiss on her little cheek. I thought my heart would burst. If only I could stop time and keep all of us here, right now.

"You did good Sis, she's a keeper!" Ron said as he admired her.

Carolyn was already trying to take her from him. "Awwwww she is so cute. This is going to be fun," Carolyn said.

"All right, you get night shift," I said.

"Oh, she has her days and nights mixed. You let her uncle fix that, we will get her straightened out," Ron said as he winked at me.

"You got it. I'll be glad for you to fix her. I'm sleep deprived," I said.

I felt a surge of relief, even though it was a joke about fixing her. Ron had that effect on us. He was the head of our family even when halfway around the world.

My shattered nerves could take a break while he was home and in charge. I already felt better, as long as I could push back the reason why he was here.

"We have to get you inside before Mom starts throwing stuff," I said. "She can't get off the bed."

We went back inside so Mom could get her hugs from Ron and Carolyn. They exchanged hugs and kisses and Ron began to inspect her cast. Of course we had written all over it.

"Here Bo, sign Aunt Genie's cast," Lisa said as she handed Ron a marker.

"Ok, let me find an empty spot," he said as he signed his name, and then handed the marker to Carolyn.

We had found Ron's stick horse from his childhood while moving things in Mom's upstairs. It was a painted broomstick, with ratty red fake hair for the mane and a plastic handle for the reins. We presented it to him out on the patio while we finished cooking on the grill. Ron rode it all around the yard yelling giddy-up and pretending to whip the stick to make the horse go. We laughed till we cried. These were the best of times. I watched my family and loved the picture we made. The panic of Ron's departure would catch me off guard sometimes, but I would push it back. The entire day was a family celebration, welcoming Ron and Carolyn, passing Angel around, eating, drinking, laughing and loving. I refused to let fear ruin the first day my daughter and my big brother spent together.

The first day came to an end too soon. It was time for Les and I to pack all the baby stuff and everything else that had migrated to Mom's in the past three weeks. By this time we had two cars, and both were packed to the roof.

We hugged and kissed everyone goodbye and pre-pared to take our baby girl home. My grandparents, aunt, uncle, and cousins were hugging Ron and Car-olyn and promising to see them in a few days, already planning our next get-together. There would be many before he left.

I would be back at Mom's the next day as there was no way I wouldn't spend every moment as close to my brother as I could for the next month. I found every excuse under the sun to be there, even though I didn't need one.

Ron seemed to have a lot of business to take care of while he was home. I didn't know exactly what he was doing as I only heard bits and pieces, but it sounded legal. I heard the name of a local attorney a few times, then mention of him and Carolyn signing papers. I was too busy with Angel and still helping Mom to even wonder what he was doing. Besides, it wasn't unusual for Ron to be taking care of business.

He had sent several big, beautiful, antique German clocks home to be taken care of in his absence. He took one to Aunt Lettie's and hung it on her wall, telling her to leave it there until he returned home. He hung one on Mom's wall and told her the same thing. The rest were in boxes ready to be stored in Mom's upstairs.

He went to Charlie's sister, Jeanette, and talked to her about something, no one ever knew at the time what it was about. Aunt Jeanette was an astounding woman and our family adored her. What we couldn't figure out was how she came out of that weird family.

She may have been one of the reasons Mom put up with Charlie for so long.

Next we had to make room for Ron and Carolyn's things in Mom's upstairs, so this was the excuse we used to clean out un-needed keepsakes of our younger life. Mom couldn't throw anything away that had an ounce of sentiment to her. She recognized that this task had to be done, but she hated it.

Ron backed Charlie's truck up to the upstairs window, took out the screen and started. Mom could hear things being thrown out the window and began to cry. She couldn't stand not knowing what was being thrown away. Ron, Jim and Les carried her up the stairs so she could oversee what was being tossed.

It took her about two seconds to get even more upset. Ron, Carolyn and I were going through boxes and Ron was tossing stuff out the window. Mom was frantic as she couldn't believe what we all thought was ridiculous to keep. At one point, Ron held up some of his first grade papers and teased Mom.

"Oh Mom, why on earth do you still have this stuff?" he asked.

"Son, it's your school papers, I can't get rid of those," she said as she blew her nose.

"Mom, you have me. You don't need these," Ron said and gave them a toss out the window and into the truck bed.

I felt sorry for Mom. She treasured our things and I couldn't help but let Ron words stab my heart. *Please God, let this be true forever.*

The upstairs was beginning to look better. Now we could fit Ron and Carolyn's boxes up there until Ron came home. The discard session ended a few hours later and new boxes now replaced the old ones. Mom had been taken back downstairs. She had settled down and come to the realization that you can't keep every paper, article of clothing, Christmas tag, or empty boxes that might come in handy.

Supper was being prepared by Carolyn and me. Angel was in her deep sleep that should have been for the wee hours of the night. I knew I was in for another night without sleep.

After we had finished eating and were still sitting around the table talking, Ron told me to bring his niece to him.

"Uh, ok," I said as I got up to get her, never questioning his request.

"Let's wake her up, get those days and nights back in order."

"Oh, ok give it a try," I said.

He took her from me and began to shake her gently, saying her name.

She showed no signs of waking up. He kissed her neck, tickled her feet softly, and sat her straight up on his lap. She was dead to the world. By this time we were all laughing at both of them. Ron was bound and determined to wake her up, but it was not going to happen. He held her up and talked to her. Her little head fell over and Carolyn jumped up and took her.

"That's enough. She's sleepy and you're not going to be able to wake her up now. That is pitiful," she scolded Ron. He gave her up as Carolyn took her back to her cradle and tucked her in. She came back to the table and tried to shame Ron.

We were still snickering at how funny Angel looked and Ron's tough guy attitude of fixing her sleep habits.

"Sorry Sis, I tried. Sam's the boss. It's her fault if you have to stay up all night again," he said as he winked at me. Carolyn swatted his shoulder like he was in trouble.

Every family interaction we had like this made me more determined that Ron would come back to us. But I never took for granted the time spent with him, secretly engraving these memories in my soul. Just in case.

We were about two weeks into his four week leave. Every time I let myself think about it, I broke out in cold sweats and felt panic like I had never felt before. I only let myself get upset when I was alone as I didn't want to upset Mom, make Ron feel bad, or let Carolyn see my fear. I also didn't share these feelings with my husband, as he would have told me not to cry. I didn't know he felt about the situation. I believed he cared, but didn't know how to show it.

Family get-togethers, house and yard clean-ups, Ron touching base with all of his friends—everyone went through the motions of pretending everything was normal.

One evening Ron, Carolyn, Les, Angel and I went down town to the street fair. Ron insisted on carrying

Angel and several of his friends thought she was his baby. He would tease me and take credit for her existence, then laugh and tell his friends that this "cutie pie" was his niece. I loved walking behind him and watching him carry Angel. I felt like I had waited my entire life to have this relationship with my brother and I didn't want it to end. I didn't want him to leave again, especially to Vietnam. I hated our government right then and whoever was letting this atrocity go on.

Please God, bring him home to us. I asked this of God many times a day. Then I would tell myself it would be ok. God would not let us lose him. I knew it.

Time was racing by with only a few days left and Ron was busy getting his affairs in order. He was organizing and preparing for Carolyn to be without him for a year, or for however long he would be gone.

It was down to one day. The extended family—grandparents, Aunt Lettie, Uncle Gene, Gina, Mona, and Lisa, had gathered for one last dinner before he had to go. There were other relatives also dropping in and out. We had a family dinner with everyone trying to be upbeat and not dwell on where Ron was going. I tried not to watch or listen as each member hugged and kissed him goodbye at the end of the day. I couldn't stand the fear in every one's eyes, or the hugs that were too tight and too long. I knew what they were thinking. Would this be the last time they looked into his eyes and held him? I kept myself busy with Angel, Mom or cleaning up from the dinner. Tomorrow I would be telling him goodbye and I didn't know how I was going to do it. One minute I was certain God would bring him home to us and the next I felt crippling fear.

It had been decided that Carolyn, Les and I would take Ron to O'Hare Airport in Chicago, where he would depart to Hawaii, then on to Vietnam. We had to leave Covington at about 3:00 pm. My grandparents, Jim, Mom and Charlie were there to see him off. No one stayed inside while Ron told Mom goodbye. Then he came outside, shook Charlie's hand and told him to take care of Mom. Next he shook Jim's hand and told him he was the man of the house and to take care of Mom and Carolyn. Then he hugged him. I couldn't watch and turned away.

All the time this was taking place, grandpa was standing with tears running down his face. Ron hugged grandma next and told her he loved her and he would be back before she knew it. He turned to grandpa and tried to console him, but it was no use. Grandpa had once been a very strong man, but that was before his heart attack and years of aging. He could no longer control his emotions or fear, and had no idea how his behavior was affecting Ron. I could see the pain on my brother's face. He loved grandpa and grandma like parents. Grandpa had been the father Ron never had. This was torture for both of them.

We got into the car and backed out to leave. Grandpa followed the car and stood in the middle of the alley crying. "I'll never see you again, Ronnie. I'll never see you again, Ronnie. This is the last time I will ever see you," Grandpa said as his voice broke into sobs.

We had to leave so Ron wouldn't miss his flight, so we drove away leaving grandpa standing in the middle of the alley, crying and repeating himself.

No one spoke for a while. I knew I couldn't speak without crying and I didn't want to start or I wouldn't stop. Ron broke the silence when we stopped for gas, asking if anyone wanted anything. No one did and I couldn't have put anything into my stomach anyway.

I just wanted to erase the image of my grandfather's pain. I wanted to convince myself he was being over dramatic and weak because of his age and ailments, but it was no use. I was petrified that he was right.

We got on the road and headed for Chicago. After a while we were talking, laughing and trying to forget what we had gone through at Mom's and what was coming in a couple of hours.

We stopped to eat dinner about halfway to Chicago. Ron got plenty of attention when he was dressed in his Army Special Forces dress greens and beret. Usually the military didn't travel in dress because of the horrible way the public treated them, but it must have been the Green Beret that still got the respect.

The stop took longer than we anticipated and put us behind schedule. Ron joked with the waitress, teasing her into hurrying up the process by telling her he had a plane to catch, they needed him in Vietnam. I turned so no one could see how his remark affected me.

Back on the road we had to make up time or he would miss his plane, making him AWOL. I secretly hoped he would, maybe they wouldn't let him go. We got into bad traffic and it was doubtful we would make it in time. I could feel Ron's tension. He and Les made a plan that we would pull up to the appropriate gate, three of us would get out with Ron's baggage and Les would park the car, then find us inside the airport.

Ron and Les shook hands in case Les didn't make it in time to say goodbye. We only had minutes to get to the gate and get him checked in. Carolyn, Ron and I ran through the airport and got to his gate just as they were closing it. He grabbed me, hugged and kissed me goodbye and told me to take care of everyone and that new baby girl. I told him I loved him and to come back to us. He turned to Carolyn and picked her up off the floor, kissed her and hugged her tightly. I couldn't watch the desperation in their embrace, so I turned so they wouldn't see me crying.

"I love you Sam," he said so sweetly I thought my heart would break.

"I love you honey," she said without crying.

He had no time to say anything else as the door was closing. He grabbed his duffel bag and walked toward the closing door. With his bag thrown over his shoulder he turned to us, raised his hand, waved, smiled his big beautiful smile and just before he disappeared through the gate, he said, "See you in a year."

Les, Carolyn and I walked without words for most of the way out of the airport. I was trying to pull it together, but my heart was breaking and I was scared to death. I prayed hard and begged God to not let this be the last time I saw my big brother. *Oh God, please bring him back to us, he is too important, we can't survive without him. Keep him safe. He is such a good person and we need good people in this world. I know you will protect him. Thank you Lord.*

We made our way to the car in silence. I looked up into the dark sky and wondered which plane Ron was on. I had no doubt he was looking down on the airport. I wondered if he was having some of the same feelings we were. Once inside the car we talked about traffic or what road to take next, only because the silence was worse.

"How do you do it?" I finally asked Carolyn. "How do you keep from crying?"

"Ron asked me not to," Carolyn said as she took a deep breath. "He said he couldn't bear it. He said it kills him when you and Mom cry when he leaves, it would be unbearable if I did."

"Oh," I said as I turned and looked out the window. That felt like a punch in the gut, but I had asked for it. I vowed that I would never cry again when he left. *Please God give me the chance to keep that promise.*

Please God...
Not Vietnam

My entire life I had endured empty unsettling days after Ron had gone back to wherever he was stationed. I never got used to it and it never got better or easier.

Now he was in Vietnam or close to it. This was the worst I had ever felt. When I was young, I just missed him. Now I was aware of the danger he was in. I had no idea how we were going to endure this for an entire year.

After the ride home from the airport the night before, Les and I let Carolyn off at Mom's, gathered Angel and all the baby stuff and went home.

Les was at work the next morning and I couldn't stop walking the floor. I wanted to be at Mom's, to be close to her and Carolyn; besides Angel made them happy. I went to Mom's to see if I felt better with them.

I talked to Mom before I saw Carolyn and asked how she was. Mom told me she could hear Carolyn crying most of the night.

"Oh, that makes me sick, Mom. She didn't shed a tear last night when he left or all the way home. How can she hold it inside?" I asked.

Mom wiped tears that had started to fall with the corner of her bed sheet. "I don't know. I couldn't do it."

I started to share what Carolyn had told me about why she didn't cry, but stopped. Mom didn't need to hear that now. Carolyn came into the room about the time I decided not to tell her.

"Hi Carolyn," I said, as I sat Angel in the middle of the table in her infant seat.

"Morning," she said. She set her coffee cup down and went right to Angel to coo and talk to her. I felt relieved that something could make her smile. I left Angel with Carolyn and went to the car to bring in the diaper bag and the laundry I had brought to wash.

I felt better being with Mom and Carolyn and it was obvious that Angel was going to be a positive factor in this equation. She was close to three months old and she was learning to coo, kick her legs and throw her arms around when we talked to her. She was also learning to hold and chew on a small stuffed giraffe that Carolyn had bought her. It fit perfectly in her hand and had become her favorite toy. Every time Carolyn went to town she came home with something for Angel. There was no mistaking how she felt about my daughter.

Carolyn had already fallen into her obsessive behavior regarding the house. It was ok by now as we had figured out that it was her way of coping and I didn't care because I needed the help. She had the house, Mom, Trixie, and Angel to keep her from going crazy.

When I came back in she was making another pot of coffee. I wondered how many pots she had consumed this morning. It seemed that she was going to live on coffee and cigarettes. She was already so thin a strong wind would blow her away; she would be invisible by the time Ron's tour was done.

Hours melted into days, and days into weeks. Angel kept me busy and helped keep everyone's mind off the fact that Ron was in Vietnam. His letters came pretty often, considering where he was. Most were to Carolyn with messages for all of us. When it came to her private messages, she would giggle and tell us we couldn't hear that part. All he would ever tell us about what was going on or what he had to do was that he wasn't in any danger and everything was ok. I knew he was trying to shield us from the truth, but I wasn't going to be the one to say the obvious.

Ron had Carolyn send an eleven by fourteen picture of her that they had taken on his leave the year before. He wrote that when he hung it in his barracks, the Montagnards, (South Vietnamese soldiers) who had become his friends and comrades, gave Carolyn a rating of #1. As Carolyn read these passages in his letters I could feel her emotion, her loneliness, her love for him and even her embarrassment over her picture hanging in his barracks. Their separation broke my heart. I just wanted to hug her and promise he would come home. How could I do that? I only believed it half of the time.

Then Ron started sending letters with strange requests. He wanted to know the name of the governor of Kentucky, saying he would explain later. He went into great detail about the little village of Pleiku where he went to buy camera film. He would capitalize certain words. We thought it was strange, but had no idea what or why he was saying some of these things. He also sent an 8x10 picture of eight guys, all Americans including himself, holding m-14's dressed in generic clothing, no names, no insignia.

Ron in Vietnam

He gave no explanation and it didn't occur to us that some of this might have had hidden meanings.

Since our communication with him was fairly often, I decided to bring a subject to the table that I should have before he left but hadn't because I didn't have the time to breathe, let alone plan ahead for my demise. Now I had time to worry about Angel's fate if something were to happen to Les and me. We discussed the matter and both agreed Ron and Carolyn was our choice of who would take Angel. I talked to Carolyn and she was quite pleased with being Angel's godmother, but told me I had to ask Ron before we took it to the legal level.

I wrote to my big brother and asked if he would take my baby girl if something happened to Les and me. I had my answer in about two weeks. Absolutely yes, as long as Sam was ok with it.

This made me feel better for two reasons. One, Angel's future was protected as Ron and Carolyn would be her godparents. And two, in my heart, this meant Ron was coming home. We were making future plans and including Ron. For some reason making these plans with him insured his existence back in the states, with us.

In September, he wrote and asked us to send canned or processed food. We couldn't get the package in the mail fast enough. I was horrified that he wasn't getting enough to eat. Carolyn baked cookies; we made fudge, and bought canned meat and cheeses. Within two days, the first box was on its way.

I started to relax a little, after much prayer, correspondence with Ron, and conversations with my cousin, Gina, who came and stayed with Les and me sometimes.

"Do you think he will come home or ..." I asked one night as she helped me give Angel her bath.

Gina looked at me like I was crazy. "Yes, he will come home. He's Ron. He's invincible." She laid Angel on the bed and began patting her dry. "I know you're right, but there are so many guys who are not coming back. I'm scared."

"You can't think like that. My Dad came home from Korea. Your Dad came home from Korea, whether you care that he did or not. Men do come back and Ron is tough. He will, you'll see." She zipped up Angel's pajamas. "All ready for bed, pooter butt," she said, kissing my baby's cheek.

"Okay, thanks, that makes me feel better. Maybe I need to quit worrying so much. He's been through lots of training, he was a cop, was in the Navy and, yeah you're right," I said, breathing a little easier.

After Gina's advice and recalling how many guys I knew who had come home, I decided to have a more positive attitude. I still prayed many times a day, but I decided to have confidence in Ron's ability to take care of himself, and trust God that he would keep him safe and bring him home to his family. We couldn't exist without him.

Where is
My Big Brother?

It was cold on that December 2nd in 1970, nearing my sweet Angel's first Christmas, and I was busy taking care of her. Les had gone into town to run errands before he went to work. I wanted to get my house cleaned and then go to Mom's to do laundry. Les was working second shift and I usually spent my time at Mom's when he worked evenings.

The phone rang and I picked up the receiver.

"Get here now," Mom said before I could even answer.

"What?" I asked, cold chills running over my entire body. "Mom, what is it? Is it Ron?"

"Now, get here, now." She hung up.

Oh my God, Oh my God, Oh my God, Please, Please, Please, no, no, no, no.

I ran to Angel's room and picked up my sleeping baby out of her crib, wrapped her in a blanket, grabbed my keys and ran out of the door and into my car. No snow suit, no diaper bag, no coat, nothing.

I drove the mile to Mom's with Angel wrapped in a blanket, lying on my lap.

I prayed harder than I had ever prayed in my life. I started to cry, and then pushed it back. *God do not let this be my big brother. You know we can't be without him, you know this. Ok. Ok, it's not Ron. I promise you I will never do anything bad or wrong again. I promise you anything in this world if you make this not be about Ron. God, please not Ron. God would not let this happen to the most wonderful brother, son, husband—the best person in the world.*

Gina's words ran through my head, "Yes he will come home. He's Ron. He's invincible."

Then what is it? Why would Mom order me to come to her house like that with no explanation, and then hang up? It's Ron, that's the only reason she would have sounded like that. NO! I won't let it be. Angel has to grow up with him. I have to grow old with him.

I turned the corner onto Mom's street. Our car was in her driveway. Les was at Mom's. How did he know something was wrong? Then I saw the military car. A government car with the official license plate was parked in front of Mom's house.

I pulled up behind the Army green car and thought I was going to throw up. I didn't know if I could stand. *How can I walk into that house and hear what I am going to hear?*

I sat motionless and could not make myself put my hand on the door handle. I held Angel tight and kissed the top of her sweet head. *Its ok, baby. God won't take your uncle away from you. You haven't even gotten to know him yet. He has to sign the papers to be your godfather. He has to be at your birthdays and send you presents from all over the world. You have to get bigger and love him as much as I do. This is not happening.*

I saw his face smiling at us, telling us he would see us in a year when he walked through the airport gateway four months ago.

Ron always keeps his promises to us, always. Whatever these government men have to tell us is wrong, it is a mistake. Don't worry baby, its ok. Ron will always come home to us, he always has and he always will.

I had to go into the house and face this. I took a deep breath, opened the car door and set my foot on the pavement. Then I wrapped the blanket tighter around Angel. I tried to stand, but my legs were too weak and I had to sit back down and gather strength. I was shaking so hard I wasn't sure I could hang on to my baby.

Somehow I made it to my Moms front door, reached for the door and stood there with my hand on the knob, trying to make myself turn it and go in. I couldn't turn the knob, it was stuck. It felt as if I was trying to turn a thousand pounds. I knew that once I entered my family home my life forever would be changed. The military didn't come to tell families their loved one was doing ok.

I walked into Mom's house and the first thing I saw were two men in Army green uniforms sitting on the couch. Their military head gear was lying on their knees. One of them had a plethora of colorful medals across his chest and on the other lapel was his name, Captain Hill.

Mom was sitting in the rocking chair, her face red and racked with pain. Carolyn was standing next to her, shaking. Les was a few feet away with the same horrid sad face, looking at me with helplessness in his eyes.

Where's Jim?

Carolyn broke the silence, "Ron is missing in action." She shouted the words.

"Les, take Angel before she drops her," Mom said as she broke into sobs.

He took her as my arms went numb. I backed up, trying to get away from their words. "No." Unimaginable pain and fear racked my entire body, things I had never felt surged through me.

I heard talking, but I couldn't understand what they were saying. I couldn't process any of it. I retreated to the stairway, lying across the stairs. Pain and suffocation clouded my head and lungs. I couldn't breathe, I couldn't speak. Tears didn't come, nothing was real. I was outside my body watching the scenario unfold in the house so familiar to me. I grew up here. I laughed with my brother in this room. We unwrapped Christmas presents and played cards in this room. Gina and I pin-curled his hairy chest while he slept on the couch in this room. Now some Army personnel were sitting here telling us he was missing in action.

I need details. Give me details.

A hundred questions were beating against my brain trying to get out. I forced myself to get up off the stairs and face these men who were saying things and talking about my brother like they knew him. I hated them. I wanted to hit them and tell them they didn't know a damn thing about Ron. They didn't have the right to even say his name. Whatever they said was wrong, he is invincible. Missing or not, he was coming home. I sucked up more strength than I knew was possible.

"Ok, I need details," I said. "How long has he been missing?"

"He went missing November 28, four days ago," Captain Hill said.

"Four days? Four days ago?"

I have been living, breathing, loving my baby, laughing with my friends, going to bed at night with my husband and my brother has been missing in action? Not possible.

"Where was he seen last?" I asked.

"That's classified, ma'am," Captain Hill said.

"I don't care. Who cares now? We're his family, we won't be talking to the North Vietnamese," I said. "Who saw him last?"

"That's classified. I'm sorry," he said.

"Well what do you know?"

"He is missing, that's all we know."

"That's not good enough. What are his chances of surviving?" I asked, glaring at him.

"That's all we know, ma'am. He is missing in action."

"What kind of action? What was he doing? Who was he with? You have to know more."

"I'm sorry, ma'am. That's all we know. We will be in touch with your family when we know anything else. When there is further news we will return and give you the information in person," Captain Hill said.

I looked at Mom and Carolyn, then at Les. I wanted someone to make them talk, to tell us more.

The two men got up, hats in hand, straightened their attire and prepared to leave. They gave Carolyn and Mom cards with their phone numbers and instructions to call if we needed anything or had questions.

"Mrs. Smith, Mrs. Reffett, again we are extremely sorry for your anguish. We can only imagine how you feel," Captain Hill said as he nodded toward Les and me.

I felt like my brain was going to explode. *Questions?* I had just asked twenty questions and only received an answer to one. *Why would we bother to call and ask again?*

Les had been holding Angel during the entire conversation. He sat her on Mom's lap and walked them to the door. I stared as they left with more apologies and heartfelt sorrow for our situation. They promised to be back when they learned any more news of Ron's disappearance. I moved to the front window and watched them retreat to their official car, remove their hats again and get inside.

They sat there for a while before starting the engine and pulling away. The car disappeared out of sight. They had come here, torn our world apart, and then vanished, leaving us with no idea what had happened to Ron.

Life couldn't go on as it had. I already felt like we had been living on some kind of suspended routine by going through the motions some days, pretending like everything was ok. Now what?

"You were there Les, will he be ok?" I asked. "Do you think he is hiding and will make it back to his base when the enemy is gone or, I don't know, what do you think?"

"I have no idea. I was in the Air Force. Ron was on the ground. It is very different. There is no way to know."

I didn't understand how he couldn't tell me more. He had been there.

Surely he had an opinion. I quizzed him on the lay of the land of Vietnam. Was it cold? Could he find food? Would shelter be available?

"I don't know, there are too many factors that are unanswered, like where he was, how big his company, what they were doing. You heard Captain Hill, he gave us nothing to go on," Les said.

"I have to know, I can't stand this," I said.

Mom was crying into her hands, and Carolyn was making coffee and lighting a cigarette.

"Oh Mom, we have to call the family."

Jim came through the back door before I started making calls. His face was panic stricken as he had passed the military car at the end of our block. We told him that his big brother was missing in action and we knew next to nothing. Jim went to Mom's side, which only made her cry harder.

Charlie had come home at some point, although I didn't even notice. He was trying to be helpful by making coffee and offering food, which no one wanted. He stood by Mom and patted her shoulder, looking helpless.

My mind was reeling and I couldn't think straight. I had to get control, somehow. I fixed Angel's dinner, and was thankful we kept food and clothes for her at Mom's because I hadn't brought anything with me, not even my purse.

I went through the motions of feeding my baby and sitting her in her playpen with a bottle. Then I prepared to make the dreaded calls.

I started with Aunt Lettie and Uncle Gene, first telling them Ron was missing and then giving them the job of going to my grandparent's house to tell them. That could not be a phone call. Aunts, uncles, cousins were called to break the horrible news. Within a couple of hours, the house was filled with our closest relatives.

It was the worst family gathering I could have imagined. Each time someone came to Mom, she broke down again. Tears, sobs, and dreadful phone calls seemed to last for hours. Carolyn had turned into stone, and coffee and cigarettes were her only staple.

We repeated over and over what the casualty officer had told us, but it still didn't seem real. Maybe it wasn't. Maybe I would wake up and this would be the worst nightmare of my life.

I prayed it was a mistake, a nightmare and it would be over soon and Ron would be ok. What if he was back at his camp right now, safe, or at least as safe as he could be in that horrendous country?

But nothing changed. I didn't wake up and God didn't back up time and give this nightmare a different ending.

That day, December 2, 1970, seemed to last for days. Goodbyes were endless and unbearable to watch. Parting was filled with more tears and false encouragement.

"Surely you will hear something soon Sis. Call us the minute you hear anything, day or night," my aunt said as she hugged her sister tight and Mom sobbed again.

Grandpa was as bad as he was when we left him in the alley crying and repeating that he would never see Ronnie again. Grandma continued to cry, but tried to get grandpa to have faith that he would come home.

"Now Tink, stop saying such awful things," grandma said. "You get some rest, you hear, Honey. He has to be all right." Grandma hugged Mom.

Gina, Mona and Lisa were quiet and played with Angel until she fell asleep, then waited for their parents to decide to go home.

By midnight everyone was gone and I helped Mom get ready for bed. Carolyn had long since locked herself in her bedroom and as soon as the noise and talking stopped, she could be heard sobbing. I hoped for her and Mom's sake that she would pass out from exhaustion.

Jim and I tucked Mom into bed and held on to her as she broke down again.

"I'll see you later. I'll be back when I get things taken care of at home. Call me if you need us or anything. Call us if Captain Hill calls," I said holding her. She nodded her head and promised in a whisper.

"Jim, call if Mom or Carolyn needs us," I said.

"Ok Sis," he said, looking like the little boy I used to take care of.

Les and I wrapped Angel in a big blanket and left the house. No words were spoken as we drove to our home and like robots; we went inside, put Angel in her crib, undressed and went to bed.

I thought I couldn't cry another tear, but I was wrong. I began to sob, letting all my emotions out that I had been holding back for Mom and Carolyn's sake. Les held me and sometime before daylight I fell into a troubled sleep. I dreamed I was looking for Ron in a wooded area. I was crawling on the ground and calling his name, my eyes begging to see him.

Reality returned when I heard Angel cry for me to get out of her crib. It took a split second before I remembered the hell we were in and I groaned as I forced myself out of bed. It had only been about three hours since we went to bed.

Angel was standing in her crib bouncing up and down, smiling when she saw me like nothing in the world was wrong. She reached for me to pick her up and begin her day. I took her out of her crib and kissed her cheek good morning.

"Hi sweet pea," I said kissing her again. "You have no idea, do you? How could you?"

Her world was safe and nothing had changed in her baby mind. *And that's how it should be.*

"I will always protect you from the pain in this world, baby girl," I promised as I changed her and took her to the kitchen to prepare her breakfast.

This was my first hard lesson of motherhood. *Your needs don't stop for my pain, do they baby girl?* I tried hard to smile for her, but smiling was not what I wanted to do. I wished that for today I had someone to take care of her, my house, Les and my responsibilities. I didn't want to do any of these everyday tasks that I was used to doing. I didn't know what I wanted to do, but being an adult was not what I needed.

What I needed, wanted and ached for were military uniforms at Mom's door informing us that they had made an enormous error and Ron was not missing. Or maybe his team had made it back to their camp and he was accounted for, he was ok. *That's what I want.*

It didn't matter, I would never have neglected Angel so I sucked it up and took care of my baby. I got my house in order, packed Angel's things and prepared to go back to Mom's as soon as Les got up and I made his breakfast. He had to go to work, crisis or not.

By early afternoon I was back at Mom's house. It was as bleak as it was when I left the night before. Mom was hobbling around on her cast; Carolyn was drinking coffee and busying herself with Trixie and laundry.

"Nothing from the Army?" I asked. I knew the answer, but I didn't know what else to say. Mom shook her head.

I sat Angel in the middle of the table in her seat. This was becoming a habit and a pleasure for Mom and Carolyn. Angel had graduated from infant seats months ago, now it was her bouncy seat or her horse she jumped up and down in. Talking, laughing and tossing her toys about for someone to pick them up and give back to her. She was a happy baby and had no idea our world had been turned upside down. She expected her Nanny and Aunt Carolyn to be as happy as they had been in the days before.

It was impossible not to laugh at her or have your spirits lifted by a happy baby, babbling, laughing and playing like nothing had changed, if only for a few minutes.

Not long after I got to Mom's the doorbell rang. Mom, Carolyn and I jumped and looked at each other, eyes wide with panic so thick you could see it. Who was going to answer this time? Carolyn had answered yesterday and when she saw who it was stood screaming, refusing to let the Army personnel in. One of us had to go to the door.

I held back looking at Carolyn, giving her the chance if she wanted. At the same time we both started to the door scared to death it was the Army again. We looked through the small window on Mom's door, and it was a guy in uniform, but it was Western Union, not Army. *Oh my God, please let it be good news this time. Don't let it be bad, please God I am begging you! Let him be found and back to his base.*

Carolyn opened the door and signed for the two telegrams—one to her and one to Mom. We walked back into the kitchen, where Carolyn gave Mom hers and opened the one addressed to Mrs. Ronald E. Smith. Her hands were shaking so hard I didn't think we would be able to read whatever it said.

I stood beside her and tried to read the yellow telegram. Its print and use of abbreviated words were not easy to understand, along with how hard Carolyn was shaking. I had become good at skimming for key words. I looked for words like rescued, found, returned to base, nothing. It was a repeat of what Captain Hill had told us yesterday. I started over and read it completely, it was not good news. But at least it wasn't anything worse than we had heard the day before.

Carolyn sat down and let out a huge long breath. Mom was crying again, not hard, but tears were running down her face. I looked at my baby and thought about how Ron was Mom's baby. It must be so hard for her to read the cold words on this paper about her child.

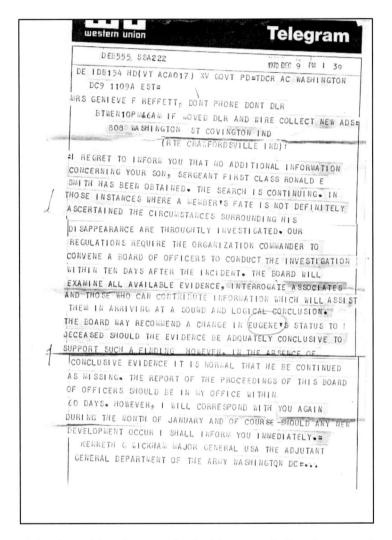

I had no idea how to help Mom and Carolyn or what to do next when Angel came to our rescue by throwing her giraffe on the floor and jabbering her baby talk. I moved to pick it up as Mom and Carolyn broke their silence by giving her attention. *Thank you God for Angel.*

We moved on by getting food out for supper preparation and taking laundry out to the line to hang up. I didn't want to do these things, but having to do daily chores kept us busy and made the hours go by.

Status Change

No one felt like decorating or putting up Christmas trees, but that wasn't a subject for debate. It was Angel's first Christmas and we would make it wonderful for her. Ron would have wanted it that way.

We put up trees at our house and Mom's, and brought out Santas, reindeer, and Frosty the snowman. Within a couple of days it looked like Christmas at our houses, but looks were deceiving.

The only time I felt like I might have a small flash of Christmas spirit was when I was praying for a miracle. I caught myself daydreaming about Ron coming back to us on Christmas Eve. He would appear at the door late in the evening, a complete surprise to all of us, creating pandemonium. We would call the entire family and have the most amazing celebration. I could even hear the laughter and feel the tears of joy. We would never let him go again. My daydream would end and the letdown was so depressing that any Christmas spirit I had mustered was gone.

Les and I shopped for our daughter and immediate family. We did Mom's shopping because she wasn't up to fighting the crowds and snow in her cast. Carolyn seemed to get the most pleasure shopping for Angel. It was obvious she was crazy about her and this made me happy. Carolyn was an extension of Ron touching my daughter. Christmas came and we did all the get-togethers, opened presents, baked, cooked and pretended. We made Angel's first Christmas a success, despite the agony we all felt.

My one Christmas wish didn't come true and my prayers were not answered.

Spring was approaching and still no word, good or bad. Even though time was dragging, I couldn't believe we had endured these many days hanging in limbo.

It was late April, and Les and I had gone to Mom's so he could do a house repair before he went to work. Mom was puttering around the house, I was preparing lunch and Carolyn was pouring over another mound of mail from the Army. I was used to seeing her go over and over the tons of redundant correspondence.

I was across the kitchen table with my back to her when she began to scream at the top of her lungs. She startled me so badly I dropped the bowl and utensils I was working with. Les and Mom came into the kitchen as fast as they could from the living room. She continued to scream and we got her to hand the letter she was reading to Les. He took it from her and as he started to read, she was able to form words.

"Ron has been shot. Ron has been shot. He has been shot in the head. They say he's dead!" she said.

I felt my knees go weak and Mom sat down beside her. Les read the letter while we looked on. He nodded his head and confirmed what Carolyn had said.

"That's what it says." Les began to read the letter out loud. "The team came under attack and Smith exposed himself to enemy fire to help the helicopter locate them for extraction.

"Sergeant Smith was hit in the head, chest and side, then when his team leader was attempting to drag him to cover they were hit again with rocket propelled grenade fire.

"The team leader was knocked unconscious. They had to leave Sergeant's Smith body because of enemy fire. The other members of the team carried the team leader out because he was still alive.

"It is the estimation of all concerned that Sergeant Smith could not have survived. The Army is changing his status to Killed in Action/Body not Recovered."

"No Les, they can't send that kind of information in the mail. Captain Hill said they would come here in person with any more news," I said holding onto the table so I wouldn't fall to the floor.

"I know, but it is here in black and white. Here, read it," he said, as he handed me the letter.

"We need to get Captain Hill on the phone," I said as I pushed the letter away from me.

Mom was opening her letter to see if it said the same, tears dripping off her chin. Carolyn sat at the kitchen table shaking and crying. Les continued to read through the rest of the mail.

"Yes, we need to call Indianapolis," Mom said.

Carolyn managed to dial the number. Captain Hill was appalled that we had received this correspondence.

"That news was not supposed to be sent to you until we came to deliver it in person," he said.

"So it is true?" Carolyn asked.

"I'm afraid so, ma'am," he said.

"Oh my God, no." She sank onto Mom's bed.

"We will be coming to your home within three hours, ma'am," Captain Hill said.

Carolyn came back into the kitchen where we were all waiting for her to tell us what we already knew.

"They will be here in a few hours," she said.

"Did he say it was true?" I asked.

She nodded her head and sat back down at the table where she had spread out all the letters. She stared at them and shook her head. "I can't believe this," she cried into her hands.

Mom was falling apart, Carolyn was turning to stone, Les looked helpless and I was numb. I made myself read the letter. *Killed in Action/Body not Recovered, what does that mean? How can they be sure if there is no body? No body. My brother's body is missing. They say he is dead with no proof. No, this is not possible. I refuse to accept this. I will make them tell us the truth this time. This is absolute crap. Jim, oh no, we have to call him home.*

"Mom do you have the number for Jim's work?"

"No, you'll have to look it up in the phone book," she said

I called the factory where he worked and left a message that he needed to come home. *He will be petrified and alone. He will know.* Next I called Charlie to come home from work.

We decided not to call anyone else until after Captain Hill talked to us. I had to get a grip so I could have half a brain and remember all the questions I wanted to ask. *Oh, Angel will be waking up from her nap soon.* I wasn't sure I could function. I didn't know I could be so terrified, feel so vulnerable, angry, sad, and yet numb. I was having another out of body experience and watching myself go through the motions.

God, I begged you to bring Ron home to us. Why? Why did you let this happen? There is vermin in this world that have no value to anyone, why Ron? He's good, honorable, honest, and loved by so many people, why? He is so vital to our existence.

And Carolyn, what about Carolyn? What is she going to do now? This isn't fair. Life isn't fair! Why should we be good, responsible and always do the right thing if this is the way we are rewarded? God, if you weren't going to answer my prayer, that's ok, I'm not the good one. But Ron is, why take someone like him who deserved to live and be happy?

My tirade to God ended when Angel woke and began chattering to get out of her playpen/bed. She was ready to have her lunch, be changed and have some Nanny and Aunt Carolyn time.

"Hi baby girl," I said as I picked her up and kissed her on her precious little cheek.

She giggled and turned to look for her Aunt Carolyn. She had already learned when she was at Nanny's house; Aunt Carolyn would be there to play with her.

"Ok Pumpkin, it's ok. Aunt Carolyn isn't feeling so good right now, so you're stuck with your Mommy." She had no idea what I was telling her, but she smiled and played with her giraffe while I changed her. I hurried to prepare her lunch so I could be ready when the Army got here.

Jim came in the back door like he was on fire while I was feeding Angel.

"Did they find him?" Jim asked. His eyes seemed to beg for me to tell him yes.

"Oh Jim, I'm so sorry. No, they didn't," I said. "Maybe you should sit down."

"I don't need to sit down, I can see by your face. What happened?"

"We got a letter, saying they're changing his status to Killed in Action. The Army said he's been shot."

"No sis, not Ron." Jim grabbed the table to steady himself and the color drained from his face. I could see him struggling to be the man he was supposed to be.

"That's what the letter said." I reached across the table to offer it to him.

"I thought they were going to come to the house if they had any more news," he said.

"Yeah, that was the story, but that's not what happened. Carolyn called Captain Hill and he should be here anytime. He confirmed the letter, but I still don't understand. I have a million questions for them."

"When did he get shot? Where is he? Is his body home yet?" he asked.

"I don't know where he is. They said his body has not been recovered, but they are changing his status to Killed in Action/Body Not Recovered."

"What? If they don't know where his body is how can they be sure he is dead?"

"Jim, I have no idea. That's exactly what I will be asking the Army as soon as they get here. I am..."

The sound of the doorbell interrupted me, and cold chills ran over my body. *Oh God they're here. Please make this right.*

We all walked into the living room and waited for Les to let the Army into our house.

Captain Hill and his staff shook hands with Carolyn, Mom and any one of us who offered a hand. I didn't want to touch him, so I stayed back.

Carolyn handed him the correspondence she had received four hours ago. He held his hand up for her to stop.

"I have read every line," he said.

"Is it true?" Carolyn asked, not even offering him a seat.

"I'm afraid so. I'm so sorry you received this letter before we could come here and tell you in person. This is not protocol. On behalf of the Army, the Special Forces and the United States of America we offer our deepest condolence," Captain Hill said. "Your husband is regarded as a brave American and soldier. He gave his life for his country and his team members. You can be very proud of him."

"I don't understand. Where is Ron?" I asked, almost cutting off his speech.

"His body has not been recovered," Captain Hill said.

"Then how do you know he is dead?" I asked.

"From the interviews of the men involved. His team members have been debriefed and it is their opinion that he could not have survived his wounds," he said.

"When did you find them?" I asked.

Mom interrupted and asked them to sit down. Everyone moved to the couch and chairs in her living room. I stood. I wanted answers, and sitting didn't seem right to me. I didn't feel polite and wasn't about to pretend.

"What do you mean?" he asked.

"When did his team members come back or when were they found?"

"They were never lost. They have been at the base since November 28."

"What? When did they tell their story of what happened to my brother?" I asked.

"On November 29th Ma'am," Captain Hill said.

I felt my face getting hot. I tried to control my anger until I got a final answer. "So you knew Ron had been shot when you here five months ago?"

"Yes, Ma'am."

"Why wasn't our family informed about this five months ago?" I asked trying not to scream at the Army Captain.

"It needed to be confirmed. I am sorry," he said.

"Who confirmed this story?" I asked.

"His team leader, another American and the Montagnards that were in his team."

"What are the Americans' names?" I asked.

"That is classified, Ma'am. I'm sorry."

"I don't see why we can't talk to his team members who survived," Mom said.

"I am painfully aware of how you must all feel. But there is nothing else that I can tell you at this time. When more information is available we will contact you."

"Like this time?" I asked, rolling my red swollen eyes.

"I can only imagine how you and Mrs. Smith must feel. We are so sorry for your loss and how this was handled. If there is anything we can do, please call." Captain Hill stood.

Carolyn sat staring at Captain Hill, twisting her tissue into fibers.

"I have more questions. What part of Vietnam was he in?" I asked.

"I'm sorry, Ma'am that is classified," he said.

"Was he even in Vietnam?" Mom asked. "Was he in Cambodia or Laos?"

I stared at my Mother. *How do you know that?*

"He was in Vietnam, but it is classified as to exactly where he was. We will release that information when it is possible."

"So what do we do now? Is the Army looking for his body? And what if you are wrong?" I asked. "What if he was not wounded as badly as you thought? Why would you give up on him so soon?"

"His wounds, Ma'am, they were too severe. We have not been able to get back into the area where he was shot. We hope to do that soon," he said.

"We should have been told all the information from the start," I said. I shook my head trying to hold back the tears. I didn't believe them and I hated them even more than I did the last time they came here and brought this hell into our lives.

They began the process of leaving and it was a re-run of the last visit, shaking hands, giving out business cards, offering their sorrow and more promises.

I didn't want their cards, their handshakes, their pity or their fake promises. I wanted to hurt someone, maybe them. Definitely whoever made up all these stupid rules and classified secrets.

I didn't want them to leave, I wanted to fire questions at them, be rude to them, and insinuate that they were hiding the truth. I didn't watch them leave this time and couldn't make myself look at the military car. It hurt too badly. I didn't want to look at their uniforms and their military posture and presence. It was too hard to even breathe. I didn't want to watch them pull away, taking all of our hope with them.

I was terrified, my heart was crushed for Mom, Carolyn, Jim and myself. I couldn't stop shaking and crying and had no idea how I was going to get through the next ten minutes, let alone the rest of my life without my brother.

One Day at a Time

The next several days were unbearable and the only thing that could have hurt as much would be if I lost my Angel. Hours felt like days, and everyday tasks were endless and meaningless. Who cared if the dishes were washed, or the laundry was done? I didn't. If it hadn't been for Angel, I don't know if I would have come through the nightmare. I had to take care of her, so I forged ahead.

Les went to work each day and tried to console me in his way, which was to hug me and tell me not to cry. I needed to cry. I couldn't stuff anymore pain down into my hiding places or on the back burner. My daughter needed a functioning mother and Mom needed me.

I continued to spend a lot of my time at Mom's house where Carolyn and Mom were trying to sort out what needed to be done. The first time someone mentioned that we had to have a service, I thought I would puke. *A service? Don't say these words, my heart can't take it.*

Someone told us that protocol was not to have a funeral when there was no body, it should be a Memorial Service. Physical torture could not hurt any worse.

The mail continued and now Mom and Carolyn were receiving sympathy and apology letters from the Army and different departments of the government. Only there was something odd about the contents. After all of the correspondence was received, we had five different scenarios of Ron's fate. They went from the team leader not being able to reach Sergeant Smith to determine if he was dead, to the team leader got to Sergeant Smith and determined he was dead, to the team leader got to Sergeant Smith and was not able to determine if he was still alive, to the team came under attack, separated and when back together, Sergeant Smith was missing. Then the last, Sergeant Smith was last seen seeking cover.

The next travesty came in more boxes of Ron's personal effects and his belongings. Among his Army clothes, pictures, and letters from us were his wallet, wedding ring, Special Forces ring, and his dog tags. I was stunned. I thought dog tags were always worn by soldiers. Wasn't that the point, identification?

Mom, Carolyn and I couldn't understand any of it. Les was at work, so I couldn't ask him. There was a matching hat and sweatshirt that none of us had ever seen. The sweatshirt was black with Smitty embroidered on the back and RT Kentucky on the front. The hat had the same. We had no explanation or clue as to what RT Kentucky meant. I was given the shirt and hat, as it didn't fit Jim. Ron's Army clothes had all the patches torn off.

"What does all this mean, I don't understand," I said, as Carolyn laid out more clothes.

"I don't know. He never said anything about taking his rank and name off his clothes," Carolyn said.

Mom shook her head. She had been an Army wife, but nothing prepared her for this.

I felt myself getting angry again. I hated the people responsible for the all these questions. Couldn't someone have called or written to tell us what to expect? I was livid. We asked Captain Hill to come to Mom's again. As far as I was concerned, he or the Army had a lot of explaining to do about all the discrepancies. All this did was put hope back on the table that Ron was alive. How could he not be? I was sure my brother was alive. After all, Ron was invincible.

A day or two later, Captain Hill and his assistant came to Mom's again, to explain the discrepancies in the letters. As always, they were polite and apologetic to a fault. I was impatient and didn't want to bother with all the formalities.

The second they werc seated I began my drill. I had the letters ready to show them, but like before, they had already read all the correspondence we had received.

"If you know, then why?" I asked.

"I'm sorry Ma'am, what do you mean?" Captain Hill asked.

"What? What do you think? Why, with all these versions of my brother's fate, why would anyone decide to change his status?"

"Ma'am, I have told you. It is the determination that your brother could not have survived his wounds," he said.

"But why are there so many versions?" I asked.

"In the heat of battle, one cannot be certain of the details."

"Exactly. That is what I am saying. That is what they are saying. So why are they giving up on him so soon?"

He lowered his head and didn't respond.

"Ok, so why did we get all of his personal things back. Why his dog tags?"

"His team went out on reconnaissance mission sterile."

"Sterile. What does that mean?" I asked

"They can have nothing on them so the enemy could identify them if captured."

"And his clothes, his name was torn off?" Carolyn asked.

"Yes Ma'am."

It was useless, just like before, robot answers. Mom thanked them for coming, Carolyn went through the motions. Again they promised to let us know if there was any further news of Ron. I wanted to ask more questions, but it was useless. I was done asking these men anything.

"Mom, do you believe what they say?" I asked as soon as the door was closed.

"I have to. The Army would not do this to us," she said.

Yes they would. They are doing it. I didn't argue with her, because I didn't think she could take it.

We were forced into accepting that Ron had been killed. Maybe someday the Army would be able to go back to the last place where Ron had been seen and try to recover his body. That's what we were left with. Nothing.

Ron was everything to our family and the Army or government had taken him and gave us nothing. No hope. No body. Only empty words that meant nothing.

A Memorial Service for My Missing Brother

I hadn't slept so I was out of bed before Angel called for me. I had to get her ready to go to Mom's house as Nance was going to take care of her during Ron's Memorial Service. The immediate family was going to meet there by noon and go to the church together. I woke Les up after I was ready. I felt so sorry for Angel, as I couldn't smile or even feel by this time.

We were ready to go by eleven and when we pulled into the driveway at Mom's house, the numbness I had experienced most of my morning left. Now I felt nausea and panic. I was starting to visibly shake and was afraid to see how Mom and Carolyn were doing.

Oh my God, please help Carolyn. My heart hurt so badly for myself, and then I would think of her, and it would break again. And my mother, this was her child. *How on earth will she get through this day? Her and Ron were so close and had been thru so much. God, will you please wake us up from this hell?*

Les got Angel, I grabbed her bag out of the car and we went into the house. Every step was harder than the last. We found Charlie in the kitchen making coffee. Mom was in her bedroom and Carolyn was upstairs. Jim was in his room dressing.

I went to Mom to help her finish getting dressed, then fixed her hair. We didn't talk much. *How are we going to get through this day?*

Les took care of Angel until Nance arrived and took over. The rest of the family was starting to gather and everyone had the same look on their faces. This was the saddest gathering my family had ever endured.

My grandparents, Aunt Lettie, Uncle Gene and the girls were coming through the front door. Walt was already here waiting for Gina. Aunt Mel and her boys were outside and Aunt Tootie and Bruce were pulling up.

We finished getting Mom ready, everyone made a last bathroom visit and filled their pockets and purses with tissues. It was time to go. Nance held my daughter and I kissed her head as she cried and reached for me. More pain.

"I'll be back soon, baby girl," I said as I tore her little arms from my neck.

I wanted the ride to the church to last forever, but since it was only four blocks, we were there in minutes. I saw the cars and flags, and started to panic. *I can't do this. Please God wake me up. Please. I can't.*

I don't remember getting out of the car, but I do remember walking up the steps to the church. I had Les' arm, Jim was beside me, and Jim's wife Karen beside him. Our uncles and Charlie were helping Mom, Carolyn was beside her. Grandpa and grandma were following behind us.

As we started to enter the church, I stopped. Lined up at the back of the pews were six Green Berets, in dress greens and berets. They were at attention, motionless, and could have been statues. Flags lined the back of the church and the color guard with guns.

The pain in my heart and head took over. Jim and I held each other to gain strength and comfort. I was told later that two of our uncles walked up to catch us before we fell. I only remember seeing one face, Max Keller, Ron's dear friend and chief of Police. He turned and looked at us as we went into the church.

I don't recall being seated, only looking up and seeing Ron's picture sitting on a flag draped coffin at the front of our church. I cannot remember one thing the minister said. I do not remember the service ending or getting up to leave. All I could feel was the worst pain and sadness I had ever felt. I didn't know it was possible to hurt this bad, to feel this lost, and to feel such panic.

I walked straight toward the Green Berets still standing motionless, eyes straight ahead and faces like steel. Their uniforms were perfect, their berets honorably placed on their heads. I don't know how I got past them, outside and into our car.

The next thing I remember was driving to the cemetery. We were going to have a service at the family cemetery with no body. It was to be a full military honors funeral for my war hero brother. He was a recipient of a Silver Star, a purple heart, and many other honors as he had exposed himself to enemy fire to get his team out. *Why didn't he get the Medal of Honor? Why the third highest? What more did he have to do, DIE?*

Someone in the backseat said something and brought me back to the moment. I was wiping my red swollen eyes and my head hurt so bad I couldn't see clearly. I reached for my purse to find some Excedrin, but had nothing to take it with. *Later,* I thought as I slipped them into my pocket.

We were pulling into the cemetery, more pain. The tent was set up with chairs for us to gather under if it rained. We wouldn't need the tent, as it was a hot sunny June day. Rain would have better suited this horrendous day.

The color guard and Green Berets were already there at attention. It nearly tore my heart out my chest to look at them. I wanted them there to honor Ron, but at the same time it was a cold slap in the face that I would never see my brother in uniform again. I would never again see him fuss with his beret, situating it perfectly on his head.

Seeing him in that uniform always gave me cold chills. Now that very uniform had taken him away from us. I would never get to touch, see, or laugh with him again. I wanted to hate the uniform, but I couldn't. I was still in awe of the Special Forces and what they stood for.

Someone opened my door and helped me out of the car. Les came around, took my arm and we made our way to the mound of flowers and the closed grave waiting for us. All you could hear was sniffling and crying.

When everyone was gathered, the minister started the remainder of his eulogy. The men looked like hell and the women were all crying, everyone except Carolyn. I didn't question why she wasn't crying, it was Ron last request. He couldn't bear to see her cry when he left and she was going to give him her promise one last time.

As the message ended, the color guard brought their guns up and began the 21 gun salute. The shots rang out and my body jerked with each shot. The powerful force of the guns made me think of how the bullets had torn through my brother's body. I was crying so hard I could barely breathe. Not a loud cry, but deep. A cry that was foreign to me and wouldn't relieve my pain. This torture was like no other. No end. No relief.

As soon as the guns were done and the shells had fallen onto the ground, the lone bugler started taps. I knew this was the most pain I would ever feel in my life. The horn made the loneliest sound I had ever heard.

A cold wind blew over the cemetery, the sun disappeared, and leaves and anything not fastened down blew away. The sound of taps seemed to bring on the wind and cold, and it circled around my legs. It was so sudden and such a drastic temperature change that I expected to see a tornado headed our way. Nothing was coming, just leaves blowing around us. The bugler finished and the cold wind was gone as fast as it came. I was too devastated to try to figure out what had happened.

After more hugs and tears from all who were there, we made our way to the cars and started the 25 mile journey back to Mom's—back to try to figure out how to go on without Ron. Would we ever feel joy again?

Being alive made me feel guilty. Loving my husband and baby gave me guilt. Ron was gone and I was sure I would never be happy or find peace in my life again. I felt it would be disloyal to his memory if I went on with my life as before, but I was a mother now and I had no choice.

Killed in Action/Body not Recovered ran thru my brain like a ticker tape on a newsreel, over and over and over.

Where are you, Bo? You can't be....just gone. This can't be all there is to this. We have to find you, but how?

Help me God. Please help me find my big brother.

Ron's immediate family receiving medals after Ron's status
was changed from MIA to KIA. 1971

PART TWO

Searching for Ron and Answers

Eighteen years later, in 1989, I was headed to Joe Taylor's house in Danville. He was the president of Vietnow, a group of Vietnam Veterans who had formed a nationwide club. Their function was to give aid to vets that needed help, help them get their VA benefits, and right the wrong that was done by our government by leaving our POW/MIA's behind.

I had been to several Vietnow meetings in the past few months and I found this group through one of my patients at the optometry office where I worked. Tony Estes was a Vietnam Veteran who found out that I had a brother who was a MIA. He gave me a POW/MIA bracelet with Ron's name and information engraved on it. I didn't know I could get one since the government had declared him KIA, but now I had one and wore it on my right wrist. I vowed never to take it off until my brother came home.

This group had stacks of government documentation and pictures of live POW's. I was infuriated. I had wasted years trying to accept what the Army had told us. Now I was hearing much different stories and there was proof that it was true. I had never believed what we were told or that all of it was factual.

Joe had invited me to come to his house and bring all of the correspondence from the Army, Ron's last letters and anything that might be helpful in connecting what we had to what he could find out. Joe had connections to Army records and people who knew things that they were not supposed to know or divulge.

Jim had gone to one meeting with me, but he didn't trust what these men had to say. After all the lies and controversy in Ron's status, he didn't want me to get hurt or excited and think I would finally get truthful answers. He also didn't want to me to go to Joe's house by myself as he was afraid the guys in the club had alternative motives.

"I'm a big girl and I can take care of myself," I said to him.

"Oh Sis, you are so naïve. Guys are pigs. Please don't go to his house."

"Jim, if this guy was not safe to be with, Tony and Linda would never let me go there." Tony and Linda Estes were patients at my office who I had become friends with. They were members of Vietnow and Tony was a Vietnam Veteran.

"Call me as soon as you get home, I mean it," he said.

"OK, I promise."

I had to shake my brother's attitude as I pulled up in front of Joe's house and breathed a little sigh of relief. The house was beautiful, well-kept and in a good neighborhood. OK, here goes. *Take care of me big brother.*

I gathered all the things I had brought for Joe, walked to the door and rang the bell. Joe answered and welcomed me in.

"Let's go to the dining room so we can spread all this stuff out," he said as he took some of my things.

We pulled out two chairs and sat. I gave him all the letters the government had issued to Mom and Carolyn. All five versions of what had happened to my brother. He took each letter and read it carefully. He got excited about one, because he knew the guy who had written it. Then he explained he was going to call his contact and start the process. He dialed the phone, waited and greeted someone. They exchanged dialogue, and then began. Joe was writing stuff down that looked foreign to me. I began to feel stupid and a wave of embarrassment flooded over me. I wanted to disappear and felt my younger brother's doubt. I saw what Jim saw. This guy was living in the past, and never completely came home from Vietnam. He either lost buddies or he couldn't leave it behind. I was going to be polite, listen, then leave and never go back to Vietnow.

"What recon team was he with?" Joe said into the phone. I watched him write down RT KENTUCKY.

I choked, then blinked, and then read it again. RT KENTUCKY.

Oh my God, there it is. They know about RT Kentucky. I had to hold myself from butting in and demanding to know what they knew about RT Kentucky. I waited for Joe to finish his conversation and hang up. He turned to me and I nearly shouted at him

"What is RT Kentucky?" I asked.

"It was his recon team," he said.

"That's the sweatshirt and hat we got back when he went missing. I have been wearing it for years and had no idea what it was."

"The recon teams were named after states, Ron's was Kentucky. Did you bring one of his last letters?"

"Yes, here is the last one he sent Mom. I can't get the ones he sent Carolyn, his wife. We don't see her that often and I'm not sure how she would react to asking for personal letters."

"Ok, let me see it." I handed it to him and he read it through, then turned and looked at me.

"What?" I asked.

"This question about the governor is telling you what Recon Team he was in. Kentucky," he said. "And this line where he is telling you he buys his camera film in the village of Pleiku. That is the village where he was closest. He was telling your family where he was."

"Oh my God, why? Did he think we could come and get him?"

"I don't know, Linda. Probably not. He knew what danger he was in and how doubtful it was that he was coming home. Whether he seriously thought you could find him, I doubt it, but he just felt the need to try and tell you where he was."

I didn't think I could hold back the tears. Survivor guilt was not new to me, but this was terrible.

"Ok, what are those numbers?" I asked, pointing to a row of numbers Joe had written as the man on the other end of the phone talked.

"Those are the coordinates where he was last seen. Did the government give these to you?" he asked.

"Are you kidding me? They gave us nothing but lies and grief."

"Well now you have them," he said.

"Yes I do. What can I do with this information? So far, all it has done is make me feel guilty and totally worthless. Don't get me wrong, I am thankful you have been a link to unanswered questions, but what can I do?"

"I don't know yet, Linda. I know a lot of guys who have connections to people who go to Vietnam. Let me work on it."

"Ok. I think. I'm so confused."

"You need to go to the Kokomo Vietnam Veterans Reunion with us this year. You can make a lot of connections."

"When is it?" I asked, as I gathered my papers.

"The third week of September. We will be talking about it at the next meeting. You need to copy all of these documents, get pictures of Ron and have plenty to give out. We will get some of the Special Forces on it that I served with him in NAM. We will find out what happened. You will be blown away when you see all the SF you can make contact with," he said.

I felt dizzy. *What have I done? What have I missed out on? Were these guys around all this time? What if Ron has been alive all this time and we didn't go get him?"*

I gathered Ron's things, thanked Joe and left with a promise that I would be going to Kokomo. My head was spinning, my stomach was churning, I felt that I might be sick. What if we could have done more? What if we find him alive? Will he ever forgive us for not finding him? I was furious with the Army and government, again.

I was pulling up in front of my house before I realized I had driven home and couldn't remember most of the drive. I called Jim to let him know I was home, unharmed, physically anyway.

I relayed all the things Joe had told me. Jim warned me again, "Don't get your hopes up Sis. I don't trust anyone."

"Well, why? Why would they lie to us? They are on our side." I said.

"I'm not sure. I just don't feel good about this."

"I'm going to the Kokomo reunion and the Vietnow meetings. I hope you go with me, but even if you don't, I'm going."

"Be cautious Sis," he said as we hung up.

This was the beginning of my quest to find out what really happened to my brother and where they had left him. I joined clubs, flew my flags, marched in protests, wrote letters to legislators, signed petitions, had articles published in the newspaper, and spouted my disgust to the news media whenever a microphone was pushed in my face.

The Vietnam travesty was beginning to surface all over our country. I had my eyes open and my ears tuned to anything related. I tried to be involved with anything where my voice would be heard and I could get Ron's name in the media.

I attended the Kokomo Vietnam Veterans Reunion that September. I took copies of Ron's information, Ron's last letter to Mom, and several copies of a picture Ron had sent Carolyn from Vietnam. It was of eight American guys standing in two lines, with M-16's and dressed in Army greens fatigues. We knew it wasn't his A-Team because he had told us that his team was made up of three Americans and two Montagnards. We didn't know what this group meant, but I was going to find out.

I had high hopes that someone there would have known Ron or someone in the picture. I met Vietnam Veterans, some regular Army and a few Special Forces. I met highly decorated soldiers, collected business cards, and received promises to help me find information. One of the most highly decorated men I met was Sammy Davis, a congressional Medal Honor recipient. I met him the first year I attended the reunion, where we talked about Ron and he gave me an autographed picture of himself. He was a highly decorated Army Veteran.

Another war hero was Bo Grits, a highly decorated Green Beret from Vietnam. He also talked with me about Ron, gave me an autographed picture, his business card and promised to let me know when he went back to Vietnam. Bo Grits was planning a trip to Vietnam with ex-military who would be searching for POWs to bring back to the US. This trip was not approved by the military, so it would be a covert mission.

I wanted him to promise to find my brother, but at the same time I wasn't sure if this was real. Ever since Ron went missing and the government had given our family so many versions of his disappearance or death, I had not believed them and always knew there was more. Now I had found the people and organizations who believed as I did. Why did I have a nagging feeling that someone would stop all their good intentions? Maybe because it had been happening since the Vietnam War. There had been military and veterans who went against the government with proof, and had been slapped down. It seemed that everyone who had gotten close to the truth or finding POW/MIA's had been shot down. That's why I was afraid to believe.

I continued to be involved with Vietnow, even though I had hit a dead end on finding anyone who knew Ron. There were plenty of people who knew of the Special Ops groups and MACV SOG, Ron's group, but no one knew anything more than Joe had told me.

The past 18 years had been filled with love, pain, struggle, the birth of my second child, Matthew, and my divorce from Les. My divorce had been the second hardest thing I had ever lived through, even though I was the one who initiated it. I would never be the same, but now I could be myself instead of the person Les wanted me to be. Even though Les had infuriated me at times and made me crazy for twenty years, I would always love a part of him and never regretted our marriage.

I had started in nursing after Angel and Matt were in school, but before I had gotten totally involved in nursing school, I got sidetracked into optometry. Matt had an amblyopic eye which had put me in the optometrist's office quite often. After getting to know his doctor and the doctor's wife, who was his optician and office manager, I was offered a job. At first it was just a couple days a week to make up for the days I was getting cut at the hospital, due to low census. After a few weeks, I was offered a full time position and nursing went by the way side.

By this time Angel was 18 and had graduated the past May, Matt was 15. Both were living with me.

When Angel was two, Les and I had purchased a house in Covington. The property had a small cottage in back of the main house. Mom had moved into our small house after she divorced Charlie. Sadly, he moved to his parents' rundown farm house and drank himself to death.

My friend Deb started a girlfriend club which eventually included four of my cousins, Brenda, Gina, Mona and Lisa. This club was one of the most wonderful experiences in my life and without these friends I probably would have been committed at some point. I had to fight tooth and nail the first few months of club to get away from my married life, but I did it and never let anyone come between me and my friends again. Club had a lot to do with my sanity staying intact throughout the years.

Jim had married Karen about a year and a half after Ron went missing.

They had two children, Scott and Crystal. Scott Ronald was born December 28th, 1973, three months to the date before Matt. Crystal was born February 14th, three years later.

Angel lived up to her name as she was a beautiful baby and had grown into a beautiful young lady. It was no surprise she was doing well in beauty school in Danville, as she had been doing hair for two years before she graduated high school. I never knew who or how many people would be in my kitchen getting a haircut when I came home from work. She was a very talented artist and I wanted her to go to an art college, but she was set on cosmetology. Her artistic ability was probably, in part, the cause for her success in hair and fashion.

My daughter and I had an amazing relationship; open, honest and fun. She was outgoing and participated in everything she could at school. Cheerleading, softball, volleyball, dance, band, baton, rifle, flag corp and gymnastics. I referred to her as the million dollar kid.

Matthew was involved with football, baseball, hunting, motorcycles and having fun with his buddies. He was a clone of his father in looks and disposition. He was also very artistic, especially in metal works. Our relationship was pretty good, but we struggled at times. I adored him and drove him crazy trying to get him to open up. Boys were definitely harder, in my experience anyway.

I adored my children and would have died for either one of them in a heartbeat. The only regret I had was that my big brother was not there watching them grow up and having his influence in their life. It hurt so bad sometimes I thought my heart was going to break for the millionth time. I had been living with this pain for 19 years, and thought it was supposed to get better with time. It didn't get better or go away. I just learned to live with it.

Starting with the horror of losing Ron, our family had three years of loss. Eight months after Ron's memorial service, grandpa had another heart attack, but this time he didn't make it. Most of the family felt that losing Ron had been too much for him. He was despondent, depressed and had no fight left.

A few months after grandpa died, my cousin Gary, Brenda's older brother, died in a freak accident in a motel swimming pool. The man who had lived his life on the edge doing all kinds of crazy stunts, cracked his skull going down a slide and died nine days later.

By that time, I was convinced that life totally sucked. Mom's broken ankle and declining health, losing Ron, grandpa dying of a broken heart, and Gary dying in a swimming pool. For a few years it felt like all we did was go to funerals and bury family members.

In the late 70s, one of my Club girls and best friends, Linda McCollum's husband Chuck, fell into a grain bin during a blizzard and suffocated in the corn. They had two children, Lori age five and CJ age one. I was devastated for her and the kids.

My high school boyfriend Gary wrapped his truck around a tree and died instantly.

Carolyn Moves On

Carolyn had moved out of mom's house just a few days before Ron's memorial and moved into an apartment about a mile away. I was petrified that she had moved so she could be alone to take her life. The morning after she moved, I had to go to her apartment to deliver a message because her phone was not hooked up. I was so afraid to knock on her door and find her dead. Thank God I was wrong and she just wanted to be alone.

Ron's disappearance ruined her health and within a year she had one medical problem after another. Stress and devastation seemed to tear her body apart.

Six years after Ron was declared KIA (1976), she met Donald Ridge. Our family liked Don and he was always respectful and caring toward us. When I took Angel to see Carolyn, Don would take her out in the yard and take pictures of her. I was happy for Carolyn and didn't want her to be alone anymore. By the time she met Don, she had moved on to the little house she bought in Covington. Ron had left her quite well off, so she never had to work. When she and Don got married, we attended the ceremony, even though my heart was breaking as I watched my brother's widow walk down the aisle with another man. The tears were not all happy tears.

Carolyn and I stayed close for several years, and then she started giving Ron's things away to her family who didn't know him or have anything to do with him. We felt that Ron's things meant nothing to her family, and these were personal things that we would have cherished. Our niece, Crystal, saw Carolyn's nephews wearing some of Ron's Army clothes at school. These boys didn't even know who he was, and this infuriated our family.

She also tried to take the clocks that Ron had placed on Mom and Aunt Lettie's walls. Neither would give her the clocks, which was not to her liking.

Carolyn and I had stayed in touch off and on and exchanged Christmas cards most years. Our relationship had been through many phases over the years, and with each phase came changes in how much we corresponded. One Christmas I received a Christmas card from Carolyn, but Mom didn't. Crystal took it upon herself to write a letter to Carolyn telling her how unfair she had been to us and especially Mom. There was no answer in response to the letter, but Mom started getting a Christmas card each year after that. Little by little we started corresponding.

Carolyn stopped by Mom's house one day and gave Jim a bag of Ron's things. It seemed like a gesture to mend the rift between us. I called her every once in a while to let her know things I discovered or ask her for addresses for Ron's friends. Slowly we mended our relationship.

A Michigan Man

After my divorce, I wasn't looking for a husband, or even expecting to find a man who I would ever trust or consider letting into my life. Single life was not as much fun as I had imagined and I wasn't enjoying it much. Dating was not fun, as most of the guys I met were pigs or had more baggage than I did.

One evening in February 1990, I had plans to watch Mary, the girl I worked with at my Optometry office, in a light opera play and go to the cast party afterwards. That was the night I met Randy, who had been in Illinois for six weeks working in a factory installing a wood working saw. He was from Grand Rapids and worked for a company that sent him all over the US installing saws, then re-visiting these plants to trouble shoot any problems.

Mary's play and Randy's farewell party happened to be at the same hotel/lounge. Randy had become acquainted with a couple whose wife, Cindy, I had graduated with. Cindy and I ran into each other on a band break and in the middle of a sentence she grabbed my shirt and dragged me to her table to meet Randy. We danced, talked a bit, and exchanged a little of our history. When he asked if he could come back in a couple weeks and visit me, I told him he lived too far away and was a bit young for me. He was 11 years younger, but he didn't care in the least that I was older.

Even after my remark, we exchanged numbers and talked at least four times a week for the next month when he came to see me. We were exclusive immediately. I told myself he was too young and lived too far away, but I wouldn't stop seeing him. He was sweet, funny, generous, refreshing, totally hot and different from anyone I had dated.

His company sent him home every two weeks, so he could fly or drive depending on his location. He started flying into Indianapolis instead of going to Grand Rapids. I was now dating a man who lived four hours away from Covington. This long distance relationship gave new meaning to my life. Phone bills were escalating and I seemed to be on the road every weekend.

Randy had been in the Air Force for six years, serving three years in Germany, close to where Ron had been stationed. He was in security, and had guarded nuclear weapons, President Reagan and foreign dignitaries. We shared the love and respect of our military and he was immediately interested in my brother's fate. He even wanted to get involved with Vietnow. Whenever possible he would attend meetings and planned to go to the Kokomo reunion that fall with me.

My children's' opinion of Randy was important to me and I was happy that they liked him. If they hadn't, I don't know what I would have done. They were 18 and 15, not babies anymore, but their feelings were first on my agenda. Raising Matt separate from Les had been a challenge, and making ends meet was hard. Watching Angel move into an apartment in Danville had been hell. The one thing that was good was Randy.

Dating someone so far away was hard, but Randy and I continued our long distance relationship throughout the summer. The first time I went to Michigan for the weekend, he drove from Grand Rapids to Covington, picked me up, and drove back to Grand Rapids on Friday evening. On Saturday, we picked up some wine and cheese and headed out of Grand Rapids going west. Forty five minutes later we came to a dead end, and parked in front of a giant sand dune covered with long waving sea grass.

Randy grabbed a blanket, the wine, cheese, my hand and we climbed the dune. As we got to the top and I could see over it, I caught my breath. There stretched out in front of me was a beautiful body of aqua marine water, glistening as the sun kissed the waves and creating a picture perfect scene. I had only been on Lake Michigan once when I was 11 and it was pitch black in the middle of the night while crossing on a ferry.

We went about half way down the dune, spread out the blanket, and sat down to have our wine and watch the sunset over Lake Michigan. Big Red, Holland's famous lighthouse, was to our left with all kinds of boats going in and out of the channel. In front of us were beautiful sail boats, motor boats and jet skis, all enjoying the water or settling in to watch the sky as the sun started to melt into the giant blue lake.

Linda and Randy

As the sun disappeared and the sky came alive with swirls of pink, I was in awe of the ambience of this new life I had stumbled into. *Am I falling in love with Randy, my new surroundings, or both?*

We had a wonderful summer together where he acquainted me with the entire shoreline of western Michigan. We visited every lighthouse we could get to and most of the quaint towns and villages along the water.

Time passed quickly and it was time to go to the Vietnam Veterans reunion. I was anxious for Randy to meet some of the guys I had met the year before. I introduced him to Sammy Davis, Bo Grits and some of the Special Forces. I had hopes that someone would know more, tell me something I didn't know, or introduce me to my next connection that would get me closer to finding out what happened to my brother.

It was great seeing all the veterans and friends I had met, but nothing was new. Everyone was still ranting about the government leaving behind live POWS with full knowledge of their actions. I had been involved with Vietnow for two years. The momentum I had felt and the hope of any solid information had peaked and was now on a downward slope. However, I still believed in what they stood for and was grateful for being involved. It was humbling getting to know so many people who cared about what our family had endured for the past 20 years.

Now the hardest part was stepping back from Vietnow, from the cliff I had been standing on since I let myself get caught up in the hope that we would find Ron, alive or dead. I didn't want to stop doing all the things I had been doing to support the cause, but at times I felt like I was wading in mud and getting no-where. I had started feeling guilty that I prayed for him to come home alive. *How can I be so selfish?* To have him come home alive would mean he had gone through torture and hell for 20 years. *Maybe it's time to start praying he did die on November 28, 1970, 20 years ago.*

Maybe.

As fall 1990 approached, I started driving to Michigan by myself some weekends, and occasionally one or both of my kids would go with me. Some weekends Randy's kids would be with us, sometimes we would be alone. Our first Christmas we celebrated in both states.

The new year had barely begun when I was taking my turn driving. On this particular weekend I was alone, glued to the radio as our country was about to go to war in Saudi Arabia.

About half way to Randy's condo north of Grand Rapids, President Bush declared war and Desert Storm began. Our troops had started bombing as I drove to Michigan that Friday night. Tears ran down my face as I tried to control my emotion. *Here we go again. More American lives will be lost. Families will lose their loved ones.* More families would have to endure the hell our family had been living for 21 years.

Randy and I were glued to the news channel all weekend. It was the first war that felt like a sporting event. The American public was kept abreast of the war on a continual basis. It was like nothing I had ever experienced, read or heard of concerning a war or military endeavor. Add to the mystery, we seemed to be kicking butt.

"Why could we not have done this in Vietnam?" I asked Randy as we listened to the reports around the clock.

"It was a different war, different time. Vietnam was a ground war and we didn't know who the enemy was half the time. Desert Storm is an aircraft and tanks war. We have better technology now."

Desert Storm was short, we seemed to have won and I was thrilled. Had our government learned a valuable lesson and was not going to put us through another Vietnam? Maybe all of the protesting had sent a message to the government that the American public would not accept another screw up like Vietnam. I prayed this was true. Only time would tell if my prayers were in vain.

Randy was laid off from his job in the spring of 1991, so we decided he would move to Indiana and see if our relationship could survive day-to-day life. We had dated long distance for a year and a half, talked about marriage and now it was time to put this relationship to the test. We had had some rough patches, but we loved each other and stuck it out. When Randy moved to Indiana, he had no intentions of staying. Before he moved, he had asked me if I would move to Michigan when my kids were old enough to be on their own or out of school and could move with us.

The plan was to live in Michigan once my kids could leave Indiana.

Matt graduated in 1992 and three years later, Randy accused me of dragging my feet. I couldn't deny it, but I was not ready to go. My daughter, Angel, was about to give birth to my first grandchild. There was no way I could leave now. I thought I could convince him to stay, but he had been sending resumes to Michigan employers without my knowledge. I found out one day when he informed me he was driving five hours north to an interview. I was shocked, but thought I could talk him out of it. I tried, but he was adamant and I could not persuade him to wait.

It was early April when we drove to Edmore, Michigan to a job interview for Randy. After the interview I cried for five solid hours, all the way home. My tears didn't work and he took the job. Within three weeks, Randy was preparing to move back to Michigan. He was going to stay with an aunt until I could get things arranged and move. I dragged my feet and anything else I could drag. I just couldn't make the move and we were back to a long distance relationship.

Our wedding date had been set for September 30, only four months away, at a log chapel in the middle of Hartwick Pines, a national forest. We then had reservations to stay in a bed and breakfast lighthouse in Michigan's Upper Peninsula on Lake Superior.

On June 1st my granddaughter Madison Claire was born. I was now a grandma and my little Angel was a momma. I stayed with Angel and Madison for a few days after she was born and it was the greatest time for Angel and me, sharing Madison's first days. I loved being able to help my daughter and spend time with my precious Madison. It would now take a bomb to get me away from this baby and her mother.

Randy and I were still planning on getting married in September, but we lived five hours apart, again. When I held Madison in my arms I felt a mixture of endless love and impending sadness. I knew what I had promised Randy and I understood why he wanted to move back to Michigan, as his kids were there and he had been in Indiana for four years. I wanted to be near Angel as Madison grew up, to be the grandma I had not had. I wanted to give Angel what my mother had given me. I was torn between my two worlds.

Randy was getting nervous that I was not going to follow him. I had put the house up for sale, but that as far as it had gone. He could tell that this was tearing me apart, and I did not want to leave my family.

Matt had moved to Colorado, Angel was settled and ran her own business and Mom was living in her own apartment near Jim. I was free to go, but I couldn't.

In August, Randy broke off our engagement. He said he was not going to be the reason I left my family. I was devastated. Now I didn't have to leave my family, girl-friends, and baby granddaughter, but I was hollow and empty. It was all I could do to get through the day, and nights were unbearable.

Randy and I had put our cars, insurance policies, and bank accounts in each other's names. It was as bad as a divorce.

A few weeks after the break-up, he came and got his things. Up until that time I had hopes we would get back together, but I decided it was time for me to move on. I tried dating, but it was worse than after my divorce from Les. No one was Randy.

My financial situation was a wreck. I quit buying food, sat in the dark and cold, and lost weight. Jim stopped by my house one night when I was sitting in the dark trying to watch TV and wrapped in a blanket. He went into my kitchen, looked into my fridge and had at fit. I tried to convince him I was ok, but he made me turn up the furnace and bought food for me. At that point I didn't care if I ate or if I sat in the dark.

I tried to recall if I had ever been so sad or pathetic. Oh yes, the loss of my brother had hurt much worse than this and the loss of Ron never would end. Nothing could compare to that pain. I would get over this man who had stormed into my life and turned it upside down. I would go on with my life and be near my family, especially my baby granddaughter.

I tried hard to be happy and went to church with Angel, Scott, and Madison. I babysat with Madison whenever needed and got together with my club girls. Nance and I went out at least once a week. It was my night to whine about how much I still missed Randy. I had quite a few dates, but only one of Matt's best friends dad's was worth my time. He took me out a few times and was a real gentleman, but he wasn't Randy.

I tried to hate Randy, remember all of his faults and be thankful I didn't live hours away, but it wasn't working. As hard as I tried to pretend, Angel saw through my pretense.

"You're here Mom, but you're not. You should have gone."

"I know, but I can't live without you and my family near me. No matter which way I turn, I lose."

Our break-up lasted about three months until Randy came down around Thanksgiving. He asked me once again if I would marry him and told me he would move back to Indiana. I didn't give him a definite answer right away, but said that if I married him, I would move to Michigan. I felt it was only fair as I had stayed in Indiana to raise Angel and Matt, and now we could be near his children. I went to Angel and asked if she could forgive me if I left.

"Mom, you have done your job. You were and are a great mother. Go. Be with Randy. We are not worlds apart. We can still have a life together on weekends and holidays. It's only four hours, not across the ocean."

"I know, but if you need me I won't be here like Nanny was for me."

"Mom, I don't want you to be Nanny. Remember, she had no life without us. I don't want that for you. If it doesn't work, you can come back. We will be here. I love you and always will, no matter what state you live in."

I looked into my daughter's beautiful brown eyes, filled with tears and wondered when she became the adult.

Randy and I re-set our wedding date for the next year, October 5, 1996 and I would move to Michigan in May. I still couldn't seem to make myself pack up the house, so my club girlfriends came to the rescue. They arrived with boxes and packing tape, and we had packing club. They pulled clothes out of closets, dishes and pans out of cupboards, and took pictures off the walls. I walked around and told them to keep or pitch. They packed, taped, and marked the boxes. About three hours into it we took a break and went to dinner. We came back to my house and packed some more. I had lived in that house for 23 years. There was a lot of stuff.

At one point Deb, Nance and I sat on my front porch and cried. It had started with these two girls when we were only 13. Our friendship had endured so many changes and tough times but here we sat, still best friends. Now I was leaving. The remainder of the club came out to see what we were doing. When they heard sniffling, everyone started talking at once.

"Don't start that or we'll never get done," Mona said wiping her eyes.

"We are not going to cry, remember, this is just another chapter," Linda said.

"I'll tape your eyes and mouth shut if you don't stop," Lisa said pretending to tape us together.

I still felt like I was going through the motions, but was not really going to go through with the move. Something would stop me, but when? My house had a for-sale sign in front of it and I had let the girls pack it up. I had quit my job and had another in Michigan starting the next Monday.

How far am I going to carry out this farce?

"Ok girls, everyone shut up and listen to me," I said.

"Just because you're the president doesn't mean you can boss us around," Nance said.

"I'm serious, you guys, listen to me a minute."

"We have been listening to you for...uhhhh, how have we known her?" Deb asked as everyone laughed at her.

They were all talking at once, laughing and carrying on as we always had. I knew what they were doing. No one wanted to get serious and have this evening turn into a cry fest. Nance and Brenda had already told me they thought club would slowly fade away after I moved. I was not about to let that happen, even if I was living in another state. I had been the main coordinator who pushed and pleaded when one of us started to slip away. That's how I got to be president, and the fact that no one else wanted the job.

"Ok listen, I mean it, this is serious," I said as I banged my tape dispenser on the steps like a gavel. They finally shut up and let me talk. "You all have to promise that you will not let club die," I said as my voice broke. "We have 24 years into this craziness, and we are not going to let it go. We have been through everything imaginable together and it's not going to die." I wiped the tears from my face.

Everyone but Nance and Brenda promised me with conviction. The two of them gave a half- hearted promise. That was enough for now, as I would work on them privately.

We wrapped up the packing and I hugged each of them with promises to talk as often as possible, and be at as many clubs and outings as I could manage. I also got to still be the president, but Lisa would take over my responsibilities as club coordinator.

I stood on my porch as each of them got into their cars and pulled away, tears dripping off my chin. I then walked through my boxed up house and wondered what the hell I was going to do now.

Three days later I had filled Randy's truck as full as I could possibly pack it with clothes and personal items. Randy and I were going to rent the upstairs at his cousin's house until I sold mine.

I was making my rounds telling Mom, Angel and Madison goodbye and could barely put one foot in front of the other. Mom was first and we held each other and cried. As I was promising her I would see her in a couple weeks, it dawned on me that I had never been away from Mom. I was having a hard time catching my breath. I left her standing in her apartment, holding onto the door, and watching me pull away.

Next I went to Angel's beauty shop. She was busy with clients, but we hugged and I cried. She didn't. She was stronger than I was and my guilt was unbearable. I felt I was abandoning my daughter even though she had told me to go. She had given me her blessing, telling me that I had been a fantastic mother and now it was time for me to do something for myself.

My last stop was to see Madison at the babysitters. I told Cindy, the babysitter, that I needed to see my sweet baby girl, then took her from Cindy arms and walked around the yard with her. She was just about to turn one and had no idea what I was saying. She chattered to me, pointing to flowers, and wanting me to lean her down to smell the blooms. She jabbered her baby talk to me like always, showing me the fake deer in the yard and butterflies. Madison had no idea my heart was breaking in two. I kissed and hugged her, trying not to let my tears fall until I was away from her. She put her little arms around my neck and hugged me back. I took her back to Cindy when I couldn't stand it any longer. Cindy, her sister and friend had been watching Madison and me. They knew I was leaving and what this baby meant to me so, they were all crying as I handed Madison back to Cindy.

"Take good care of her, please," I whispered.

Thank God Matt was in Colorado, as I couldn't take another goodbye.

I got into the truck and started driving north. I cried for the entire five hour trip and have no idea how I got to my destination. In between crying jags, I kept asking myself, "What the hell am I doing?" and "How am I going to live without my heart and the core of my being?

Alone Again?

I had only been in Michigan a few days when Randy received a job offer in Holland. It was 90 miles south, closer to Covington and an answered prayer. Within two weeks, Randy was working in Holland and living on the boat we had purchased the previous February. We stored it in a marina in Muskegon, 35 miles north of Holland, much closer to his work. So here I was, alone again, living in his cousin's upstairs apartment. I needed to quit my new job and find another in Holland or nearby. I was thrilled at the prospect of moving to a town on Lake Michigan, but not sure how to get from point A to point B.

I would put in my 40 hours at work, and then head to the boat on Friday night. There I would feel alive and be with Randy, the reason I was living in Michigan. During the week I felt like I had been plucked out of my life and put in some foreign town with strangers. It was bad enough when Randy was there, now it was horrid.

I wasn't thrilled with my job, and the town was filled with friends that were not mine. I felt so alone. The only saving grace was Randy's cousin Terry who was a sweetheart and tried to make me feel at home. I wanted to quit my new job, but I was so embarrassed that I had just started that I kept putting it off. I decided to confide in a co-worker one day that Randy was working in Holland. She asked my intentions and I lied, telling her we were looking at houses in-between Holland and Mt. Pleasant. They fired me a couple days later, stating they knew I was going to leave and they needed to start training someone.

I went to Covington the last week of June and brought Angel and Madison back with me. On Wednesday morning we packed my car to the top, filled the gas tank and screamed out the windows as we streaked towards Muskegon, my boat and the real start of my life in Michigan.

We settled into marina life and made new friends. Randy suggested I take a break from job hunting and enjoy our boat life. My days were filled with beach and pier walking, sun bathing on the front of my boat or at the pool, cleaning the boat, reading, people watching, and of course missing my family. The new boat and marina life dulled part of the ache.

My new life felt like I was on vacation 24/7, especially since I wasn't working. My life had changed so drastically that I felt like I was having an out of body experience most of the time. There were several different groups of boaters—fisherman, partiers, dock people (ones who never left the dock), Sea Doo lovers and sailboat people. It was addicting and there was even a new language to learn. The ropes that hold the boats were not ropes, they were lines. It wasn't a bathroom, it was the head. Kitchen was a galley. A bedroom in the back of the boat was an aft cabin; the front was the V berth. By the end of the first summer I could talk the talk and hold my own in a conversation.

I learned about the Great Lakes and that the weather could be dangerous and change in an instant. We learned to respect the lake and be aware of the dangers that could be deadly.

Randy was in heaven. We fished on Lake Michigan, watched sunsets off our boat, listened to concerts from the water, watched fireworks on the water, and tried to be a part of my family from 250 miles away.

Angel, Madison, Scott, Angel's husband at the time, Randy, and Randy's youngest son Charlie, spent the Fourth of July weekend on the boat. I was in heaven, but the Fourth of July vacation was over too quickly and it was time for Angel, Scott and Madison to leave for Covington. Their departure spiraled me into a depression and a crying jag that lasted for days. Having my daughter and granddaughter with me for those few days was wonderful and I didn't want to give them up again. What headway I had made, was shot to hell. Nothing made me happy and I tried not to resent Randy for taking me away from them. *Why does life have to be so complicated and hurtful?* It made me think of my big brother and what I had lost. Now I was giving up my

Angel and Madison. It would take days for me to come out of the funk.

Angel had made me promise that I would not cry in front of Madison when we parted. It ripped my heart out, but I tried hard not to show my pain. As they drove out of sight the tears would pour.

I had a couple weeks before club girls came up for a four day stay and had reserved the Harbor House Bed & Breakfast in Grand Haven. We were going to slip our boat in the marina for whenever we wanted to hang out on the boat or go for rides on Lake Michigan when Randy was not working.

Saying that we had fun was ridiculously understated and Michigan summer club had started. When it was time for them to leave, I went into my depression again. I loved Grand Haven, Muskegon, my boat life and all the new things I was being introduced to. Why couldn't I get my family and friends to move up here? *Quit your jobs, uproot your kids, leave your parents, sell your houses, and move up north!*

I also missed my Mom and worried about her every day. I had put a burden on Jim, being responsible for her by himself. She was still living by herself, and he repeatedly told me it was ok but I still beat myself up.

My family and friends tried to convince me that I was right to have gone with my heart and moved, if that was what I wanted to do. Some days I believed they were right, some days not so much. One day I hoped to rid myself of the guilt.

After the girls left I started to finalize our wedding plans. We were going to get married in a log chapel in the middle of an old logging camp at Hartwick Pines, a national park, in the northern part of Michigan.

Two nights of our honeymoon was going to be spent in a Bed and Breakfast lighthouse on Lake Superior, named Big Bay Point, near Marquette. After that we were going to the very top of Michigan's Upper Peninsula, Copper Harbor.

I spent hours on the phone making plans and reservations, without the internet. It was frustrating, but worth it. On October 5, 1996, I would join the ranks of married people again.

It was late July when I began job hunting. I took resumes to several Optometry offices from Holland to Grand Haven. I had no idea where to begin, which offices had a good reputation or which doctors were good ones. So I dropped off resumes at several offices along the main highway between Holland and Grand Haven. By the time I got back to the boat, I had messages from one of the offices wanting me to come for an interview. Within a week, I had a position in an office in Holland. I negotiated a week off for my wedding and honeymoon and life seemed to be falling into place. If we could chop off the northern half of Indiana and the southern fourth of Michigan and push them together, my life would have been perfect.

Even though I was working, I still felt like I was on an extended vacation. My life was nothing like I had ever lived. The six years that Randy had brought me to

Michigan for weekends and vacations were mostly spent near the lakes, lighthouses, and parks. So living on a boat in a marina giving me access to Lake Michigan seemed like a long holiday.

The summer was winding down and our wedding date was fast approaching. By September, boats were being pulled out of the water and the camaraderie between the boaters was slowing down. I was beginning to tire of living in such close quarters. I longed for a house and the ability to walk more than 26 feet and be from one end of my dwelling to the other. Randy worked second shift, so my evenings were lonely.

Throughout the summer there was always something going on and many of our new friends were at the marina all week long. Now I was alone many evenings until Randy got home around eleven. The days were shorter and the sun was gone much earlier, so pier walking was not as pleasurable.

As October 5th approached, I decided I wanted to come home to a structure on dry ground. I told my future husband that if we didn't rent an apartment before we left for our wedding and honeymoon, I was going back to Indiana when we returned from up north. He could have stayed on the boat until it froze in the water, I was tired of it.

Once we decided to rent an apartment it only took me a few days to find one, pack up our things from the boat and move myself in, while he was at work. My furniture was still in my house in Indiana so it was more like camping, but it was heaven to me. It was a two bedroom, with a nice size living room, small kitchen and attached garage. I had brought my TV from the boat and all my clothes. I bought a blow up mattress, a couple bean bag chairs, a dish drainer and a few kitchen things. I was a happy girl.

It was October 3rd, Thursday night, when Angel, Scott, Madison and Matt arrived at our barren apartment. Early the next morning we left for Traverse City, stopping to pick up Randy's boys, Joe and Charlie. Randy's brother Ken and cousin Terry were the only other family members that were going to be at our wedding. I wanted my Mom to be there, but her health prohibited it. My club girls, my brother Jim and his wife Karen, were also invited, but none were able to come.

Randy and Linda at wedding chapel.

Overwhelming sadness flooded over me as I thought of my big brother. I had let someone else influence me into a decision that kept him from my first wedding.

Now so many years later and he wasn't here again. My heart ached. I wanted to share my life with him, ask him for advice. Ask him if I was making a mistake moving away from my family. But I couldn't. All I could do was imagine what he would say to me, like I had for the last 26 years. Tears trickled down my cheeks. Would I ever run out tears to shed for him? Doubtfully. *I miss you Bo, sure wish you could be there tomorrow.*

The chapel at Hartwick Pines was a short hike into the woods and very rustic with no electricity. We brought our jam box so we could have music, but no one remembered to check the batteries. Angel brought candles and flowers. It was private, simple and perfect. Madison decided to chatter during the ceremony, but no one cared. She was my sweetheart, so she could say whatever she wanted.

After the ceremony we drove to the Mackinaw Bridge, then back to Traverse City. The next morning my kids took Joe and Charlie back to their house on their way back to Indiana. Randy and I headed north; to places I had never visited in Michigan.

We went to every lighthouse we could get to by land or boat, along with Tahquamenon Falls, Whitefish Point and Sceney National Wildlife Refuge. We saw deer, eagles, huge woodpeckers, blue heron, porcupines, coyotes, and it seemed like every fish that inhabited the Great Lakes. The next two nights we spent at Big Bay Point, a lighthouse Bed and Breakfast on Lake Superior, near Marquette. I had dreamed of staying in a lighthouse since my first visit to one not long after I met

Randy. The mystic and ambience of the lighthouse gave me goose bumps. I felt like I had gone back in time and was a family member of the old lighthouse keepers. I read the stories and poured over their old pictures and diaries. Their existence was lonely and the winters proved to be deadly at times. As badly as I wanted to live in a lighthouse, I couldn't imagine doing so in the 1800s.

After our stay in Big Bay Point, we kept going north until we couldn't go any further. A couple days later we reached Copper Harbor, at the very top of the Upper Peninsula of Michigan. Randy was disappointed because it had become so commercialized, but I looked at him like he was crazy. We drove through the entire village in two minutes or less. Again, I felt like I had been plucked out of my existence and this time placed back in time about 100 years.

The motels were replicas from the 1950's and the grocery store had a front porch with stuffed bear, deer, fox, and other critters. The gift stores were wooden shacks and the town smelled of wood smoke. We were told that it was not unusual to see bear or moose walk through the middle of town. My cell phone had not worked for the last hundred miles and the motels didn't have phones. We were definitely up north.

We had dinner one night at the Harbor House Inn, on the rocky shore of Lake Superior facing the Copper Harbor lighthouse, across the bay. As evening approached, the blue light in the tower beckoned to any boats still on the water. We bought gifts made by Native

Americans, hiked, and tried to find the Copper Harbor lighthouse by land, which was not possible. One night we sat on the golf course at Keweenaw Lodge at three o'clock in the morning and stared at the moon. My honeymoon was unlike any other vacation or trip or I had ever been on.

All too soon, it was time to start south. We had wandered around through the UP until we had no time left. It was late Saturday night and I had to be at work Monday morning. We drove all day and into the night, when I finally had to get some sleep while Randy drove. My honeymoon was one of a kind and I would always treasure the moments.

Ken, Randy, Linda, Charlie & Joe

Matt, Ken, Randy, Linda, Angel & Madison

My Third Child

In May of 1999, Randy's Dad became sick and within two weeks he passed away. We stood by his bedside while the nurses turned the machines off and he took his last breath.

We had found the house we wanted and had started the process of getting financed, while his Dad was dying. It was hard to be excited about our house and sickened by the death of his father. It seemed like every time life gave you something good, it took something away.

Five months before Randy lost his father, in the fall of 1998; he called me at work one morning and informed me that his ex-wife was bringing his youngest son Charlie, to live with us full time. No warning, no discussions, it was a done deal. I knew it was the best for Charlie, but I was only thinking of the years of child rearing he still needed. I wasn't sure I was up to the task.

Charlie was five years old when Randy and I started dating. He was a cute mischievous, energetic, full of life little boy. Now he was twelve and he was a bigger version of his five-year-old self.

The remainder of my work day was distracted by a million thoughts of what lay ahead for me. I was also worried about Charlie's state of mind as it had been a decision made without his input. My head ached from thinking of whether I was up for this challenge and then to knowing this life was better for Charlie.

Randy had to go to work before I got home, so Charlie was alone at our apartment for a little while before I got there. When I walked in the door and looked at his face, all doubts vanished. He was sitting in the corner of the couch watching TV and looked like a lost little boy. My heart melted and any hesitation faded. I had to let him know he was wanted and help him be the happy carefree boy I had known for the past nine years. My mother instinct took over as I made our dinner and talked with him.

The next few years were filled with school schedules, football, wrestling, drivers education, sex talks, girlfriends, big rowdy guys, all mingled in between Randy, my kids in two other states, our jobs and our boat life.

We weren't the Brady Bunch, as we had plenty of family stress, but it was worth it. As the years passed, Charlie became my son and I never regretted him coming to live with us for one second.

False Hopes

In the spring of 1997, I received a call from the Army requesting DNA from our family. I couldn't speak.

"Mrs. Winters, are you there?" The voice on the other end of the phone asked.

"I'm here, but it's Mrs. Cope. I re-married," I said as I tried to control my breathing. "Why do you want DNA? Did you find someone who you think is my brother?"

"No, it's just routine. We're trying to collect DNA from all the families who have a loved one Missing in Action, Prisoner of War or Missing in Action/Body not Recovered.

"Number one, there is no routine when you call a family who has a loved one missing and ask for DNA," I said. "Why would you want it if you don't think you found him?"

"We are trying to get DNA from everyone, before it's too late. Sorry, Ma'am. Is your Mother still alive?"

"Yes she is. Before it's too late?" I asked.

"Your mother is the best person for DNA, and if we could get you and your siblings, it would be great. The parents of this war are aging and we need to get their DNA before we lose them."

"Oh," I said. "Ok, I think. I'm sure my mother and brother will be willing to do this for Ron. How and when do we go about this?"

"We will be in touch within the next couple of weeks and give you instructions. It will probably be done at the nearest lab."

"Ok, just let us know what to do next. Are you sure there is not more to this?" I asked, disappointment settling in.

"Someone from our office will be calling you. Thank you, Mrs. Winters, uh sorry Mrs., I'm sorry; what did you say your new married name is now?"

"Cope, C O P E, please just hyphenate my name, so you don't forget who I am. Please change it to Linda Winters-Cope," I said.

"You will have to do that legally."

"Of course I will. Thank you." I hung up the phone and sat motionless. *Here we go again.* I wondered if anything had changed. Would this be as messed up as the last time we dealt with the government. *Is this the truth? Have they found him and won't tell us until they identify his remains? I have to tell Jim and Mom.*

I called my brother and it sounded like a recording of the conversation I had a few minutes before. He asked the same questions and had the same hesitation I still felt. Yet he surprised me with his response.

"I'm not giving them anything," he stated.

"What? You won't do this?"

"No, I'm not going to do anything for them."

"Jim, it's not for them, it's for Ron."

"They're probably lying. That's all they know how to do."

"I agree, but I will not refuse if it means identifying Ron's body."

"They will screw it up and I don't believe a word they say."

"I know, but we can't not do this, and you know it."

"I know," he said in a whisper.

We agreed we would give them our DNA and explain to Mom what she had to do. Jim said he would tell her in person, as over the phone was not the best idea. I would wait for the Army to call and tell us the next step. I was sure we had not been told their true motives, just like last time.

It was at least a month or longer before I heard from the Army again.

"Hello," I answered into the phone.

"May I speak to Mrs. Winters? I am from the Department of the Army," he said.

"This is Linda," I said, giving up on explaining my new married name. "We are calling on behalf of Ronald Eugene Smith. We need to speak to the primary next of kin. That would be you, correct?"

"Yes, this is Linda Winters-Cope. Ronald is my brother."

"We are calling back to ask for the families cooperation in getting DNA on file. We would like to ask why your family has decided not to give DNA."

"What are you talking about?"

"We contacted you sometime back and you said your family was willing to cooperate with giving DNA."

"And we still are. You are the ones who dropped the ball. You were supposed to call and tell us where and when. I have heard nothing."

"Oh, I'm sorry ma'am. Someone in another department must not have called you back," he said.

"Evidently, again. Where and when?"

"Someone in that department will contact you."

"Are you kidding?"

"I will leave notes that your family is ready and willing. What hospital or lab do you and your family want to go to?"

"To start with, again, it won't be the same facility. I live in Michigan, and my brother and Mom live in Indiana. Can we go to separate ones, or will that confuse your department?"

"Oh, uh, I guess that can be arranged," he said.

"Well if you can't manage to get that worked out, just let me know. I will go to Indiana and go with my brother and make it easier for you."

"That won't be necessary, we will work it out. We will be in touch Mrs. Winters."

"Whatever," I muttered under my breath. I hung up the phone and dreaded my next call. Jim would have even more doubts about dealing these people.

I wanted to talk to someone who could tell me if this was standard procedure. Did they really get DNA from families before they found, or thought they found, their loved one? I wanted to call someone, but whom? I had lost touch with the guys from Vietnow. Captain Hill, Ron's Casualty officer, came to mind, but I was sure he was long gone from the job he held in 1970, and I didn't have his number.

After I reported the ridiculous phone call to my brother, I waited for him to respond. He said nothing.

"Jim, are you still there?" I asked.

"Yes. Sis, do you see now? Would you honestly believe anything they would tell us?"

"Not really. But I can't not do it. I have an idea. If they ever find Ron, let's have whatever body parts are left, tested ourselves."

"OK, that's the only way I'll do it."

"Thank you." I took a long breath.

"Sis, you don't have to thank me. I wouldn't have refused you or Ron. I just hate those people and I don't trust them as far as I could throw them. Look at the idiotic way they are handling this DNA thing," Jim said. "Look at how they screwed up when Ron went missing. If we ever find out what really happened to Ron...well, the only way we will is if he comes home and tells us."

As the tears streamed down my face, I told my little brother I would let him know as soon as they called back.

Three months later I answered my phone to be asked insane questions once more of why our family wouldn't cooperate with the government and give our DNA. This time I went off on the woman on the phone. I cursed, cried and held nothing back. I reminded her of how our family had been treated and ignored when my brother went missing. I knew she had nothing to do with what happened 27 years ago, but I couldn't stop myself. I asked her if everyone who worked for the government was as incompetent as what our family had dealt with for all these years.

She apologized over and over again.

"I'm not going to tell you it's ok, because it's not. Just leave us alone, I'm sick of it," I said.

"Mrs. Winters, please accept my apology and let me fix this mess," she said.

"If I tell you ok, you'll just tell me someone will call in a week and arrange for us to give our DNA. Then no one will call, and then someone else will call and start all over again and if it happens again I may shoot someone," I said.

"Oh Linda, don't say that. I know you don't mean it, but you can't say things like that. Not to government people."

"Whatever."

"Listen to me. I will personally handle this myself. I will not turn this over to the next department. I will make the arrangements and call you back myself."

"Seriously? I'll believe it when I hear it."

"OK, I'll call you back in a few days myself. I promise."

"If you call back, I'll do it. But do me a favor, don't call my brother, let me do it. I don't want to have to visit him in prison. He will say things worse than I did. He didn't want to do this even before you all screwed this up so badly."

"May I ask why he wouldn't want to identify Ronald's body?"

"That's not the case. Of course he wants to identify our brother's body.

He doesn't trust anything any of you do or tell us."

"I see, I'm sorry. I guess I don't blame you. But I will fix this, I promise."

I hung up with her still promising and apologizing.

I called Jim and reported the insanity. He was silent, but I swore I could hear him shaking his head.

The DNA woman called me back within a week and informed me she was setting up the appointments. I could go to the lab of my choice. I gave her Jim's number so she called him. We would give our DNA to help identify Ron, if he ever came home.

From the time I got the first call to the time we gave our blood for DNA matching, it was nearly a year. I couldn't understand how messed up their program was. If someone didn't do something to straighten out the confusion, it would fail.

While we were waiting for our DNA to be taken, I received a package with a military looking return address and thought it was something to do with the DNA testing. It wasn't. I took out a huge medal and laid it in my lap while I opened the letter that came with it. It was a medal issued to personnel who had been in Vietnam and was given in Ron's name. I thought it was strange since we had already been given a shadow box full of medals in 1971.

The second page explained that we could buy as many as we wanted. *Ok, I missed something, what did this say?* As I read the price list I started feeling a burning sensation through my body. I was livid, incensed, and fuming. *Who would think of such an insult? They want us to buy medals?* I called and told them it was an insult to be asked to pay for medals after losing Ron. They said they were sorry I felt the way I did and would take me off their mailing list. *Will this insanity ever end?*

It was 2004 and had been two years since Mom, Jim and I gave our DNA to be filed into the data bank for identifying Ron, and we had heard nothing.

I missed my connection with Vietnow and the military guys I had become acquainted with. Randy decided to find me a group I could become involved with and he found a Vietnam Veterans group in Holland. I attended a meeting one evening while Randy was working and felt lonely and out of place. It had been hard enough getting into these groups several years ago, now I just didn't have what it took to go back. I had made friends with many of the people in Indiana and kept in touch with them. At this time, I just didn't have it in me and I didn't go back even though I felt guilty. I told myself I didn't have time because of work, Charlie and my new house.

In reality, I didn't want the promises that these groups wanted to make to me when they found out I had a brother who was MIA. Their hearts were in the right places and I loved them all for their compassion, but I had run into so many dead ends in the past years that I couldn't seem to get past the disappointment of yet another.

When I got into Vietnow in Indiana, I was so sure they were going to find Ron that I was daydreaming of his homecoming. I had seen pictures and governments reports of live sightings of hundreds of Vietnam Veterans. I had sat down with families who had pictures of their loved one sitting in villages in Vietnam in the present day. It had been confirmed that the person was indeed the lost solider, POW/MIA.

Our group, other groups, private citizens, and family members had protested, wrote letters, tried to get on the news, screamed and cried. Nothing ever brought them back. I had run out of energy to do it again and couldn't stand the heartbreak.

That didn't mean I had not forgotten my big brother. I thought of him every day and still had many sad days and crying jags. I wrote dedications on Veterans Day and most of the time the newspapers or radio stations printed or read them. I read books and articles about Vietnam, Special Forces, and how badly the government had handled Vietnam, left our men behind and lied about it. I flew my flags, American and POW/MIA. I just couldn't join the Vietnam group.

What Is
Rolling Thunder?

In mid-summer of 2005 Mom called one day. "Who is Carol Smith? And what is Rolling Thunder?"

"Uh, Who? I don't know, I don't think. Rolling Thunder is a group that is dedicated to POW/MIA's, why?"

"Let me read this article to you I found in the paper," she said. She began reading an article from the newspaper telling of an Indianapolis woman, a Rolling Thunder member, who had been riding to the Vietnam Wall in Washington DC in honor of Ronald E. Smith, leaving a set of dog tags at The Wall. This organization rode and spoke for soldiers who couldn't speak for themselves because they were still Missing in Action from Vietnam. Carol Smith stated she had ridden with Rolling Thunder for several years and placed Ronald's dog tags on a wreath at The Wall along with the other Indiana men still listed as MIA. By the time Mom finished reading the article, tears were streaming down my face.

"Mom, do we know this Carol Smith? Does it give her address or phone number....oh, of course it wouldn't," I said.

"It says she lives in Indianapolis, and that she would like to be in touch with his family if they would be interested in meeting or talking. It says they have tried to find us but no one knows who his family is."

"What? How can that be? We all live in the same town, but me. You all have the same phone number. Evidently the list Ron is on doesn't have any of us listed," I said as my mind raced. "I'll call the paper and see if they can get her number. I'm betting there is more than one Carol Smith in Indianapolis."

"Don't you think it's weird that her name is Smith?" Mom asked.

"Yes, I do but it's probably a coincidence. Anyway, I'll find her, it will be interesting. I'll let you know when I talk to her."

"Ok, do you want me to send this article to you?"

"Yes, I do. I'll talk to you tomorrow. Love you Mom."

"Love you too. Bye bye."

I sat motionless for a few minutes. *Someone else is paying respect to my brother, riding to The Wall for him.* I felt a warmth toward this woman I didn't even know existed 20 minutes earlier, but I couldn't shove back the guilt I felt that it wasn't me riding to The Wall.

The next day I called my hometown newspaper and convinced them to give Carol Smith my phone number, since they wouldn't give me her number. Three days later, Carol called and we talked for over an hour. I thanked her for honoring my brother and told her how appreciative we were. I ask if her last name had anything to do with her choice. She said when she looked at the 63 names from Indiana still missing she had a feeling about Ron, so she chose him to ride for and place his dog tag at The Wall.

I asked Carol if she knew anything about Ron. She told me she had read his bio that came with the dog tags Rolling Thunder had made for the members to leave at The Wall. Other than that, she was unable to find anything else. The bio gave his rank, what Special Forces group he was in, and how he went missing. She didn't even know how old he was or what he looked like.

I asked her for more information about Rolling Thunder. There was no doubt she was proud to be a member of this organization and more than willing to educate me on their mission.

Their actual mission statement read:

The Major function of Rolling Thunder, Inc. is to Publicize POW-MIA issues. To educate the public that many American Prisoners of War were left behind after all past wars and to help correct the past and to protect future veterans from being left behind should they become Prisoners of War or Missing In Action. We are also committed to helping American veterans from all wars. Rolling Thunder,

Inc. is a non-profit organization and everyone donates his or her time because they believe in the POW/MIA Issue.

This organization believed there were live POW still being held in Southeast Asia. I had at one time, but it had been so long that I assumed there was no possible way they could have lived this long. Rolling Thunder did. Besides that, Rolling Thunder lobbied for better Veterans benefits, better pay, assistance after deployment, assistance for families at home, better VA benefits, and faster results for VA claims. They gave countless donations, donated to the HVAF, (Hoosier Veteran Assistance Foundation), helped to feed and clothe the Veterans, celebrated some holidays with them, and the list was endless.

I was humbled by the fact that these people were so active and I had let that slip through my fingers. Carol invited Randy and me to go to a Rolling Thunder meeting. I thanked her and promised we would come.

We exchanged numbers and promised to be in touch. I thanked her again and we said goodbye.

Again I sat motionless with tears streaming down my face. I had two calls to make. Mom and Jim would be blown away. Would Jim feel as ashamed as I did?

I waited to tell Mom everything until I was with her. Her hearing was getting bad and I wanted her to understand everything I had learned. I didn't think Jim felt as I did. He was interested in the chapter and what they stood for and what this lady was doing in Ron's honor.

As far as my guilt over the fact that I wasn't doing anything lately for the POW/MIA's, he didn't say much. He had not gotten into Vietnow partly because of his job as a truck driver and being out of town all the time. The other issue was because he was protective of me and didn't want me to get hurt by people taking advantage of my vulnerability when it came to Ron.

I sent Carol some information regarding Ron and we talked again. She invited us to a meeting once more and I made excuses—Randy was working, I worked some Saturdays, and we had responsibilities with Mom. I came up with anything I could to put it off and I wasn't sure why. Carol called me after a few months and asked if she had done anything to offend me.

"Absolutely not, why would you think that?" I asked, my mind raced to come up with excuses.

"Well, we invited you to a meeting and so hoped that your family would come. We are all excited that we found the family of a POW/MIA. That doesn't happen very often. Of all the chapters that we know members personally, none have family members."

"Carol, you have done nothing in the world to offend me. You have to believe me. We live in Michigan and it is harder than I thought to get back into the military, POW/MIA thing. But we will come to a meeting, I promise."

I hung up the phone and questioned the lie I had told Carol. This woman was paying tribute to my brother. She was doing what I wished I was doing. I was envious, ashamed and I wasn't sure why I kept putting these people off.

When I first got involved with Vietnow, I had let some the members convince me I was going to find Ron; some even seemed to believe he was alive. I had tried to keep that notion out of my head, but it crept in when my guard was down. I became so involved with finding out the truth that I let myself believe it, even when I told others I didn't think there was any possibility he had survived. My subconscious fell hook, line and sinker.

My move to Michigan had made it easier to ease away from Vietnow and that intensity. I used distance for my excuse to step back. My heart couldn't take the disappointment and I had needed a break.

Now I had found a group, or they had found us, that intrigued Randy and I both. I had such respect for them, their cause and dedication. They were paying respect to Ron and they knew no one in our family. These people were awesome, and their organization was unbelievably selfless.

So why am I holding them at arm's length?

A flashback of me standing under the enormous American flag at the Kokomo Vietnam Veterans reunion, arm and arm with the Special Forces guys and Vietnow members, listening to the Brit Small Band sing the heartbreaking song, "He Ain't Heavy, He's my Brother," flooded my heart. Heaviness came over my soul. Depression and disappointment felt as if it might suffocate me. The awareness of my actions was rising to the surface of my conscious.

Ron, I'm not sure I can do this again...

Less than two weeks after my conversation with Carol and my promise to make it to a Rolling Thunder meeting, she called back. I was all set to assure her we would make it soon, when I learned that she had a different request.

A director of documentaries, Jeff Shea, had become interested in Rolling Thunder. He had been filming Chapter One of Indiana for several months and had made the trip to Washington D.C. the previous year. Carol and her boyfriend had been featured members in his film.

When he chose Carol and Eddie (Scooby, Eddie's nickname), Ron became the featured MIA. This brought Ron's family into the story line. When the director discovered that Carol had been in contact with us, he asked if we would be in his documentary. If we agreed, he wanted to know if we would be willing to meet Carol and Eddie on film.

His request was to interview Jim and me on camera telling Ron's story. He wanted to know what happened and how it all went down. He wanted the entire story, what the government did, said and how they handled our 35 year battle of trying to find out what had happened and where we felt Ron was now.

"Are you serious, Carol?" I asked

"Yes, I am. This guy is great. He rode to D.C. with us last year, filming everything," she said.

"I've wanted to let the world know what happened and how the government handled this for 35 years, but I felt like no one cared, that is until I met Vietnow and now you guys. Now someone wants us to tell it on film?"

"Do you think you can do this?"

"I know I can. Jim will be another story and I won't do it without him. I'll talk to him and get back to you. Would he like for Mom to be with us?"

"He didn't say, but I'm sure that would be another plus."

We hung up with promises to talk the next day. I couldn't wait to call my little brother and tell him what Carol had asked.

Jim was a little hesitant at first, as he was not comfortable in front of a microphone. Plus, he was always more cautious than I was in these matters. When he consented he repeated his usual response, "You get to do the talking. You always have been the mouthpiece for the family."

I called Carol the next day to let her know we were on board. After several phone calls back and forth, we had plans set for our meeting and the interview with Jeff. We would have the meeting at Jim's house in Covington and Jeff's people would bring all the equipment for filming. I feared it would be someone with a home video camera, a small tape recorder and a dream of something bigger on the horizon. I hoped for more, but it seemed too good to be true.

The day had arrived for our filming with Rolling Thunder. I was nervous and hoped we would be able to get our message across. Would meeting Carol and Eddie be spontaneous and believable? Would this be something to be proud of? I was having doubts.

The family had gathered at Jim's house—Jim, Karen, Scott, Scott's wife Karen, Crystal, Mom, Brenda, Gina, Lisa, Mona, Angel, Randy and myself all waiting to see what was about to happen. I hoped the filming crew didn't mind having an audience. Everyone had been advised to stay inside so the crew could set everything up for our first meeting with Carol and Eddie.

Jeff knocked and the introductions began. As the lights, microphones, recorders, and miles of cords were brought in, I knew this was what I had hope for. This was professional.

I heard a Harley pull up, but Jeff stopped us from going to the door. Carol and Eddie would be staying outside until everything had been set up. The next task was hooking Jim and I up with microphones and then testing them.

Jeff had the rest of the family stand back in the dining room and instructed them to be very quiet. He explained that the microphones would pick up every little movement and noise. He had us seat Mom in Jim's recliner in the living room. Jim and I were to stand near the door, ready to answer when Carol and

Eddie came in. The only thing missing was the black and white board that movie people click together and yell Action.

Jeff motioned for Carol and Eddie to come into the house and pointed at Jim and me and said, "Go."

Carol and Eddie walked through Jim and Karen's front door and I was immediately back in. The flag waving, protesting, letter writing, demonstrating and screaming my brother's story and our hell.

They were leather clad, with POW/MIA do-rags on their heads, dog tags around their necks and riding on a Harley with an American and POW/MIA flag attached to the back of the bike. At one glance, I could see into their hearts. Their Rolling Thunder vests were full of the patches professing their beliefs, and mine. There were POW/MIA patches, American flags, and Vietnam Wall patches. There were patches that professed their disgust of the government leaving our soldiers behind, patches of all the years they had been to D.C. for the Run to The Wall, and patches in memory of men who they had been lost from Indiana Chapter One. As one of them turned sideways I saw the bright yellow patch cursing Jane Fonda's name, calling her America's Traitor.

How had I not known these people existed? The United States had chapters full of these awesome people. People who cared so much for the men left, lost and the families that endured years of hell not knowing what had happened to their loved ones. I held back the tears as we introduced ourselves to each other. There were hugs immediately, not just handshakes, but hugs. These people had been honoring my big brother and they had no idea who he was or what he was all about. All they knew was his name, rank, service, his bio from the internet and that he had been left. They had no idea how much he was missed and mourned. When Carol had chosen to ride for Ron, she had no idea he was the best big brother ever and that he was a loving son who honored his mother and took care of her. She had no idea he was a fantastic husband and that his widow had nearly lost her mind and her health was ruined when she lost him. All of these thoughts were running through my mind while I was trying to sound sane on camera. I wanted them to know these things about Ron. I wanted them to know that Carol had chosen one hell of a man to honor.

Slow down Linda, all in good time.

As the introductions and hugs slowed, Carol said she had something for us.

"Linda, Jim we have brought something for you," she said pulling out two sets of dog tags, one for each of us.

Jim and I stood there, looking dumbfounded.

They brought gifts for us? Shouldn't this be the other way around?

"Oh Carol, thank you so very much," I said, as a tear ran down my face.

"Thank you Carol, Eddie," Jim said as he took his tags.

The tags had Ron's name on them, the panel and line that Ron's name was located at on The Wall, and Rolling Thunder printed on the last line. These tags were the same as the ones the chapter members took to The Wall each year.

Next they brought out a POW/MIA flag and handed to us. I was having a very hard time not falling apart.

"Thank you both so much, but you have already done so much for our family, this is over the top," I said.

"No, your family has given more than any one should have to give. It is our turn to give back to you," Carol said, as Eddie agreed.

I couldn't hold back the tears and had forgotten we were being filmed. Jeff calling "Cut" and the filming stopped, brought me back. He wanted to end this segment and resume talking to Mom. This part didn't go as well because of her lack of hearing. Regardless, she was Ron's mother and she needed to be a part of this. A couple of times Jeff had to stop the filming and remind our cousins and kids that the microphones were picking up everything they were whispering. When it was time for Jim and I to have our interview with Jeff, the rest of the family had to be motionless. I had been waiting 35 years for someone to ask me these questions, to have my answers filmed and out there for someone and everyone to hear.

Jeff asked Jim and I questions for over an hour. Questions about how the government handled Ron's missing status, reporting to the family, where Ron was left, and if we believed them. He asked if we thought we were told the truth, and if we believed he might still be alive. It was brutal but satisfying at the same time. After about four hours of taping, Jeff wrapped up our session and talked with the five of us while the family listened.

"We will review all the footage and decide what we will keep and what we will leave out. If we need anything else, will all of you be available?" he asked.

"Absolutely. Just call and let us know, but I can only be here on weekends. You know what, forget that, I'll be available anytime you want or need," I said.

"Weekends will be ok with me," Jeff said.

Carol, Scooby and Jim all agreed.

"Ok, thank you, Linda, Jim, very much. It has been a pleasure to meet you and hear the story about your brother. I will be in touch. After the film is finished, there will be a viewing in Indianapolis. I would really like for you both and all of your family to be there," he said.

"We will be there, you couldn't keep us away," Jim said as he shook Jeff's hand.

We hugged Carol and Scooby again, thanked them for all they had done and promised we would be coming to Rolling Thunder meetings. This time I knew I meant what I had promised.

It was clear what had been going on in my head and heart. Getting back into one of the military groups hurt like hell, but it was like falling in love with someone who was not available. I wanted to be a part of Rolling Thunder whether it hurt or not. I wanted to jump back on the band wagon, whether it would do any good or not. I wanted to scream injustice, whether it helped or not. I wanted to protest the government for leaving my brother behind, for leaving over 2500 men behind after the Vietnam War and lying about it. I wanted to shame the American public who had treated our Vietnam Veterans so badly. I wanted to keep searching until I found the answers, whether it hurt or not. I was back, I was in and I was ready to fight.

I'm coming back Ron. I'll find you or die trying.

In early April 2005, I received a call from Carol that the documentary was finished. She gave us an invitation for our entire family to attend the debut which was to be held at a dinner theater in Indianapolis.

Jim and I called the family and offered invitations, and about 25 members of our family attended the viewing of documentary. Pictures of our family were taken outside the theater with Carol and Eddie, and they introduced to us to many members of the Rolling Thunder chapter.

Everyone was very welcoming.

We were ushered inside, offered tables near the front and seated together. There was quiet talking for a few minutes before Jeff came out and introduced himself, gave special thanks to our family and started the documentary.

The beginning of the documentary was Jeff's explanation of how he became interested in Rolling Thunder. He then interviewed other veterans about their experiences in Vietnam.

Ron's face appeared on the screen and it took my breath away to see him being portrayed as a war hero on that huge movie screen. Several members of our family had the same reaction and I heard quiet gasps. As Jeff narrated Ron's disappearance and other pictures flashed across the screen, you could hear the sound of sniffles and soft crying from members of our family. It was 35 years late, but my brother was getting the honor and recognition he so deserved. It was long overdue but much appreciated.

Jim and I were next in the film with Jeff asking us questions, in Jim's living room. This was a first for both of us and I had a hard time looking at myself. The important thing was that Ron's story was being told.

When the film ended, many of the chapter members thanked us for coming and invited us to attend meetings anytime we pleased. I was overwhelmed and felt as if I was going to wake up and this would only be a dream. Jim and I were each given a copy of the documentary, and we purchased copies for Mom.

We said our goodbyes and started back to Jim's house in Covington. Mom looked tired and we needed to get her back to her assisted living apartment. She wasn't as vocal as she had been and I wondered what was going through her mind and how she processed the day.

I wasn't sure to what degree I would become involved with these people, but for now I wanted to learn more, catch my breath and then jump on their band wagon. It didn't take much to get me excited on this subject and I was now on overload.

Memorial Day 2005 was fast approaching and it was time for Rolling Thunder's annual Run to The Wall. Scooby and Carol extended an invitation to us and anyone in our family to ride to D.C. with them. That meant Randy and I had three weeks to get vacation time approved, and with it being a holiday, it wasn't enough notice. The trip would have to be put off until the following year. I was hooked. That Memorial Day weekend I spent half the day on my cell with Carol who kept me updated on what they were doing on the trip.

Every Memorial Day, Randy and I spent four days on our boat at the Marina with our boat family. Some years our kids came to visit. This year I had my cell phone stuck to my right ear and the other hand over my left, walking back and forth on our dock, listening to Carol telling me everything they were doing.

Randy, Linda, Carol & Scooby 2007

My Brother's Name on The Wall and On Me

One year later and we were ready to go. Randy got off work at ten p.m. and we were on the road to Indianapolis by 11:30 pm. We were going to drive to Washington D.C., following the bikes of Indiana Chapter One. I was finally going to see the Vietnam Wall and touch my brother's name.

We arrived at Carol and Scooby's house in Indianapolis about four in the morning. I slept for a little while, but Randy and Scooby never laid their heads on a pillow all night. Scooby explained that he never went to bed the night before they took off, as he was just too geeked to sleep. He was in their garage preparing the bike, packing, re-packing, checking flags and re-arranging everything.

Around 7:00 am we made our way to Harley Davidson North of Indy, the staging location for Rolling Thunder to begin their ride to The Wall. There was a program with speakers from the Indiana Department of Veterans Affairs, mayors, decorated war heroes and politicians. TV and radio stations were there to film and interview.

Randy and I were feeling rather out of place, especially since we not clad in black leather, Rolling Thunder tee shirts and Harley boots. Most everyone had on jeans, and black leather vests with pins and patches that resembled what Carol and Eddie had on their vests. Hats, doo-rags, ponytails and braids were the main head gear. We stood out like sore thumbs.

Not knowing for sure what we should be doing, Randy and I mounted the big flags we had bought onto the back of the truck. Randy had made extensions from the trailer hitch to hold 3x5 American and POW flags. Along with the magnets Eddie had given us to put on the truck side doors, we started to look as if we hadn't arrived at the wrong event.

As bikes were lined up, we were instructed on where to park our truck so we could pull out directly behind the bikes. The program started with the pledge of Allegiance, a prayer from a man they all called Big Daddy, and then Rolling Thunder's mission statement was read.

The guest speaker gave a speech professing the never ending quest to bring our POW/MIA's home—alive and deceased. Next they passed out bright neon green buttons with the letters FNG printed boldly across them, to the people who were going on their first run to The Wall. They were to be worn at every Rolling Thunder event they attended for a period of one year. The initials stood for Fun New Guy or Girl. It was a play on words from the military when new guys were called FNG's. Only difference was the F stood for a different word, so the chapter had cleaned it up quite a bit.

Toward the end of the program, Carol and Scooby walked up to the front where John Brinkley, the chapter president, handed Carol the microphone. Carol called me to the front and I froze. *Oh no, what is she going to say?* I hadn't been given a clue that I would have to talk or be pointed out. I didn't want to be any more of a spectacle than I already felt. I took a deep breath and proceeded to the front of the group and stood beside Carol.

She introduced me to the group and then she and Scooby presented me with a leather vest. It had POW/MIA silhouette on the back and on the front was another patch that said Linda Cope, and under it Smitty's little sister. I had shared with Carol that I had grown up hearing Ron's friends call me that.

Tears trickled down my cheek from behind my sunglasses. I had vowed not to cry in front of anyone but family because I had seen too many fake expressions of pain and sorrow. I never wanted to be one of those people.

I sucked it up, took the microphone and thanked Carol and Eddie for the vest and inviting us to ride with Rolling Thunder to Washington. I didn't say everything I wanted because I couldn't compose my thoughts and I didn't want to cry. The chapter applauded and welcomed us. I still couldn't believe I had found these people.

Next the squad leaders and sweeps, the men that rode last bike in each squad, lined up in front of the group and began the roll call. John Brinkley called out each man's name from Indiana that was still missing. Every time a name was called, one of the squad leaders or sweeps would step forward and say "Still Missing, Sir." At that time, there were still 63 unaccounted for from Indiana, my brother included.

A pastor performed a blessing of the bikes, and the program ended with prayer.

At 10:00 am, the chapter began the Ride to The Wall. We had a police escort to the county line and police bikes raced around us stopping traffic. There were bikes as far as I could see, our truck decked out with flags and Rolling Thunder magnets, and then three chase vehicles behind us.

I was glad Randy and I were alone in the truck because I couldn't control my emotions. With members' welcoming words, Carol and Eddie's gift, the sight of 105 bikes stretched out in front of us, all the POW/MIA flags, patches, clothing, and the anticipation of where I was going. I couldn't stop the tears.

Each leg of the trip was about 90 miles and we stopped for gas, bathroom breaks and snacks. Terry (Flash) Sanderson was our road captain, complete with a bull horn for bellowing instructions. At these stops, we started making friends with the members.

The first day ended in Athens, Ohio at a Best Western hotel. In those years, there was a lot of parking lot partying and members brought coolers full of beverage, food and snacks. It was evident these people had a lot of history together, but it didn't detract from how welcome they made Randy and me feel.

Bikes were in and out of the hotel parking lot, gassing up, going to dinner and making sure they were ready for the next leg the following morning. I thought most members would want to make this an early evening, but I was wrong. The camaraderie continued way past any sensible hour considering we had early wake up call.

The next morning, the rule was kickstands up at 7:30 a.m. and we were off. It was a hard and fast rule, not one minute after, be there or be left. Randy and I were up and ready to follow the bikes. Most everyone had nicknames, mine started out to be little sister, and our truck got stuck with the name flag pole. It fit since we were sporting two giant 3x5 flags.

Friday was a crazy ride through the mountains and into D.C. by five or six P.M. When we got within 30 miles of the hotel, the traffic was so heavy we sat in the 95 degree heat, sometimes without moving an inch for long periods of time. Our hotel was enormous and a very welcome sight after two days of traffic, hot weather, and some close calls from drivers who had no respect for bikes. Other motorists waved and gave thumbs up when we passed each other, they seemed to know what we were doing and where we were going.

We checked in, showered and rested. At 9:00 p.m., we staged outside our hotel for the ride to the Vietnam Wall for our candle light ceremony. Carol and Scooby rode in our truck instead of on their bike so we wouldn't get lost and I could be present for the Gold Star Mothers ceremony. Gold Star Mothers were the Moms that had lost a son or daughter in one of the many wars. This ceremony took place about an hour before RT Chapter One had our ceremony and left our wreath and dog tags at The Wall.

Poster made by Matt of Ron's dog tag.

I had waited for 20 years to come to the Vietnam Wall to see and touch my brother's name. We had planned it many times, but something always prevented the trip. Angel had been here on her senior trip and brought flowers to lay under Ron's name. She took pictures and her classmates had taken pictures of her with Ron's name. Many people had brought me rubbings. Now I had a feeling I was supposed to come the first time with Rolling Thunder Chapter One, my new family.

We gathered at the National Mall at the west end of the Vietnam Wall waiting in a crowd of mothers who had lost their sons. I was allowed to walk with them this one time, being a Gold Star sister. I was shaking at the thought of touching Ron's name and Randy held my hand, with Scooby and Carol right beside us. After a few minutes, the line of people started walking.

All whispering had stopped and the only sound was footsteps. I looked to my left and realized we were walking beside the first names on The Wall. I had waited so very long to come here and I felt as if we were walking on sacred ground. I don't think it's possible to describe in mere words the feeling of walking past the names—all the lives destroyed, the families torn apart and a country nearly divided over this war. Now I was walking past all their names. There we so many, so damn many American lives lost, for nothing. People had told me about the mystic this memorial held, but you can't feel it until you are here and the spirits of those lost souls surround you.

We walked to the center of The Wall where the top was above our heads, names filling up panel after panel. By the time we stopped, I was pretty sure we had passed Ron's name. I wanted to break away and find him, but knew I needed to wait until the ceremony was finished. By the time the Gold Star Mothers ceremony concluded, the rest of our chapter had arrived and it was time to present the wreath from Chapter One. Our Chaplin, Tom Ransdale (Big Daddy), led the ceremony and prayer.

Big Daddy talked about our mission, Randy and me being there that year, and how our family was what Rolling Thunder was all about. We then placed the dog tags of the missing men and a simulated candle each of us had brought, on our wreath. Our wreath blinked in the dark all night, with a dog tag for each man still missing from Indiana. Big Daddy concluded our ceremony with prayer.

Randy and I made our way to Ron's name. I had known his panel and line numbers since Angel went in 1988—panel 6W, line 89. Since we were at the center, Randy and I made our way six panels back, with Carol and Scooby following. We found panel 6 west and my eyes were racing over the names, trying to find Ron's name on that black granite wall. I was looking so hard I couldn't see it. Then Randy reached up and pointed to his name—

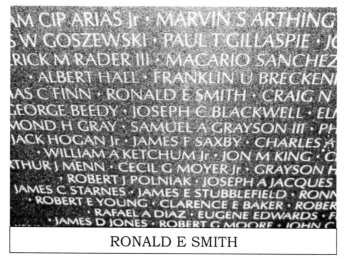

RONALD E SMITH

My heart was pounding, I caught my breath and I whispered, "Oh God, help me to not fall down."

I reached out and touched his name as tears ran down my face. Randy's arm reached around my shoulders, and Carol slipped her hand into mine. There was my big brothers name on the black granite wall in Washington DC. I was finally touching Ron's name surrounded by 58,282 lives lost or missing from Vietnam.

I was mesmerized by his name as I stared, touched, cried and once again broke my vow to never cry in public. I sat down in front of his name, with Randy standing behind me and pushed the rest of the world away. I just wanted to be with Ron. I wanted to talk to my big brother. I wanted to know where he was and exactly what had happened to him. I wanted him to hold me and brush the tears and pain away as he had done when I was six years old and wrecked my bike in the gravel. I felt his love, but didn't get answers. I would have to get those another time.

I felt so close to him, but I also felt the same sadness and loss I had felt many times over the last 35 years. I thought of times and events I hadn't thought of in years, times with Ron, Jim and I. I felt us riding in his convertible through the streets of Covington, exchanging Christmas presents with him the year he gave me a plastic corvette and I gave him a check for a million dollars. I saw him riding his stick horse on the patio at Mom's before he left for Vietnam, the stick horse that now sat in my bedroom. The love I felt for my brother filled my heart and soul and I thought I couldn't stand the pain and loss for another minute. I reached for Randy's hand, he helped me up and as we stood in front of Ron's name. A lone bugler started to play taps. I thought I couldn't feel any more pain, I was wrong.

The young man playing the bugle was from our chapter, and was playing taps in honor of Ron and for me. The sorrow, loss and raw pain was just as hurtful as it had been 35 years ago. At that moment, I felt as if I could never move away from that spot or stop the tears from falling, ever.

Randy, Carol and Eddie helped me place the things we had brought as close to his name as we could. I had red silk roses with his name on the ribbons. Matt had made a gigantic metal dog tag with Ron's name and a POW/MIA silhouette on it. I brought a letter written about Ron that a radio station back home had asked me to write for Memorial Day.

Several of the chapter members hugged us and told us how sorry they were for our loss. Big Daddy stayed, prayed and comforted me. Some of the members asked if I wanted them to take pictures of me and Randy in front of Ron's name. Their interaction helped bring me out of my desperation. These people were unbelievably kind. *Where were they 35 years ago?* Not so much these people, but people like them, who cared. We had felt so alone and now I was surrounded by strangers who felt like family. *I will never walk away from this.*

As we started back to the hotel, Scooby, Carol, Randy and I stopped at a restaurant near our hotel. It was after 2:00 a.m. before we got back to our room and I was drained, numb and exhausted. I fell asleep with the impression of Ron's name still on my fingertips.

In 2006, when we joined Rolling Thunder I saw that many members had tribute tattoos. Some were small and simple, with a name or branch of service or a date. Others were large, sprawling down an arm or across backs, some on the calf of a leg. They had names, dates, faces, flags, eagles and haunting reminders of someone lost.

I wanted one, but knew I would probably never be able to bring myself to go through with it. I didn't have any tattoos and the only time I toyed with the idea was after I met Randy and fell in love with lighthouses. I wanted a small lighthouse on my ankle, but never got serious enough to do it. The problem I saw with tattoos was the fact that they were very permanent. I would see one that really touched my heart, play with the thought of getting one, then dismiss the idea. This went on for a couple of years.

Then Randy began asking questions about tattoo artists whenever we met one, or asking who the artist was when we saw a really great tribute tattoo. I was surprised at his interest as I had assumed he would not be in favor of me getting one, since his body was tattoo free.

In 2009, Crystal got a Green Beret with angel wings tattooed between her shoulder blades. Below the beret was Ron's name. It gave me chills to look at it and I was amazed once again at her dedication to the uncle she had never met. She was extremely involved with the issues of Veterans and POW/MIA's, and became a member of Rolling Thunder. I looked at her tattoo with envy and pride.

In late 2010, Angel excitedly called to tell me she had rented one of the spaces in her building to a tattoo business, American Tradition. She knew I was getting serious about getting a tattoo of Ron's portrait. Not every artist could do faces and I did not want a botched face of my brother etched on my body for all of time.

"Are they good? Can they do portraits?" I asked.

"I don't know Mom, let's wait awhile and see what they do. I have seen pictures of their work and it looks good. At this point I don't know who does what. There are two artists, let me check them out."

A couple months later I met with tattoo artist James and we talked over what I thought I wanted. I gave him pictures and ideas that were swimming around in my head. I thought I would have it put on my shoulder, but James said it would work better if I had it put between my shoulder blades, like Crystals.

I worried that would upset her so the next time we were in Covington, I contacted her.

"OK, Crystal. You have to tell me the truth, no matter what. Truth, OK?"

"Aunt Linda, you are freaking me out. What is wrong?"

"Well, I talked with James Komando, you know the tattoo guy at American Tradition."

"You're going to do it?" she asked, smiling at me.

"Uh, well, yes, but I might have a problem."

"Why? What are you talking about?"

"Umm, you know how I had planned on getting it on my shoulder, even thought about over my heart. Well, James said it won't work there. He said it would be better on my back between my shoulder blades."

"And what? What is wrong with that?"

"It's the same place as yours."

"What? I'm not following." She stared at me for a few seconds with a blank expression.

"I don't want to copy you. I want it to be original, but James says it will be better between my shoulder blades."

"Aunt Linda, that is absolutely crazy." She looked at me for a few seconds and shook her head. "Get your tattoo and put it wherever you want and wherever James thinks it will look the best. It doesn't bother me in the least. Is that what's bothering you?" She laughed. "I thought it was something bad. All is good. I think it's great, besides they won't look anything alike."

I took a deep breath and smiled.

I gave James a picture of Ron taken in Vietnam, with a bandana tied around his head, holding an M-16, and standing with seven other Green Berets. We had scanned this picture and used it for many things and events. As much as I loved him with his beret on, this picture was my brother.

For a couple months, each time we went to Covington, I stopped in and checked out what James had come up with. It took three changes before I said, "That's it. I like it. Now, how much can you shrink it?"

"Shrink it? No darlin' I can't. That is the size it will be or it will ruin his face," James said.

"Oh, wow. I'm not sure I can put anything that big on me. Did you notice I don't have tattoos?"

"OK, you think about it and let me know. If you want it done before you go to D.C. in May, we have to get on it soon. It has to have time to heal.

You don't want to be riding in the sun before it heals."

"OK, I'll let you know," I said.

I left with a sad resolution that I would not be getting a tribute tattoo of my brother. It was going to be from my neck down past my bra strap, then from shoulder blade to shoulder blade. I told Randy that I was giving up on the idea of a tattoo.

"Why, didn't it look good?"

"Uh, yeah, it looked great, but it was so big."

"Well, what did you expect? You gave him a book to put in it."

"Yeah, I know, but I thought he could shrink it."

"Shrink it? What are you talking about?"

"You sound like James. I haven't decided. I am going to think about it.

Do you care if I have a tattoo that big?"

"It's your back, it's your decision."

"I know that and I will do what I want. I just want to know if you are going to hate it."

"Do what you want to do."

He would not give me an answer either way.

For three weeks I tried to forget about the tattoo. I wanted it the way it was, but I was apprehensive about getting a tattoo in the first place, let alone one the size of Texas. I kept trying to push it out of my mind, but it haunted me. I kept picturing this collage of patriotism, flags, Green Berets, dolphins, and Ron's face etched across by back.

I wanted it.

I called Angel and told her to let James know we were on. We were to start early afternoon on Saturday. Randy was at work when I called Angel and I forgot to tell him I had made my decision. We left for Covington early Saturday morning. About halfway there Randy looked at me and said, "I forbid you to do it."

"What?"

"I forbid you to get the tattoo."

He thought by ordering me I would be sure to defy him. I started to laugh at him, as he was so obvious. I loved that he had finally given me the answer I had tried to get from him for the past year.

For the tattoo, I was seated backwards on a chair that resembled a massage chair. I wore no clothes from the waist up, except a robe which I was wearing backwards. About four hours into the torture, Angel slipped me some shots of rum, then wine. I'm not sure I would have made it that long if not for the alcohol numbing my brain and senses. My family came in and out checking on me during the process. Angel and Randy were there, Crystal came for part of it, and Jim came by for a while. Madison was there for most of it. Everyone was trying to take my mind off the pain. James asked me to tell him about Ron which created more tears.

Every hour or so, I would take a bathroom break and walk around a bit. Angel and Crystal took pictures and posted them on Facebook where the responses were fantastic. By the end of the evening around 30 people had made remarks about my new tattoo. Most of my friends and family thought my tribute to Ron was beautiful. It looked amazing, even with the red swollen skin, which matched my red swollen eyes.

Seven and a half hours later, James and I decided it was time to quit. It wasn't finished, but he had done enough for this time. He put some gooey stuff on it, and then covered it with cellophane. I hugged James, my new friend and tattoo artist, said goodnight and we went up to Angel's apartment.

I was in pain, exhausted, and hungry, remembering I hadn't eaten all day. Angel, Randy, Crystal, Madison and I sat around the dining room table for a late dinner. I felt like I had been through one long emotional, torturous ordeal, one that I had asked and paid for.

By this time I felt like I had known James a lot longer than three months. He was an ex-Marine and had served his country which made our connection even stronger. Even though this procedure hurt like nothing I had ever endured, even childbirth, James had a gentle touch. There was something personal about letting someone tattoo a permanent etching on your half nude body, for all those hours. I wouldn't let just anyone carve art on my body, but I trusted James and now he would become a lifelong friend.

The next day was our Rolling Thunder monthly meeting and Randy was showing off my tattoo like it was his. At his request, I must have shown my back to half the members there. No one could believe that I sat for seven and a half hours for a tattoo, let alone my first. Huge men were bowing to me. The longest session of anyone there was three hours. No one could understand how I could take it for that long, but I did it for Ron. When the pain was so bad I thought I couldn't stand it any longer, I would think of what he must have gone through. This was a walk in the park compared to whatever he experienced. And now I had him with me always. My big brother had my back.

Four weeks later, we were back in Covington to see family and go to our Rolling Thunder meeting on Sunday. James was going to finish my tattoo. He said it would be about an hour, to an hour and half. It ended up being another three and one half hours which I cried through most of.

My back was still tender and I think I was just in a bad place that day. When he finally said, "OK enough for today," I cried again. I went through another three days of sunburn-like pain, then a week of itching until I thought I might dig the tattoo off my back if I could have reached it.

Three and a half weeks later we were back in Covington. James wanted me to stop in to see how my back was healing. Upon seeing it he wanted to do some touch up work. I wanted to cry, as it had just stopped itching and was starting to feel normal. I assumed the position on the backward chair, back exposed. This time it was only an hour and a half. It was a snap compared to the previous eleven hours I had spent having the skin on my back carved on with needles.

Once more James made the claim that we were done. I gasped and squealed with excitement.

"Really? Are you sure? If it has to be touched up, that's ok, but really?"

"Really darlin'." James laughed.

I looked in the mirror and stared in disbelief. Even though I had been wearing most of it on my back for the past month and a half, I couldn't believe this enormous tattoo.

The background was an American flag with the caption MY HERO written across the top. Ron's portrait in his rag tag look from Vietnam was in the center. On one side of his face was a Green Beret, the other side was the patch which was on his beret. Under his portrait were his dolphins from his submarine in the Navy. At the bottom was the date he went missing, November 28, 1970.

I did it! I had a tattoo of my big brother all across my back. Tears of sadness, pride and relief welled up in my eyes and all I could say was "Wow!"

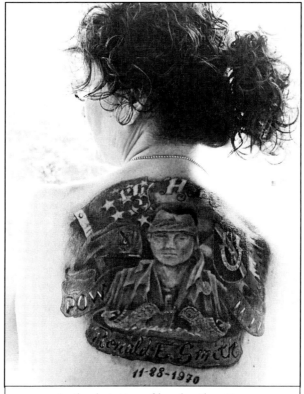

Author's tattoo of her brother Ron

So Much to Do, So Little Time

The day after our visit to The Wall, the four of us made our way back to the National Mall, to go to Thunder Alley. This was a street blocked off, across from the Vietnam Wall, where vendors had stands to display their merchandise. Leathers, tee shirts, hats, pins, patches, bike accessories, pictures, food and drink were for sale. I was like a kid in a candy store, grabbing up everything I wanted that had to do with Ron or Rolling Thunder. There were so many people you could barely walk. Carol had tried to describe all parts of this trip prior to our departure, but it couldn't compare with what I had imagined.

I needed to go back to the Vietnam Wall, so we made our way across the street to see Ron's name again. It was a different feeling in the bright sunlight, still somber, but nothing like being there at night. At night it seemed more private and the dark made me feel like my pain was more personal. I could close out the hundreds of people and pretend I was there alone with my big brother.

We walked slowly down The Wall looking at the things left for the lost soldiers. There were letters, packs of cigarettes, beers, army shirts with a soldiers ashes in the pockets, newspaper clippings of men's bio's, death or MIA status, and once a Harley Davidson motorcycle was left at The Wall.

There were hundreds of people walking back and forth in front of The Wall. The things we had left the night before were still below Ron's name. We were told on a normal day all things left at The Wall were collected each night, categorized, and stored in a warehouse. A museum for these items was in the making. Someday, I hoped to be able to see the things I have left for Ron.

Next, we were off to find a restaurant and after that we went to a bar owned by a WWII POW, now deceased, but handed down to his daughter who turned it into a POW/MIA tribute bar and restaurant. She sold tee shirts with a new logo every year for POW/MIA's. The entire bar was geared to the issue and every Friday, Saturday and Sunday a live band played. This band didn't look like they had enough money to buy their instruments, but when they started playing we discovered looks were deceiving as they were extremely talented.

The bar was very small, but somehow Flash managed to find room to show off his dancing skills. He danced over to a lady who was eager to show him he had met his match on the dance floor. For a while, I forgot my pain.

Sunday morning came and we left our hotel at 7:00 a.m. and staged at the Pentagon. Since we couldn't get into the ride or Pentagon parking lot in our truck, it had been arranged that I would ride on the motorcycle with Flash, and Randy would ride with Scooby, leaving Carol to hop on with one of the guys who was riding solo. The staging took about five to six hours and around 800,000 bikes participated in the ride. We lined up for six hours, in straight rows, as close to one another as possible. I could not believe the number and kinds of bikes, or the paint jobs or tribute paintings on them. Just about the time I thought I had seen it all, another would catch my eye and I would have my camera out snapping pictures.

The military and veterans were just as interesting and colorful as the bikes. Tattoos were abundant and clearly patriotic. A deuce and half truck was parked at the beginning of the ride, filled with Gold Star Mothers.

Following the mothers was the bamboo cage carrying the simulated POW from Vietnam. I had seen this bone chilling exhibit at the Kokomo reunion many times and it never got any easier. The first time I saw this man in the cage, I nearly threw up. He was skin and bones and had long straggly white hair. He looked exactly like the pictures of POWs. He would reach his long thin arms out of the cage toward the crowds of people, as if to beg for help. It made me sick to think of how many Americans had endured this torture and what if Ron...I had to turn away.

There were gigantic semis painted with the POW/MIA logo, the field cross, The Wall, soldiers, Arlington Cemetery and every sad, heart breaking sentiment imaginable.

The demonstration ride started at 12:00 and lasted five to six hours. There were so many bikes that it took that long just for all to file out of the Pentagon parking lot. The ride route was approximately four miles, which took about a half hour to get through. The streets were packed on both sides with people of all ages, children waving flags and sitting on their parent's shoulders, and veterans of all ages.

The ride ended at the Reflection pool by the Washington Memorial. Set up between the Lincoln Memorial and the reflection pool were several stages and tents where Rolling Thunder National held their program. There were speakers, singers, politicians, movie stars, active military personal and Wounded Warriors.

Over the following years, I met and had pictures with John Amos, and got within a few feet of Sarah Palin the year she rode with us from the Pentagon to the Reflection pool. I listened to pleading speeches from Matt Maupin's parents. Matt was MIA for four years before his body was found and returned to be buried in his hometown of Batavia, Ohio. I met, cried, hugged and talked to Bowe Bergdahl's father in 2012, who still waits for his son to come home alive.

Among the celebrities have been Gary Sinise, John Amos, Nancy Sinatra, and Paul Revere and the Raiders. In my opinion, Gary Sinise was the most sincere actor involved in our issue. Some years he was there not only as a speaker, but playing in his band, The Lt. Dan Band, which originated from his character in Forrest Gump. He donates the proceeds from the concert to the POW/MIA issue, needs of the veterans or the Wounded Warriors' aid.

During the time we were listening to the speakers, we could hear the thunder from the bikes still in the demonstration ride. The roar of the bikes could be heard and felt 30 miles away.

After listening and watching the program presented by Rolling Thunder National, we made our way back to our hotel, showered and went to dinner. The evening should have ended early since we would leave for home the next morning at 7:30, but even after eight years, it has never ended early for Randy, me or the members that we hang out with. It has been a time for review, reliving and relishing in the events of our trip.

Through connections I had made in Rolling Thunder I was able to find author Jason Hardy. He had been researching and studying Special Forces and Special Ops for years, and had published eight books by the time I found him.

Jason informed me that John Plaster, who was in the same Special Ops group my brother had been in, had written four books about SF Special Ops groups.

Plaster had written about Ron in <u>Secret Commandos,</u> <u>Behind Enemy Lines with the Elite Warriors of SOG</u> that had been published about four years earlier.

I had never heard of either of these men, but both had written books that had passages or information about Ron. Needless to say, Jim and I purchased at least 15 copies of Plaster's book.

In my conversations with Jason, he asked me what the government had told us about November 28, 1970, the day Ron went missing. I shared with him all the versions the Army had given us regarding Ron's MIA status. I told him I felt Ron was no longer living, but I wasn't sure about anything. He then shared information that John Plaster had written in one of his books.

"Linda, I'm sure your brother died that day. I have known John Plaster personally for several years and he writes the truth," Jason said.

"Did this man know my brother or see what happened? Was he there?" I asked.

"I think he was in Nam at the same time. I don't know if he knew your brother, but if he wrote about it I know he interviewed the men involved and was sure, or he wouldn't have put it in print."

Instead of feeling some kind of comfort that my brother hadn't been a prisoner and tortured, or had suffered in some horrible place without medical attention, I felt the same old sadness and dread I always did when I learned something I had never been told about Ron. What if John Plaster had known the incident and

said he wasn't sure what had happened to Ron? That
would feel even worse and would mean Ron definitely
had been captured and tortured, or lived and was still
there, unable to come home. That was even less acceptable.

Since John Plaster didn't see anything happen to
Ron, I chose not to confirm anything in my heart. I did
the same thing I had always did with information about
my brother, I filed it under speculation.

Jason gave me more information about Plaster, including what he did in Vietnam. He was a covey in an
OV10 Bronco, the planes that monitored what was
going on the ground. They would help helicopters when
extracting teams and men behind enemy lines. The
covey would be in contact with the extraction team
trying to get teams out from behind enemy lines.

Jason gave me as much information as he could,
including the name of Clete Sinyard, another SF Special
Ops veteran who was in John Plaster's book. Jason also
suggested that I go to the Special Ops reunion in Vegas
in September.

"That would be awesome," I said. "Do you think I
would be able to find anyone who knew Ron?"

"You won't get any closer. Call Clete and tell him I
gave you his number. Tell him about your brother and
that you're looking for someone who can give you
information. I'm sure he will invite you to the reunion,"
Jason said. "Just tell him I invited you and your husband."

Randy was ready to re-pack our suitcases and head to Vegas and we weren't even unpacked from attending Matt's wedding in Vegas. Besides the time off and the cost, could we go back so soon? Instead of moving heaven and earth to go to an event that I had worked toward for 37 years, I had every excuse in the book to prevent this from happening. I wasn't sure why, but I knew I wasn't ready to attend Ron's reunion. I used these excuses to put it off until the next year.

Special Forces Reunion

We planned all year to attend the Special Ops reunion in Vegas in September. I had kept in contact with these men and told everyone we were coming. As the time approached I began to come up with excuses again. I had no idea why I was backing away from this trip.

"We are going, Linda. I have helped you work towards this since I have known you, 18 years," Randy said. "You have been looking for answers for 38 years.

I didn't argue.

At the airport, Randy and I took our shoes off, emptied our pockets and handed our drivers licenses to the security at Gerald R. Ford International in Grand Rapids. I still couldn't believe I would be meeting some of the guys that knew my brother while he was in Vietnam. These guys saw him, touched him, talked with him, ate with him, and laughed with him. After our family cried and let him slip out of our arms to go off to that damn war, they became his family.

After settling into our seats, I looked out the window and waited to fly over our house. I couldn't see it, but I knew we were close because I could see Lake Michigan and the shoreline. Our house was up the dune and across the road from Lake Michigan. Randy pointed out landmarks as we rose higher above the earth. Finally we were above the clouds and I could no longer see Michigan. I could also no longer push back my thoughts or fears of what I would learn about my big brother. I was flying closer and closer to answers. Like a light turning on, it came to me.

What if I learn things I don't want to know? What if they tell me things that end my quest?

I had been told horrific things about what might have happened to Ron's body. Things like animals dragging him away from the last place he had been seen, the North Vietnamese Army (NVA) taking him to get information, him lying there and dying alone, or his body being blown totally apart, with no body to recover. All these scenarios were possible. But what if these men that I was about to meet put an end to the speculation?

I had spent my adult life looking for my big brother, or answers to what had really happened to him. *What if they tell me he really did die on November 28, 1970?* What would I do then? I had said many times that I wouldn't want him to live all this time as a POW being tortured and living with the knowledge that his country wouldn't come back for him. But was that what I really wanted? *Oh dear God, do I really want him to be alive?*

Another fear crept into my mind. What if some of the men didn't think I had a right to be at their reunion? *Why did I let Randy talk me into this?* Clete and Jason had told me I would never get closer to the answers I sought. Then it hit me. What if they told me something so concrete that I knew it was the truth? I didn't know how to not look for Ron. That's what I did. What if they told me something that ended my search?

If they gave me solid evidence, then our family could have some kind of closure. Yet I knew that there would never be complete closure unless we brought his body home, alive or deceased.

My quest for answers about Ron had become a part of me, like the air that I breathed. I wore the pain and injustice like a badge. I had learned to live with Killed in Action/Body Not Recovered, even though that was not certain.

This was why I didn't want to face the answers. As long as I didn't know for sure, I could hold some hope that we might get him back—as selfish as that hope was.

As we flew through the clouds and I half slept, I thought about the scenario I feared—that the SOG men who had not invited me would not welcome me. After all, they were a very elite group of men with many secrets still buried within their souls. How could they talk about these secrets if outsiders were there? What if I made them uncomfortable?

I took a deep breath and tried to relax, telling myself not to borrow trouble. I went over in my head what I wanted to ask them. I had years to prepare for this and had imagined what I would say or ask. Now I had no idea where to start or what I was going to say.

Randy and I arrived at our hotel very early Saturday morning. We checked into our room and fell into bed for some much needed sleep. Hours later, we showered, dressed and by early afternoon, we were ready to explore. By this time, I was anxious to see if I could identify any of the SOG guys. I remembered how they looked when I visited Ron at Fort Bragg. As we walked through the hotel, I caught myself scanning the crowd for Green Berets.

As Randy and I sat in one of the restaurants inside the hotel, I couldn't take my eyes off the crowd of people meandering about.

"Do you think he is one of them?" I asked Randy, pointing at a well-built man walking by.

"What? That guy? "Randy said "Are you kidding?"

"Uh, well no, why?"

"Cause he is about 20 years or more too young," Randy said.

"Oh."

"Honey, these guys are in their sixties and seventies. Have you forgotten how old your brother would be?"

"Yes, I mean no. I mean, I don't know. I wanted to see them as they looked when Ron was with them and when he left," I said. "I guess I didn't want to think about how they look now. I wanted young, fit, arrogant, proud Green Berets."

We ate in silence while I changed gears, now looking for much older men not wearing Berets.

Randy and I caught a shuttle to the strip and made our way to the middle of the bus where we found an empty seat. We sat down I couldn't help but look at the couple sitting in front of us. The man was older than me, and his wife looked a little younger. At one point, when the man turned and pointed something out to his wife, I caught the pin he wore on his shirt collar. There it was like a neon light, slapping me in the face—an SOG pin.

"There's one of them," I whispered as I elbowed Randy.

"How do you know?"

"The pin, it matches the ones on Ron's Green Beret. The one I have on my Rolling Thunder vest."

"Oh yeah. Yep, you are right. Talk to him."

"No, I can't just start talking to him. No."

He elbowed me and urged me loud enough that the guy heard him. Now I had to say something.

"Uh, hi, my name in Linda, this is my husband, Randy," I said, extending my hand. "Uh, I'm here to attend the SOG reunion. I see you are a SF SOG member."

"Yes I am. How did you know?"

"The pin," I said, as I pointed to his SOG pin in his lapel.

"Oh, yes Ma'am." He looked at Randy and asked, "Are you SOG?"

"No, my wife's brother is still MIA from 1970. We're here to find answers, or men, who might have known him."

"Oh, I am sorry, Ma'am. I hope we can answer some of your questions. We're glad to have you and your husband here. Anything we can do to help, just ask," he said.

I felt a sigh of relief, at least one of them understood and didn't feel I shouldn't be here. We continued to talk until we reached the strip, then we shook hands and promised to have dinner with them at the reunion. As Randy and I walked in the opposite direction as the couple, I reached for his hand and fought back tears.

We spent the remainder of Saturday and Sunday back and forth to the strip and wandering around our hotel. I got pretty good at picking out the SF SOG guys and I felt a little better about being at Ron's reunion.

On Monday, I was so nervous that I woke hours before I had to. I changed my clothes three times before I came to the conclusion that it didn't really matter what I was wearing.

Randy and I made our way out to the second floor and as we turned the corner, my heart skipped. Above the long table where people were gathering was a giant sign that said Special Forces, SOG Special Ops Group, with insignia that was on Ron's things—the patches and pins I wore on my Rolling Thunder vest.

Randy and I waited our turn to check in and get our badge, which would let us in and out of the hall for the SF reunion.

"I'm Linda Smith-Cope, this is my husband Randy," I said, as Randy offered his hand.

The lady checking us in began a conversation and I asked, "I'm looking for Clete Sinyard. I talked to him a few times the past year and I was hoping to meet him."

Before she could point him out, I heard a voice that was unmistakable. I turned and looked for the face that belonged to the voice I had been talking to for over a year—the southern drawl with a sweetness that couldn't belong to anyone else.

"Clete, there you are," I said, as I walked toward the man who didn't look anything like I had imagined. For some reason I had imagined a tall thin man. I got thin right, but not the tall part. "I'm Linda Cope and this is my husband Randy," I said, as we extended our hands.

Clete came toward us with a big smile, handshakes and a very warm welcome. He then turned to the lady who had been helping us check in and introduced us to his wife Debbie. We talked to Clete, Debbie and some of the other men who were standing close. As he introduced us, he also explained why we had come to the reunion and started the quest to find men who knew Ron. I held a briefcase full of Ron's information, bio, pictures, and my business card—with Ron's name, rank, and missing date on the back. Within an hour, there was an 8x10 photo of Ron pinned to a bulletin board that was visible to all who approached the check-in table and banquet room. Beside the picture was my card and an explanation of Ron and that his sister was at the reunion. I knew within that hour that all my fears about not being welcome had been wasted. I couldn't have felt more welcome and special. These men opened their arms and hearts to Randy, me and my journey.

Next I wanted to find Jason Hardy, the author I had talked to for the past year. I called his cell phone and he answered right away. He told me he was in the banquet hall and invited us to come and talk to him. Randy and I followed his directions to the side of the room where tables had been set up with books, old pictures, shirts, bags, hats, guns, and memorabilia. The other half of the room was set up with tables, a bar, and snack food.

We found Jason at a table of the books he had written, pictures of men in Vietnam, and Green Berets that had been embroidered by the Montagnards in Vietnam. Randy and I introduced ourselves and before we had a chance to talk to him or look at his things, he interrupted with news for us.

"You're in luck," Jason said. "John Plaster is here this year. I am going to introduce you to him."

"You mean the guy who wrote a book with Ron in it. He's here?" I asked.

"Yes, he doesn't come every year, this is good," Jason said as he scanned the room. "His table is right there and that's his wife. Let's go see when he will be back."

While Jason introduced us and explained why we wanted to talk to John, I felt the uneasiness creep back into my body. John Plaster was a retired Special Forces

SOG member and wrote books about what these heroes had done and been through. He had written about Ron and I was going to meet him. My nerves were on full alert.

Randy and I walked around looking at the bags, shirts and hats for sale, waiting for John to arrive. We picked out shirts for the family and a SF bag for me. Randy looked at the firearms and bought a raffle ticket for some rare gun. We hung out close enough to see if a guy came back to the table that belonged to John Plaster.

When I saw a man approach the table, go behind it and talk with the woman, I knew it was him. We headed over there, but before we could reach the table someone else came up to him and began talking. People started lining up.

"This is going to take a while," I said.

"That's ok, we don't have any place to go," Randy said.

We stayed close, but not too close. After a couple minutes, I heard John excuse himself and walk toward Randy and me. I nearly fainted. I couldn't believe he put me in front of all the people waiting to talk with him. I felt like such a bother. *Who am I? No one.* I was just a sister of one of the guys he served with.

"Hello, I'm John Plaster." He walked up to us, extended his hand and introduced himself.

"Hi, I'm Linda and this is my husband, Randy. I hope I'm not bothering you. I just wanted to ask you a couple of questions about my brother. Jason Hardy has talked about you and gave me the name of your book, <u>Secret Commandos: Behind Enemy Lines with the Elite Warriors of SOG</u>."

"Yes, I'm aware of your brother's status. Jason filled me in and there are some things I want to share with you that I didn't put in the book."

I caught my breath and tried to prepare myself for what he might say. Somehow I knew this was not going to be good, because I already knew the good things.

John began by telling me he was sorry that what he wrote about Ron in his book was so vague. He explained he left out the name of Ron's team leader purposely. In his estimation, the team leader was not a good soldier, and John was trying to get him court martialed at the time he and Ron were in Nam. It proved impossible since the only people who knew the Special Ops teams existed were the president of the United States and the Secretary of Defense. He felt that Ron's team leader was responsible for the death of his best friend, Fred Kruppa.

I felt myself freeze up, stiffen and fight the tears. Whatever was coming was going to be so bad. He told me what the returning men had reported once they were interrogated. They said that the team leader got my brother killed. It was his fault. They were on a recon mission, search and report. Not blow things up. He stated they had found water lines that went to a village. There was no way the team leader should have blown anything up behind enemy lines.

I was stunned as he continued by telling me that attention should not have been brought to the five guys. That's why they had 400 NVA shooting at them.

I had not taken a breath the entire time he talked as I sucked in air and tried not to fall apart. I knew that if I let this man know how I felt, he might not finish and I wanted every detail.

He indicated that this team leader was responsible for the death of at least two very good soldiers, and John detested him.

John's wife had walked over to us and stood beside him. She reached out and touched his arm. "John," she said. It seemed like she wanted him to stop telling me these things.

"It's alright," I said to her. "I want to hear this. I've waited 37 years to hear the truth."

John told us he wasn't sure why Ron had stayed with RT Kentucky, his Recon Team. He also said Ron could have refused to go out with this team and got on another one.

"I'm not sure why he didn't. My guess is that he was trying to protect the other guys from the team leader. Maybe he thought he could help the situation. Ron and the team leader were about 30 and that was older for being in Special Ops and doing what they were doing. Maybe that is why Ron stayed with him, I don't know."

"I have questions. May I ask?" I said.

"Yes, whatever I can answer I will," John said.

"If you don't trust this guy, why are you so sure Ron was dead when they left him?"

"Because we interviewed the Montagnards and the other Americans who lived. They all said your brother could not have survived. He died that day, Linda. He was a brave and honorable soldier and you can be proud of him," John said.

"Oh, there is no doubt about that. I have been proud of him my entire life, no doubts there," my voice trailed off. I had barely enough strength to make a voice. "Why can't I talk with Ron's team leader? Why hasn't he come to our family and told us firsthand what happened?"

John answered by saying he believed it was because the team leader was a coward. He stated that the man didn't come to any of the reunions or see any of the guys. "He knows what he did," he said. "He is the reason I left the details about the day your brother was shot out of my book. I wouldn't give him any notoriety."

I tried to collect my thoughts and make sure I didn't forget to ask him everything I wanted. My mind was spinning and I could have had dozens of questions, but I wouldn't have been able to think straight enough to ask.

John pointed at his book I was holding onto. "You should have the guys sign your book. A lot of the ones I wrote about are here."

"Really? I'll do that. Would you sign it also?"

"I would love to." He reached for my book. He wrote for a couple of minutes, then handed it back to me and again told me what a brave man my brother had been. Randy asked if he would have his picture taken with us. We had a bystander take our picture, thanked John

Special Forces Reunion

again and let him get back to the people who were standing in line.

We walked away a few feet before I told my husband I had to get some air. I handed him the book, ran out of the room and into the restroom.

As I ran, all I was thinking was that Ron had died for nothing, twice.

First the government's poor handling of that stupid war killed him for nothing. Now I found out a hot headed idiot that should never have been an SOG member was ultimately responsible for death.

I closed myself behind the door of one of the bathroom stalls and sobbed into my hands until I could get control. *Will this nightmare ever stop?* I had been so apprehensive about this trip. I wanted to know, but I didn't want to feel the pain. I didn't want to feel the desperation of yet another ugly truth about my brother's demise. He should have come home. According to this guy, if he had been in another team he might be here instead of me. *I will find him and tell him face-to-face what a worthless coward he is and what he took from our family.*

Many times I had asked myself and family members why the man who was with Ron when he was supposedly shot hadn't come to our family and told us what really happened. Now I knew.

I pulled toilet paper off the roll, blew my nose and wiped my eyes. At the sink, I splashed cold water over my face. I had to get back to Randy.

"Are you ok?" he asked, when I walked up to him.

"Not really, but I will be. I have to be. I have more information to get," I said. "You would think I would be numb to this by now, but I'm not. Randy I can't believe he died for nothing. It's like friendly fire."

"I know honey, it stinks."

"We've only been here two hours and I can't imagine anything worse."

"Let's go meet some of the other people. Maybe we'll find someone who was there who knew him personally, not just knew of him." He took my hand and we walked to the other side of the big room.

Over the next week I told and re-told Ron's story a hundred times. I met Special Forces guys and their wives, exchanged numbers, addresses and promises to keep in touch. A few of them knew of Ron, only two knew him personally. One couple we met, Ron and Marge Workman, were from Australia. Randy and Ron hit it off and I felt unusually close to him.

On Thursday night, there was a formal dinner and program. Randy and I were seated at a table near the front of the room. By this time I had made friends with many of the SF guys and become their little sister. Our new friend, Ronald Workman, had a part and speech in the program. He made special mention of my brother and introduced me to the entire room. After the ceremony of the Missing Man Table, he presented me with the vase and long stem rose.

The Missing Man Table Ceremony was a ceremonial tribute to those heroes who had not returned from war or a foreign land and whose whereabouts are unknown.

The ceremony went as follows, with a table set with items mentioned:

The table set for one is small, symbolizing the frailty of one prisoner alone against his oppressors.

The tablecloth is white, symbolizing the purity of their intentions to respond to their country's call to arms.

The single red rose displayed in a vase reminds us of the blood they shed in sacrifice to ensure the freedom of our beloved United States of America.

The vase is tied with a red ribbon, a symbol of our continued determination to account for our missing.

A slice of lemon on the bread plate is to remind us of the bitter fate of those captured or missing in a foreign land.

The spilled salt symbolizes the tears endured by those missing and their families who seek answers.

The candle is reminiscent of the light of hope which lives in our hearts to illuminate their way home, away from their captors, to the open arms of a grateful nation.

The glass is inverted symbolizing the inability to share in this day's toast.

The American Flag reminds us that many of them may never return...and have paid the supreme sacrifice to ensure our freedom.

The Bible represents the strength gained through faith to sustain those lost from our country, founded as one nation under God.

The chair...the chair is empty...they are not here...

How could I ever think these men wouldn't have wanted me here? Many of them told me I was now part of their family and was welcome back every year if I wanted to come.

Now I had to go home and share what I had learned with Jim.

A Home Town Honor

In 2009, Crystal drove to D.C. for the Run to The Wall. Before she left, she had Ron's picture printed and placed in both of her back seat windows for the ride. After the ride she couldn't bring herself to take the pictures out, so his pictures stayed on her car windows.

One day she came out of a gas station to find Max Keller standing at her car staring at Ron's picture. She walked up and stood beside him, he appeared deep in thought.

As they stood beside each other, he became aware of her presence.

"That's Smitty," he said.

"Yes it is," Crystal said.

"How do you know him? He was my very good friend. We were on the force together."

"He is my uncle. Jim is my Dad."

"Jim? You're Jim's daughter? Damn, Smitty was a hell of a good man. I miss him," he said. "Why do you have his picture in your car windows?"

Crystal explained she had the pictures placed there for the Ride to The Wall for Memorial Day, the Rolling Thunder protest ride.

"Really?" Max said, staring at Ron's face. "Well, Crystal, I'm glad I ran into you. Tell your Dad I said hello." He strolled away.

"I sure will." About three weeks later we learned that Max had been busy planning Ronald Eugene Smith week, which would coordinated with Covington's 4th of July celebration.

Max and the Mayor of Covington, Brad Crain, had decided it was time to honor one of Covington's heroes. Ron was to be the main event of the parade and the weekend long celebration.

The coordinators invited our family and Rolling Thunder to ride in the parade. Jim's truck would drive in front of the bikes. He had magnets made with pictures of Ron, his face over an American flag. These were on both sides of the truck, along with Rolling Thunder, Support your Troops and POW/MIA magnets.

Flying from the back of the truck were three, 3 x 5 flags—an American, POW/MIA, and a flag sporting Ron's face. We each had a flag that we flew behind our bikes in Washington D.C. on the demonstration ride, with a giant picture of him, some of his credentials and the caption at the bottom that read BRING MY BROTHER HOME.

Our town was honoring Ron and I couldn't believe it. I had to switch the gears in my head regarding a parade. In Rolling Thunder, it had been ingrained into my brain that the rides we did were not parades, they were demonstration rides voicing our disapproval of the handling of POW/MIAs. Other rides were escorts bringing a recovered MIA solider home. This was a parade to honor Ron.

It was Fourth of July for Covington and although it was a sad event for us, for most it wasn't. During the parade, people were waving, smiling and yelling to our family. I wanted Max Keller and Brad Crane to know how much we appreciated their efforts to honor my brother, so we smiled, waved and thanked everyone concerned. I kept my tears hidden behind my sunglasses.

Later that year I received a call from a Dana Jefferies from Covington. Dana had become interested in Ron after talking with Max Keller and seeing what our town had done on the Fourth of July. He commented that my brother was probably the most decorated war hero to ever come out of Covington and he had also been on the police force in our town.

He thought it was a shame that he had never been recognized.

"Well I agree Mr. Jefferies, but that's not something our family felt was our place to do," I said.

"Agreed, that's why I am doing it. I need all the information you can give me with dates and pictures," he said.

"Ok, I'll be glad to do anything I can. As soon as I have the things you need, I'll bring it or send it. You can call my brother Jim or niece Crystal for anything you want, they are closer."

We hung up and I sat speechless.

"What?" Randy asked.

"That was a guy from Covington who wants to have a memorial for Ron.

His name is Dana Jefferies and he was a state cop, was in the military in Iraq, and is now a county deputy Sheriff. He said he learned about Ron from Max Keller.

"Well that's cool, when?" he asked.

"Huh?"

"When?"

"What? Oh I don't know. He didn't say when. I can't believe this. A memorial?"

"It's happening in other towns. The Vietnam veterans got a raw deal and people are trying to make up for it."

"I guess. I'm glad Mom is still here to see this, even though it will be hard on her."

"It will, but it's also a long awaited reward for her son that she needs to receive."

"Yep, you're right," I said. "I still can't believe it's going to happen. Maybe I should wait to get excited or nervous until I see if it really carries through."

"That's probably a good idea."

I didn't hold my breath because I had learned not to believe things were going to happen until they did. I felt that Dana Jeffries was sincere in his intentions, but would other people feel the same? Would others needed to make this memorial happen feel the same as Dana?

Over the next few months I had a few conversations with Dana, then my niece and Jim took over with what Dana needed from the family.

By March 2010, the plans for Ron's memorial were nearly complete. Companies, organizations, the Indiana State Representative, the Mayor, military personnel, and many friends had stepped up to the plate and were going to make this memorial happen. One of Indiana's State Representative's, Dale Grubb, had been a grade ahead of me in school and Ron had worked on his dad's farm when he was between the Navy and Army.

Triguard, a division of Greenwood Plastics of Danville, donated the bronze marker with pictures, while Kelly Vault of Danville donated the granite. The other monument came from Maus Memorials in Attica, Indiana, with the granite donated by Nathan Maus.

My niece Crystal's landscaping business donated the work around the stones. The VFW donated the space for the memorial and food for the dinner for our family. The VFW Color Guard would perform the 21 gun salute and taps. My friends Nance and Marlea were going to sing God Bless the USA and The Ballad of the Green Berets.

Our entire family was notified and two chapters of Rolling Thunder, Indianapolis and Lafayette, would attend. Ron's classmates and friends were invited. One of the hardest invitations was Carolyn, Ron's beloved Sam. I felt she should have an invitation, but wasn't sure how she would handle this. I just hoped it was going to be as wonderful as it sounded.

I was asked to write something our family would like written on Ron's stone. I had written many things about Ron for many occasions, but this was epic. I sat down at the computer, preparing myself for hours to make this piece just right. I felt like it had to perfect as it would be there for years to come.

I laid my fingers on the keyboard and the words came out of my heart and onto the page without stopping. I had it done in fifteen minutes. I didn't have to think or re-write, it was just there, coming out of me like I had thought about it for years.

A Hero Walked Among Us
Adored by his family
Respected by His Peers
Honored by His Military

Ronald not only served his country once, but twice. He served in the US Navy and as a Green Beret with the United States Army Special Forces. Behind enemy lines in Laos, he gave his life to save his Team Members and Honor his country.

We miss him, honor him, love him, and salute him.

May God Bless You, Ron.

I ran it by Jim, Angel, Crystal, and Randy. They liked it. I then faxed it to the company who was donating Ron's stone.

Jim, Karen, Crystal, Randy and I went through hundreds of pictures for the VFW's part of the presentation. We gathered Ron's medals, Green Berets, and his dress Greens Mom had hanging in her closet and prepared them for the Memorial.

Between all of this, work and my life in general, I was trying to decide what I would say at the Memorial Service. Someone in our family was asked to say a few words and we needed to thank all of the people and organizations who had worked and donated time and money to see this materialize.

Again, my little brother gave me the honor, reminding me I was the mouthpiece for the family. This was not as easy and I worked on it for days. I could write anything, but to say it in front of a crowd was another story. I had done it many times, but it always made me second guess what I should say, then panic if I didn't get the entire message out, especially now.

The day of the memorial, April 10, 2010, a day I had secretly yearned for, for many years, was here.

Randy and I came down from Michigan the night before and all was in place. The VFW was only three blocks from my brother's house and when we pulled up to it, I couldn't believe my eyes. There was a lighted sign in the front of the VFW announcing the event with Ron's name running across the screen over and over. Plus, there were two giant tents with chairs set up for the family.

The color guard had already arrived and were preparing for their display. There was a podium arranged in front of the chairs with electrical wires going to the building. Directly in front and next to the door was a big draped cover over the Memorial. My heart quickened and my mind went to mush. Would I be able to talk when it was time for me to say my speech?

We got Mom out of the truck and walked her to the front where the family was to sit. Then we began greeting people, talking and answering questions. We were introduced to people we had never met who had worked hard on this day for many weeks. The State Representative, Dale Grubb, who I went to school with came up and gave me a hug. The mayor, Brad Crane, who I also went to school with, came to me with another hug. Nance, who was going to sing, came beside me and now I had a giant lump in my throat. *I have to keep it together.* Dana introduced Jim and me to Sergeant Major Marsh, a Green Beret who was going to present medals and honors to Mom, Jim and I. He was there from Fort Knox. *Oh God, help me not to cry.* He was in his dress Greens, shiny boots and his beret was situated proudly on his head. My heart was breaking, but I refused to let anyone know. I had always been in awe of the stringent behavior of military personnel, especially when they had a Green Beret on their head. He was so respectful, polite and sorry for our pain. *How will I ever speak or say the words I have prepared?*

Jim, Karen, Crystal, Randy and I had decided to wear our Rolling Thunder vests for the occasion. I knew any second that the roar of Harleys would take precedence over anything else. They had a way of making an entrance, without even trying. I heard the roar before I saw them. Rolling Thunder was approaching. The thunder gave me cold chills even though it was 85 degrees. I turned and watched them coming up the street and turn into the driveway of the VFW.

Steve and Kim Barrick of the Lafayette chapter were in the front. Steve was the president of Chapter Four and very close friends of our family. He and Kim had huge 3x5 flags flying behind their bike. I was so overwhelmed with love for these people who had come here today to honor my big brother, and so proud to be a part of this organization. Tears were streaming down my face. Before I could hug everyone and tell them how much we appreciated their presence, I heard the roar again. Chapter one was approaching. Our chapter was here with bikes, flags, respect and love. Randy, Jim, Karen, Crystal and I mingled with all of them giving hugs, kisses and thanks.

Crystal Smith and Karen Smith

It was time for the program to begin and as I walked toward the chairs, I heard someone in my family say that Carolyn was here. I turned and saw her and Don making their way to the tents. Jim and I welcomed her and made sure she was seated with us. She looked exactly the same, just 38 more years of life on her face.

The program started with a speech from our State Representative. He talked about Ron working for his dad on the farm when he was in between the Navy and Army and working in a factory. He said he had looked up to my brother and told how hard-working and honest he was. I didn't even remember that Ron worked for Mr. Grubb. *Oh Ron, you were so special.*

The mayor of Covington talked about Ron being on the police force. Jim and I had gone to school with both of these men.

Dana stepped up to the podium and spoke how he had been touched by the things Max Keller had said about Ron the past year when Covington honored him on the Fourth of July. He explained how he had decided there needed to be some kind of honor given this man who had served his country twice. He felt this was way overdue.

About halfway through the ceremony, the memorial was presented and we gathered around it. A prayer was said and someone pulled the cover off. I had whispered in Carolyn's ear to be prepared, as it was chilling. As the cover came off I heard several gasps, with Carolyn's being the loudest. She made a haunting sound, covered her mouth and wept out loud.

The two stones were magnificent—one with full color pictures and one with his service and credentials. In one picture he was in his Army uniform and Green Beret with a more serious expression. The other was in his Navy dress blues, smiling his beautiful smile that we missed so much. It was the one he flashed to us the night he walked out of our lives.

There were two smaller pictures in each corner, one with him sitting on the back seat of one of his convertibles while was stationed in Hawaii. The other was a high school picture in his basketball uniform. In the background were faint pictures of Airborne guys jumping out of a plane.

One was Ron, but we didn't know which paratrooper he was.

If you ran your fingertips over it, you could feel his face, the flags, the parachutes, his car, and basketball. I had never seen anything like this memorial. After everyone had a chance to look at the stones, we took our seats and the program resumed.

Nance and Marlea sang the Ballad of the Green Berets and God Bless the USA. I couldn't hold back the tears as I sat beside my Mom, holding her hand.

Mom's hearing was almost gone, so we had explained what we could to her before the day of the Memorial Service so she would know what was going on and who was speaking. Everyone gave her printed copies of their speeches and remarks so she could read what was said. I was amazed that she seemed to understand what people were saying to her as she read lips very well.

It was now my turn to stand in front of these strangers, family and friends and try to say what I had prepared. I started by thanking everyone who was there and all the people and organizations who had made this day possible.

Next, I talked about Ron's departure 38 years ago and the devastation our family felt losing him, as well as the circumstances surrounding how we had lost him. I always made sure the uncertainty of his status that had haunted us for all these years was mentioned. It was the hardest speech I had ever made regarding my brother.

As I scanned the crowd, I looked into the faces of my brother, mother, cousins, aunts and uncles, my lifetime club friends and Carolyn. We were all together again, mourning the loss of my big brother 38 years later. The tears, sniffling and sad faces of my family and lifetime friends made it nearly impossible to form words.

I made it to the end of my speech with most of what I had intended to say, thanked everyone again, and then sat down beside Mom and Randy.

I realized I had gotten a little stronger, as I would have never been able to say even one word at his first memorial service.

Sergeant Major Marsh went to the podium and talked about Green Berets. He talked of the bond and family relationship they felt for each other. He told us our family was, and always had been, in that circle of family. He praised Ron's military career, his bravery, and his willingness to die for his Team members and country. He told us again how sorry he and the Special Forces were for our loss and the heartbreak of his MIA status. He walked to Mom, knelt down on one knee in front of her and presented her with a medal in honor of Ron, then gave Jim and me one. His presence haunted me. I wanted to close my eyes, shake my head, and then open my eyes and make this young Green Beret turn into my brother.

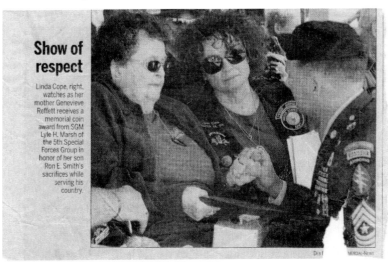

Show of respect

Linda Cope, right, watches as her mother Genevieve Reffett receives a memorial coin award from SGM Lyle H. Marsh of the 5th Special Forces Group in honor of her son Ron E. Smith's sacrifices while serving his country.

The ceremony closed with the 21 gun salute and taps, once again breaking my heart and nearly bringing me to my knees. Mere words could not describe how our family felt and how much we appreciated what our town had done. Some of these people we had known most of our lives, some we had never met.

We were then invited inside where a table had been set up with pictures, Ron's shadow box full of medals, one of his green Berets, his uniform, other honors and memorabilia. A dinner the VFW had prepared for our family was presented and I spent most of the time talking with Sergeant Major Marsh, Max, Dana, Dale, members of Rolling Thunder, and trying to thank everyone involved.

After a very long day, I took Mom back to her apartment. As I got her ready for bed, I asked her if she had any questions about the events of the day. She shook her head and looked at one of Ron's pictures as tears welled up in her eyes.

"I can't believe the work all those people put into the memorial. Linda, did those people know Ron?"

"No, none of the people from Maus, Kelly Vault or Triguard knew him, which I know of anyway. Dana didn't know him either, but he got all these people involved and interested in Ron," I said. "I know Mom, it's hard to understand after all these years. In 1971, no one but family seemed to care, now this. It's so incredible."

I sat on her bed, holding her hand and waiting for her to fall asleep. As I pulled up her covers and leaned down to kiss her goodnight, I saw she was holding the medal Sergeant Major Marsh had given her. I kissed her forehead, asked God to watch over her, and as I turned her light off, I felt my brother's presence.

"Stay with her tonight, will you big brother?" I said out loud.

I drove back to Jim's house where we sat for hours and re-lived the day. I felt like Ron had been honored, no doubt about that, but questions still remained.

As I sat on Jim's deck with him and other members of our family, I couldn't keep bitterness from creeping back into my conscious. There were two generations of family here that Ron never lived to see. Two generations of our family that never got to experience firsthand what an extraordinary person their uncle was. Jim and I had kept his memory alive so the kids felt like they knew him.

The day had been filled with sorrow and tears, and now there was laughter and kids playing in Jim's yard. For me, it only made Ron's absence more prominent. I could almost see him joking with Angel, Matt, Scott and Crystal, or giving the little ones horsey rides around the yard. Would I ever have complete and final peace? Maybe if I felt his death had not been in vain and if he wasn't still Missing In Action, I wouldn't have the unsettled feelings...maybe.

Rolling Thunder. Randy, Linda, Jim & Karen

Epilogue

In the spring of 2014, I was able to obtain Ron's Army military records.

After many requests and help from Mike Clark, our president in Rolling Thunder, I held the CD in my hands, while chills ran through my body.

Reading Ron's personnel file almost felt like spying. I was alarmed to read that he had broken his back while in Germany when his parachute didn't open. We knew he had hurt his back, but he had kept from us the fact that it was broken. He was hospitalized and had months of physical therapy.

What upset me the most was an argument between two officers, handwritten on memo paper, discussing Ron's condition when he was left in Cambodia. One told the other that "Smith's condition" was not certain, and that his Team Leader had not even checked for a pulse. The other stated they should change his status to KIA. The first man then wrote that he wasn't going to KILL Smith on paper.

Another entry in this mass of contradicting stories, is that he was receiving aid from the enemy when he was left.....

Forty-four years after it happened, I learned that my brother could have been alive when they left him. My anger and frustration for the government and Army raced to the surface again, while survivor guilt flooded my body. My endless and agonizing journey has taken me places I never would have gone, if not for my continuous search.

I have met a plethora of people, most I treasure. These people have come and gone, but some have stayed in my life to date.

A woman in the VFW in Athens, Ohio who discovered my brother was MIA, gave me her POW/MIA hat and necklace. She took these things off her body and gave them to me with tears in her eyes.

In Kokomo, Indiana, while buying a POW/MIA bracelet with Ron's name on it at the Vietnam Veterans Reunion, Linda Estes, a dear friend, nearly took off a vendor's head when he took my money knowing the bracelet I was buying was my brother's. Her husband Tony, a Vietnam veteran, gave me my first POW/MIA bracelet.

Wild Bill in Rolling Thunder offered to drive me to California to find Ron's team leader while in Vietnam.

One day while at a stop light in Holland on our bike, a man (Bruce Johnson) rolled his window down and thanked Randy and I for what we do. We had our Rolling Thunder vests on so we assumed he meant our

Epilogue

involvement with the POW/MIA issue and veterans. During one short red light, we exchanged names, and got enough information to keep us connected. We learned that this man's father was still Missing in Action.

Gord, my friend and patient, shared his Vietnam story with me after knowing him for over eight years. He is a Bronze Star recipient from Vietnam. In 1970, his company was in a horrendous battle and lost men. He survived and he was given a Bronze Star for his efforts in defending our country.

While exchanging our stories, I told Gord my plans to go to California and knock on Ron's team leader's door, demanding his firsthand version of my brother's condition when he left him.

"Let it go," he said, looking into my eyes. He said it with such conviction it gave me chills. He told me that I knew my brother was gone, and talking to this man was not going to change anything.

I think he might have been right and I have tried to put it out of my mind, but I haven't been able to completely let it go.

In the late nineties, while working at my first Optometry office in Michigan, I was pre-testing a man (Jeff) for an eye exam. He saw my POW/MIA bracelet and asked about it. I told him about Ron and his status. He asked about his branch of service and what he did. As usual, I was proud to tell him anything I could.

A few weeks later, he came back into my office and asked to talk to me. He held a book in his hand and asked if I really knew what my brother was doing in Vietnam. After hesitating I told him I thought I did, but looking into his eyes I had doubts. He held out the book and told me I should be extremely proud and that men like my brother didn't come any better, smarter, or tougher. He said he was in awe of what these men did. He gave me the book and said to keep it. He walked away and left me with tears in my eyes and the fear of what I was going to read. That book was SOG, Special Ops Group, by John Plaster. This was about eight years before I met John Plaster and read the book he had written with a segment about Ron.

Matt Maupin, from Batavia, Ohio, was the first MIA in Iraq and went missing in 2004. Our Rolling Thunder chapter became close with his parents, supporting the movement to keep Matt in the news and pushing our government to continue the search for him. Each year on our journey to Washington D.C. for the Run for The Wall, we visited the Yellow Ribbon Society, which Keith Maupin, Matt's father, had established. Almost four years to the date of Matt being missing, his body was recovered. Our Chapter attended his funeral in Cincinnati at the Red's baseball field. It was an incredibly sad, somber day, but at least his family received his remains and was able to bury him on American soil.

Four years ago, Bruce Kulman, a Green Beret buddy who was at Fort Bragg with Ron, called me. Ron, Bruce, Carolyn and Bruce's wife spent many evenings together while they were stationed at Bragg. He was planning a trip to D.C., on a Run to The Wall bike trip so we made plans to meet while in D.C. We ended up hanging out together at the Pentagon parking lot waiting for the demonstration ride to begin. Then we met at Ron's name at The Wall where Bruce gave me a challenge coin he acquired in Ron's honor.

While we were walking between The Wall and Thunder Alley, where vendors have stands and sell their goods, we met a guy who exchanged greetings with Bruce.

"That is one sweet Marine," Bruce said. It took a few seconds for his remark to sink in.

"What? You mean THE MARINE? Is that him, the MARINE?"

"Yes, that's Tim."

"Oh my God, please introduce him to us," I asked.

Bruce introduced our family to Tim Chambers, the Marine who stands at attention in full dress Marine garb, saluting a field cross, for the duration of the demonstration ride. The ride lasts anywhere from five to seven hours in 100 degree heat. I had been in awe of him since the first year Randy and I went to D.C. with Rolling Thunder. Bruce and Tim are friends, and thanks to Bruce, our family had the opportunity to not only meet Tim, but have our pictures taken with him as well.

In 2011, while sitting at Logan's Roadhouse with his brother Ken, Randy was approached by a young man named Jeremy. He had overheard their conversation regarding Rolling Thunder. Jeremy was intrigued with the issue and Rolling Thunder's mission. He wanted to contribute in some way so being an engineer and artist, he created a breathtaking piece for us to leave at Ron's name in 2012.

Many times I have answered the phone to hear a stranger ask me if I knew Ronald Smith. It always runs cold chills into my core, but it has always been someone from the Virtual Wall on the internet where I posted a memorial and left my number and email. Sometimes it was someone who knew Ron in school. A teacher called once and asked me to send information so they could educate students on Vietnam that history books do not.

In 2004, I became friends with Becky McNinch, the manager at the lab where my offices have our glasses lenses made. She was a strong supporter of veterans, making sure her lab makes glasses for veterans who can't afford them. In 2007, I gave her one of Ron's POW/MIA bracelets. She lives near Traverse City, Michigan, seven hours away, but on September 3, 2013 she went to Covington and visited Ron's memorial.

Becky races drag cars and recently she asked if I cared if she had Ron's name printed on her dragster. I assured her I would be honored for Ron's name to be on her car. At the present time she is planning on going to Washington D.C. with Rolling Thunder in 2014. Becky has become more than a friend and co-employee. She has become a spiritual connection to Ron. Neither of us has any idea how this came about but we feel God connected us for a reason.

A very good friend of Crystal, Lisa Crews, was our photographer for this book. She has taken hundreds of pictures for and of our family, Rolling Thunder, POW/MIA'S, and military. Photography is her job, but she does these things for our family for no personal gain. Her 13-year-old daughter, Mariah, is in a group called Young Marines. They are preparing for the military when they are of age and do a lot of community work. It is refreshing to know young people who are so selfless and understand the importance of our military.

Bowe Bergdahl, an Army private stationed in Afghanistan, was captured June 30, 2009. He was 23 years old. The government and his parents have received four or five videos of Bowe, alive as recent as January 2014. The Taliban's demand for Bowe's release is several terrorists that we have imprisoned at Guantanamo. Memorial Day weekend in 2012, Bowe's father spoke at the Run for The Wall. After his heartfelt speech, I made my way to the area behind the stage where he had just finished speaking, determined to meet and talk with him. Our Rolling Thunder Chaplin, Tom Ransdale, is the Rolling Thunder National's Chaplin. He saw me coming toward the stage and knew my mission. With determination I told our Chaplin, "I have to meet him, please get me back there."

"Ok, Linda, give me a minute."

He came back in a couple of minutes and brought Randy and I to meet Bowe's father. We talked, exchanged stories, phone numbers and hugs. We had so much in common. I told him we would pray for Bowe's safe return and encouraged him never to let Bowe's capture turn into the years of hell we had endured for Ron. He was adamant that he wouldn't let that happen.

On June 1, 2014, Bowe was released from the Taliban into the arms of our military. His release held much controversy and the media, as usual hung him and his father in their one sided views. The deal made by the president was not a favorable one. Most Americans did not wait to hear what Bowe's side to this story was. I for one am glad he is home. If he has wronged his military, it is their job to figure this out and decide his fate, on American soil.

Jay Norris, Ron's best friend from high school, shared a special memory with me.

Linda,

My most dominate memory of Ron goes back to High School. Out of boredom I read many library books, too many according to the teachers. Ron read only one. It was a history of all the Medal of Honor winners from the Civil war thru the Korean conflict. He read and re-read this book over and over. I remember looking at the check our card once and he was the only person who had checked the book out.

Years later, when I asked Ron why he was going to join the Green Berets he pulled this old dog eared and worn book from his pocket and said he wanted his name in a book like this. I asked if he had stolen the book from the school library, he just smiled and said, nobody ever read it but me anyway.

I love this memory Jay shared with me and will treasure it always. It depicts my brother's dreams and his mischievous personality.

During Jay and I's last conversation, he shared with me that Jack Lightle, the other musketeer and Ron's friend from high school had passed away a few months prior. Then his wife Judy, died only two weeks later. This saddened me deeply and brought back so many memories, along with the realization that an entire lifetime had passed since my brother left us. These two men had come home, married, had children, grandchildren and even one of them had passed, and Ron still seems thirty years old to me.

Ron's absence has changed who I am or might have been and I will always feel cheated out of growing up and old without my big brother. My children and grandchildren were cheated out of knowing him and feeling his special love.

One thing I am sure of is there was no other brother like him, and no son or husband as special...and missed so much.

Ron took the place of my father. He was my protector, my teacher, my friend, my hero, and the only thing that helps me deal with the pain and loss all these years is knowing that I will see him again someday.

Killed in Action/Body not recovered...I want to throw up every time I hear or read those words. How could they do this to Ron, or our family? And how many other families are going thru this nightmare?

Body not recovered...body not recovered...where is my brother's body?

Where is he? I can't stand the thought of his body in some third world country, never to come home. Has he been dead all these years? Was he wounded or captured? What if he was waiting for us to rescue him? Did someone take him to safety?

I can't stand this. My brother's body that I am so familiar with...His strong hands and his hairy chest, his beautiful smile...rotting in some jungle, maybe animals tearing at him while he was still alive? Or he was he tortured by the North Viet Cong for information, or just because they are inhumanc animals. Oh my God, I can't live with this unknown.

Does the Army or the government understand how we feel? He went to defend his country and he never came home. Apparently they just decided he didn't survive, even though they can't come up with a single story of what happened to him.

Killed in Action/Body not Recovered...

Epilogue

Big Brother I miss you, I salute you, I love you.

Your promise to see us in a year was 45 years ago.

I am still waiting.

Update

In the fall of 2015, I answered the phone to an unknown voice, asking for verification that I was Linda Smith-Cope, sister of Ronald E. Smith. Hearing the person use my brother's name, I struggled for my next breath.

It had been nearly 45 years since my brother went missing, and I was still waiting for a call that would tell me he had been found.

"I am calling to tell you that your brother, Ronald Smith, is one of the 18 inductees for the Indiana Military Veterans Hall of Fame for this year, 2015."

In that moment I was overwhelmed with emotion and kept repeating "thank you" and "I can't believe this." Tears and a bittersweet sensation rushed over my body.

The man on the phone continued by telling me that an entry had been made by Rolling Thunder.

A few months before at a Rolling Thunder chapter meeting, a gentleman had brought information of the

Indiana Military Hall of Fame, in which we could nominate a solider or veteran.

After the meeting, Flash (Terry Sanderson), emailed me to request all the information and documents required to enter Ron as an inductee. Within a couple days I had emailed all the necessary paperwork needed to Flash.

I had thought about the Hall of Fame a little, but within a few days I had let it go. I knew my brother should be one of these men honored, but I didn't think he would make it. I figured it would be some high-up personnel or famous name.

Now I was getting a call saying he had made it.

Tears streamed down my face as I continued to thank the voice on the phone and try to retain all he was telling me about the ceremony, banquet, who would accept for Ron, where we would sit, how many family members the venue could hold, and on and on. I'm sure I repeated many of my questions, but I couldn't concentrate.

I was on the phone, Facebook and texting as soon as I hung up. I couldn't wait to tell Jim and all the kids.

As quickly as my excitement escalated it plummeted...Mom. She was now in a nursing home and her condition no longer allowed us to take her out. She wouldn't be able to attend.

How can this happen without her? I ran many scenarios thru my head, but none worked. I would just have to show her pictures and try to help her to understand.

Mom's health and living conditions were another ache in my heart. I had promised her since I had worked in the nursing home where she now lived, that I would never let her go to a nursing home. Now I had to eat that promise. I knew she understood that I wanted to take her home with me, but her care was too critical and I couldn't lift her anymore.

The ceremony was to take place on Friday, November 13, in Indianapolis at the Renaissance Hotel. As the date approached our family made our final plans. There would be seventeen family members attending; Jim and me, our spouses Randy and Karen, our children Angel, Matt, Scott, Crystal and Scott's wife, Karen. Also attending would be my grandsons, Matt's boys, Gavin and Ethan, Aunt Tootie, my cousin Bruce and his wife Cheryl, along with our cousin's Lisa, Gina and her husband Steve, and Brenda and her husband Gary.

Jim and I were so appreciative that our four children were there to share in this honor. One of the biggest aches in my heart was that they did not get to grow up with Ron's influence and love in their lives. They say they feel like they know their Uncle Ron and my grandsons, nine-year-old Ethan and

Randy, Linda, Karen & Jim

twelve-year-old Gavin are very interested in Ron and what happened to him. They have asked hundreds of questions and wear his dog tags. Jim and I have tried to keep his memory alive, for us and for them.

Lisa Cope & Brenda Stanley

We arrived in plenty of time for social hour, and then the banquet room was opened for us to find our seats. We had an hour to take pictures and mingle with other families.

Farrel (Bud) Utterback, another Rolling Thunder member had been chosen as another one of the inductees. While in Vietnam, Bud had been wounded in a battle. Ignoring his injuries he went back to rescue a fellow comrade and was wounded again. Another time he went back to bring more men out. He was wounded three times while rescuing his men. He was awarded a silver star for his gallantry. He and his daughter, Shawn, were there to share Bud and Ron's honor. We were thankful he returned to receive this honor himself.

The master of ceremonies took the stage and the room quieted. Jim and I had taken our seats with the other inductee's and family members accepting for their soldier.

We listened as each inductee's story was told and he/she received their pendent, plaque and challenge coin.

Then it was Ron's name being announced. Jim was going to accept for him as I felt it was perfect for my little brother to have this honor.

As the announcer told some of Ron's military history, including the story of his brave actions as he exposed himself to enemy fire to save his team. His picture, with his silver star, was lit up on the wall in front of the room. He looked so young.

Tears fell as the mayor of Lawrence, Dean Jessep, put the blue ribbon with the large pendent, around Jim's neck. He then handed him an 11x14 plaque with the honorary words stating Ron was now in the Military Hall of Fame.

Linda & Jim

We now had a plethora of medals, honors, pins, patches and written honors giving Ron his due for being a military hero, and for that I felt pride in that my brother's worth was finally being celebrated and acknowledged. Yet, memories flooded my soul, and I still felt that pain of loss again.

The audience began to clap and our family stood, cheered and shouted their pride and excitement at what had just been awarded to Ron. It brought me back to the present and I cheered along with everyone.

We ended the evening with hugs and thank yous for our family members, and then Randy, Jim, Karen and I made our way back to Jim's house to spend the night.

The following morning I went to see my mother. I tried to explain the honor that had been given to Ron the night before, and prayed she wouldn't ask me why we hadn't taken her.

Her hearing was so bad, I repeated myself over and over, yet she seemed confused. I kissed her and told her I would be right back. I drove back over to Jim's house and retrieved the medals and framed certificate they had given us the night before. *Why didn't I take these in the first place?*

Lisa Cope, Jim, Gina Sager

I went back into the home and found Mom in the dining room. I sat down beside her and held up the 11x14 frame. She read it and tears and a look of disbelief came across her face.

"Are you serious?' she asked in her feeble voice.

"Yes Mom, we were at the ceremony last night. Ron was awarded this."

She read and re-read it as her chin quivered and what tears she had left welled up in her eyes.

"Linda, I just can't believe this," she whispered as she ran her thumb, the only digit that wasn't constricted into a fist, over and over the words.

When I felt she had embraced and understood what honors Ron had received, I hugged and kissed her. I promised her that I would have the certificate copied and hung on her wall.

Then as we did every visit, I leaned in and touched my forehead to hers. This is how I left her each time, but today was worse. Today we were losing Ron all over again. These years there was no little Angel sitting on her kitchen table jabbering and throwing her giraffe for someone to retrieve, only the reality that I was leaving her in a sad and lonely nursing home with nothing to look forward to.

After I left, I drove a couple blocks and pulled into the VFW and up to Ron's memorial. The loss of my big brother was weighing heavy and Mom's pitiful face as I left her haunted me.

Back at Jim's house, we hung Ron's award on the

Jim Smith - 2015

wall, stood back with pride and silently lost him again.

The Hall of Fame is an honor that I and my entire family will treasure forever, yet nothing has changed, he is still missing. We still do not know for sure what really happened to him. We still are not able to put his remains to rest on American soil.

Closure has not come to us.

We are...Still Waiting

Linda and Jim at The Wall

Biographical Information

**Sammy Davis joined the Army from Indianapolis, Indiana, in 1965. By November 18, 1967 he was serving as a private first class with Battery C, 2nd Battalion, 4th Artillery Regiment, 9th Infantry Division, in the Republic of Vietnam. On that day, his unit was west of Cai Lay when they fell under heavy mortar attack by the North Vietnamese Army as around 1,500 NVA swarmed the area. Upon detecting an enemy position, Davis manned a machine gun to give his comrades covering fire so they could fire artillery in response. Davis was wounded, but ignored warnings to take cover, taking over the unit's burning howitzer and firing several shells himself. He also disregarded his inability to swim, due to injuries, crossing a river on an air mattress to help three wounded American soldiers. He ultimately found his way to another howitzer site to continue fighting the NVA attack until they fled. He was subsequently promoted to sergeant and received the Medal of Honor the following year.

Major John Plaster, born 1949, is a retired U.S. Army Special Forces soldier regarded as one of the leading sniper experts in the world. A decorated Vietnam War veteran who served in the covert Studies and Observations Group (SOG). Plaster co-founded a renowned sniper school that trains military and law enforcement personnel in highly specialized sniper tactics. He is the author of The Ultimate Sniper: An Advanced Training Manual for Military and Police Snipers, The History of Sniping and Sharpshooting, and Secret Commandos: Behind Enemy Lines with the Elite Warriors of SOG, a memoir of his three years of service with SOG.

Ron's Family

The family who, in honor of Ron, still wears his dog tags, still protests for him, still loves him, and is...

...Still Waiting.

Gavin, Matt, Ethan

Matt, Angel, Crystal and Scott

Crystal, Jim, Karen, Karen and Scott

Angel at The Wall

Madison at The Wall

Bruce Lutes (cousin)

Scott Smith

About the Author

Linda J. Smith-Cope was an Army kid, born in Tacoma, Washington, at Fort Madigan Hospital. Leaving Washington at the age of two, she was shuffled from Army base to Army base, settling in Indiana. After her parents divorced, Linda lived with her mother, older brother Ron, and younger brother Jim. She grew up in Covington, a small town in western Indiana, where she met her first husband, fresh out of the Air Force, and had two children, Angel and Matthew.

After what Linda refers to as her first life, her 20 year marriage ended and a year later, she met Randy Cope from Grand Rapids, Michigan. Six years later he convinced her to move and they were married in Northern Michigan. By then, Angel had married, had her first child, Madison, and owned her own business. Matt eventually settled in Michigan. He married and gave her two grandsons, Gavin and Ethan.

Linda and Randy now live in Holland, Michigan to be near Randy's sons, Joseph and Charles. Charlie moved in with them permanently when he was 12 years old.

Linda works as an optician at LEC in the daytime hours, leaving her evening and weekends to do what she loves—writing. She hopes to be considered an author before she leaves this world.

Author 2006